CANADIAN ANNUAL REVIEW OF POLITICS AND PUBLIC AFFAIRS 2002

Canadian Annual Review of politics and public affairs 2002

EDITED BY DAVID MUTIMER

Published with the support of York University by
University of Toronto Press
Toronto Buffalo London

Toronto Buffalo London
Printed and bound by CPI Group (UK) Ltd, Croydon, CR0 4YY

ISBN 978-0-8020-9819-1

Canadian annual review of politics and public affairs.

1971–
Continues: Canadian annual review, ISSN 0068-8215.
Issue for 2002 edited by David Mutimer.
ISSN 0315-1433
ISBN 978-0-8020-9819-1 (2002 issue)

1. Canada – Foreign relations – 1945 – Periodicals.
2. Canada – Economic conditions – 1945– – Periodicals.
3. Canada – Politics and government – Periodicals.

FC2.C36 320.9′71′064 C71-2093

University of Toronto Press acknowledges the financial assistance to its publishing program of the Canada Council for the Arts and the Ontario Arts Council.

This book was published with the support of York University.

University of Toronto Press acknowledges the financial support for its publishing activities of the Government of Canada through the Book Publishing Industry Development Program (BPIDP).

Copies of the *Canadian Annual Review* published annually for 1992 to 2001 are available.

Contents

Contributors

MELVIN BAKER, Archivist/Historian, President's Office, Memorial University of Newfoundland

EMMANUEL BRUNET-JAILLY, Assistant Professor, School of Public Administration, University of Victoria

PETER E. BUKER, Independent Scholar and Writer, Corran Ban, Prince Edward Island

KEN COATES, Adjunct Professor of Political Studies, University of Saskatchewan

ROBERT DRUMMOND, Associate Professor, Department of Political Science, York University

ROBERT EVERETT, University Secretariat, York University

ROBERT G. FINBOW, Associate Professor, Department of Political Science, Dalhousie University

JOSEPH GARCEA, Associate Professor, Department of Political Science, University of Saskatchewan

CAREY HILL, Post-doctoral Fellow, Department of Political Science, University of Western Ontario

HAROLD JANSEN, Assistant Professor, Department of Political Science, University of Lethbridge

GEOFFREY LAMBERT, Professor, Department of Political Studies, University of Manitoba

WARREN MAGNUSSON, Professor, Department of Political Science, University of Victoria

PETER NEARY, Professor, Department of History, University of Western Ontario

GREG POELZER, Associate Professor, Department of Political Studies, University of Saskatchewan

DANIEL SALÉE, Professor of Political Science and Principal of the School of Community and Public Affairs, Concordia University

CHRISTOPHER SPEARIN, Assistant Professor, Department of Defence Studies, Canadian Forces College, Toronto

RICHARD WILBUR, Fundy Promotions, St Andrews, New Brunswick

DAVID MUTIMER is the editor of the *Canadian Annual Review of Politics and Public Affairs*, Associate Professor of Political Science at York University, and Deputy Director of the York Centre for International and Security Studies.

GEOFF READ was formerly the managing editor of the *Canadian Annual Review of Politics and Public Affairs* and compiled the Calendar and Obituaries. He is an Assistant Professor of History at Lakehead University.

SHANNON STETTNER is the managing editor of the *Canadian Annual Review of Politics and Public Affairs* and can be reacted at carppa@yorku.ca.

Canadian calendar 2002

JANUARY

1 Ottawa allows life insurance companies to take over mid-sized competitors, and Sun Life Financial Services of Canada launches a friendly bid to acquire Clarica Life Insurance Co. for $7.3 billion.
– Europeans in twelve countries begin to cash in their nations' currencies for Euros, as the European Union adopts a common currency. EU members Britain, Denmark, and Sweden do not adopt the Euro.
2 French citizen Zacarias Moussaoui is charged in the U.S. state of Virginia with helping to plan the 11 September 2001 attacks in the United States.
4 Pakistani-Canadian Shakir Baloch is charged in the United States with illegal re-entry, having been detained without charge in New York since 20 September 2001.
7 Canada commits 750 more combat troops, from the Edmonton-based Princess Patricia's Canadian Light Infantry, to the stabilization force in Afghanistan.
– Stockwell Day joins the race for the leadership of the Canadian Alliance Party.
8 Moncton City Council votes to request that the Province of New Brunswick allow Sunday shopping; other municipalities soon follow suit.
9 Jon Grant, former chairman of Canada Lands Co., alleges that Public Works Minister Alfonso Gagliano asked him to hire a personal friend and improperly interfered in the sale of Crown lands in Quebec.
10 James Bartleman is named Ontario's twenty-seventh

lieutenant governor. He will be the first Native person to hold the position.

11 Ford Motor Co. of Canada announces the closure of a truck assembly plant in Oakville, Ontario, putting 1,500 people out of work.

– Statistics Canada announces that employment was down by roughly 18,000 in December 2001. This, combined with an increase in labour force participation, pushed the unemployment rate up by 0.5 per cent to 8 per cent, the highest level since the spring of 1999.

14 The Ontario Court of Appeal rules that parents may spank their children with reasonable force.

– Minister of Industry Brian Tobin resigns.

15 Prime Minister Jean Chrétien shuffles his cabinet, sending Public Works Minister Alfonso Gagliano to Copenhagen to serve as Canada's ambassador to Denmark.

– The Bank of Canada cuts interest rates by 0.25 per cent to 2 per cent.

– Toronto mayor Mel Lastman is photographed shaking hands with a member of the Hell's Angels.

18 Minister for International Cooperation Susan Whelan announces that the Canadian International Development Agency has delivered $1.5 million to support the Afghan Interim Authority. CIDA has now delivered over $16 million in humanitarian aid to Afghanistan since the Taliban were ousted from power.

– Acting Sergeant Kenneth Deane of the Ontario Provincial Police, who shot Native protestor Dudley George in 1995, is given until 25 January to submit his resignation by an adjudicator at the Police Services Board.

– Justice Dennis O'Connor releases his 700-page report from the Walkerton inquiry, placing the blame for the May 2000 tragedy on the Harris government's cutbacks to the regulation of the province's water systems, as well as on the incompetence of local officials, including Stan and Frank Koebel.

21 The Canadian dollar falls to a record low of 61.84 U.S. cents.

– Defence Minister Art Eggleton is informed by the military that Canadian special forces in Afghanistan have captured prisoners.

24 Justice Minister Martin Cauchon appoints Judge Fred Kaufman to review the Steven Truscott case.

– A two-day summit of the provincial premiers and territorial leaders on health care begins in Vancouver. It concludes the next day with demands that Ottawa increase spending on health care.

25 Statistics Canada reports only a 0.2 per cent rate of job growth in 2001, ending a four-year period of sizeable employment expansion. The number of those active in the workforce increased by 2.2 per cent.

27 The Liberal government in British Columbia passes legislation allowing it to break public sector union contracts, in order to impose a new contract on the province's teachers.

28 40,000 British Columbia teachers and some 8,000 social workers stage a one day strike to protest the government's legislation allowing it to violate public sector union contracts.

– Prime Minister Jean Chrétien, responding to a reporter's question, claims that Canadian troops have yet to take any prisoners in Afghanistan.

29 U.S. president George W. Bush gives his State of the Union address and declares Iraq, Iran, and North Korea to be an 'axis of evil.'

30 Defence Minister Art Eggleton reveals that he was first informed of Canadian soldiers' taking prisoners in Afghanistan on 21 January.

– The Canadian Democracy and Corporate Accountability Commission, co-chaired by Ed Broadbent and Avie Bennett, calls for the government to ban contributions to political parties by corporations and unions.

31 Canadian Alliance member and former Reform Party leader Preston Manning retires from the House of Commons.

FEBRUARY

1 The first contingent of Canada's 750 additional troops leaves for Afghanistan.

4 Finance Minister Paul Martin announces that there will be no spring budget.

5 Contrary to Finance Minister Paul Martin's promise in the fall to place the money under the control of an independent agency, Deputy Prime Minister John Manley assumes direction of more than $2 billion in Strategic Infrastructure Foundation funds.

– Solicitor General Lawrence MacAulay announces that a national registry for sex offenders will be established.

6 Statistics Canada announces that an estimated $39.9 billion worth of building permits were taken out in 2001, just shy of 1989's all-time high.

7 Police investigating the disappearance of dozens of Vancouver prostitutes raid Robert and David Pickton's farm in Port Coquitlam, British Columbia, and charge Robert Pickton with three firearms offences.

– Former New Brunswick provincial court judge Jocelyne Moreau-Bérubé, dismissed for referring to Acadians as mostly "crooks," loses her fight for reinstatement in front of the Supreme Court of Canada.

– Air Canada reports losses of a record $1.25 billion in 2001.

8 The Salt Lake City Winter Olympic Games open.

11 MCJC Holding Ltd., owned by former chief executive officer of Corel Corp. Michael Cowpland, pleads guilty to insider trading and is fined $1 million in an Ontario court.

– Raymond Bréard, director general of the Parti Québécois, resigns over allegations of improper ties with Oxygène 9, a lobbying firm.

12 Quebec's Natural Resources Minister Gilles Baril of the Parti Québécois, follows Raymond Bréard in resigning over his own close ties to Oxygène 9.

14 The Supreme Court of Canada rules that Gerald Regan, former premier of Nova Scotia, can be tried on seven charges of indecent assault stemming from incidents involving young women in the 1960s and 1970s.

– Statistics Canada announces that Canadian motor

vehicle sales in 2001 were up 0.7 per cent from 2000, setting a record high.

15 Ari Ben-Menashe, president of Dickens and Madson, a political consulting firm based in Montreal, acknowledges that the firm filmed a video showing Zimbabwean opposition leader Morgan Tsvangirai discussing a plot to assassinate Zimbabwe's President Robert Mugabe, but insists that the footage is authentic.

– Alberta premier Ralph Klein, in Moscow as part of the Team Canada trade mission, at a news conference produces a letter signed by every premier, except Quebec's Bernard Landry, urging the federal government not to ratify the Kyoto Protocol.

18 Sears announces the closing of the seven remaining Eatons stores.

– Finance Minister Paul Martin rejects a call from Canada's mayors to give cities a share of the federal tax on gasoline.

19 Ontario premier Mike Harris launches a $15 million lawsuit against the *Globe and Mail* over a December 2001 article that he claims suggested he ordered the Ontario Provincial Police to forcibly remove Native protestors from Ipperwash Provincial Park in 1995.

– Statistics Canada announces that shipments from the manufacturing sector fell by 5.2 per cent in 2001 following strong increases during the previous two years. New orders also declined by 6.3 per cent.

21 Statistics Canada reports that in 2001 retail sales increased by 4.5 per cent over the previous year.

22 Robert Pickton is charged with two counts of first-degree murder.

24 The Salt Lake City Winter Olympic Games close.

27 Statistics Canada announces that in the fourth quarter of 2001 corporate profits fell by 5.6 per cent (to $33.8 billion), the fifth decline in the past six quarters.

28 Convicted sex offender Karla Homolka is denied early parole.

– Statistics Canada reports that gross domestic product grew by 0.5 per cent in the fourth quarter of 2001. For the year, Canada's GDP grew by 1.5 per cent, spurred mostly by consumer spending.

MARCH

4 The Canadian Institute of Health Research issues new federal guidelines allowing scientists to perform stem cell research using human embryos that are left over from infertility treatments.

– The Royal Commission on the Future of Health Care in Canada holds the first of its nineteen public consultations.

6 The Haida Nation files a lawsuit in the Supreme Court of British Columbia, claiming ownership of the Queen Charlotte Islands.

– Statistics Canada announces $2.4 billion worth of permits for housing construction were taken out in January, an increase of 24.9 per cent over December 2001, and the best monthly performance since January 1990.

9 Omani authorities arrest Canadian citizen Mohammed Mansour Jabarah for allegedly plotting to blow up the U.S. and Israeli embassies in Singapore. Jabarah is turned over to the Canadian Security and Intelligence Service.

12 Statistics Canada releases information from the 2001 census revealing that Canada's population grew by 4 per cent between 1996 and 2001, matching the previous lowest recorded growth rate for a five-year period (1981–6). The population of Canada in 2001 is given as 30,007,094, with 79.4 per cent of Canadians living in urban areas, up from 78 per cent in 1996.

13 The Ontario Court of Appeal upholds a ruling that the federal government mismanaged the pensions of mentally and physically disabled war veterans.

14 Strong motor vehicle sales continued in January 2002, according to Statistics Canada, with 146,288 vehicles sold that month, the highest monthly total in twenty-five years.

15 British Columbia's attorney general Geoff Plant announces plans to hold a referendum on Native land claims between 2 April and 15 May 2002.

19 Russian diplomat Andrei Knyazev is convicted of involuntary manslaughter in a Moscow court for hitting and killing Canadian Catherine MacLean in

Ottawa on 27 January 2001, while driving drunk. He is sentenced to four years in a penal colony.

20 Stephen Harper is elected leader of the Canadian Alliance.

22 Talks break down in the Canada–U.S. softwood lumber dispute, and Washington levies penalties of up to 29 per cent on Canadian timber.

23 Ernie Eves is elected leader of the Progressive Conservative Party of Ontario and becomes premier-in-waiting.

26 British Columbia Supreme Court justice Duncan Shaw rules that John Robin Sharpe's collection of stories about sex acts with young boys has artistic merit and is therefore not illegal. The 67-year-old Sharpe is convicted on two other counts of possession of child pornography.

APRIL

2 Three more murder charges are laid against Robert Pickton.

– A federal tribunal settles the boundary between Newfoundland and Labrador and Nova Scotia at about 170 kilometres from the shores of each province, giving roughly 75 per cent of the oil-rich Laurentian subbasin to Newfoundland and Labrador.

5 Unemployment fell by 0.2 percentage points to 7.7 per cent over the first quarter of 2002, according to Statistics Canada; 170,000 jobs were created during this period.

8 Statistics Canada reports that municipalities issued roughly $2.4 billion worth of building permits in February, almost matching January's record total.

9 A sixth murder charge is laid against Robert Pickton.

15 The Bank of Canada raises its interest rate by 0.25 per cent to 2.25 per cent.

– Ontario premier Mike Harris steps down. Ernie Eves is sworn in as premier.

16 Pakistani-Canadian Shakir Baloch is deported by the United States to his home in Toronto, after seven months of detention.

17 Crown prosecutors drop the eight sex-related charges against former Nova Scotia premier Gerald Regan.
18 Four Canadian soldiers are killed and eight wounded by fire from a U.S. F-16 fighter jet in Afghanistan.
– Canadian motor vehicle sales cooled somewhat in February 2002, Statistics Canada reports, decreasing by 0.4 per cent from January. Despite this, February's sales figures were still quite high compared with those of previous years.
19 The Ontario Superior Court of Justice blocks the privatization of Hydro One.
– Statistics Canada reports that national net worth rose by 4.8 per cent in 2001, reaching $3.5 trillion or $112,800 per Canadian.
26 The Supreme Court of Canada rules that unlicensed satellite dish providers allowing Canadians to decrypt satellite television signals from foreign sources are violating the Radiocommunication Act.
29 Bernard Ebbers resigns as chief executive officer and president of WorldCom Inc.
30 Stoddart Publishing Co. Ltd. and General Distribution Services Ltd. file for bankruptcy protection.

MAY

6 The high demand for new housing declined slightly in March, as contractors' building permits were down 1.2 per cent from February, as Statistics Canada reports.
7–8 Canada continues to push for clean energy credits under the Kyoto Protocol, at a UN–sponsored summit on global warming, held in Whistler, British Columbia.
11 Canadian Mohammed Mansour Jabarah is handed over to U.S. authorities by the Canadian Security and Intelligence Service for interrogation.
13 Seven federal by-elections take place, with the Liberals winning four, the Canadian Alliance one, the New Democratic Party one, and the Progressive Conservatives one. The new Alliance MP is leader Stephen Harper, representing Calgary Southwest.
– Canadian Natural Resources Ltd. bids $2.4 billion for

Rio Alto Exploration Ltd. The proposed merger would create the fourth-largest independent natural gas producer in North America.

14 Statistics Canada reports that in March new motor vehicle sales declined for the second month in a row, down 3.8 per cent from February. Despite this, sales reached an all-time high in the first quarter.

15 Teleglobe Inc., a subsidiary of Montreal-based BCE Inc., files for thirty-day bankruptcy protection with debts of $6 billion.

– Statistics Canada announces that the 2001 Census of Agriculture counted 246,923 farms in Canada on 15 May 2001, down nearly 11 per cent since 1996.

16 Russian president Vladimir Putin signs a pact with North Atlantic Treaty Organization foreign ministers in Reykjavik, establishing a NATO–Russia Council to consult on a range of sensitive issues.

21 New Canadian Alliance leader Stephen Harper debuts in the House of Commons.

– Ottawa rejects Alberta's alternative to the Kyoto Protocol, at a meeting of energy and environment ministers in Charlottetown, PEI. Alberta then refuses to sign the meeting's joint communiqué.

– Defence Minister Art Eggleton announces that the approximately 850 Canadian soldiers in Afghanistan will return to Canada in July, leaving a Canadian contingent of only forty commandos and snipers, from the elite Joint Task Force 2 in the region.

22 A federal advisory council finds that the decade-long moratorium on fishing for northern cod has failed to rebuild the cod stock off of Newfoundland.

– Native groups in Labrador strike an impact benefits agreement with Inco Ltd., designed to spur development of the Voisey's Bay mineral project.

23 Justice Dennis O'Connor issues his final report on the Walkerton water disaster, making ninety-three recommendations.

27 A forest fire in northern Alberta, which began on 17 May, forces the evacuation of 1,200 people.

28 News breaks of a US $2.7 billion compensation offer from Libya for the families of victims on Pan Am

Flight 103, blown up over Lockerbie, Scotland, in 1988.

30 The Canadian Radio-television and Telecommunications Commission rules that rates for local telephone service cannot be raised until the CRTC holds public hearings.

– British Columbia doctors end a work-to-rule campaign and sign a three-year deal with the province.

31 Statistics Canada reports that gross domestic product jumped by 1.5 per cent in the first quarter of 2002, buoyed by the hot housing market, a slowdown of inventory depletion, and a rebound of exports and manufacturing.

JUNE

3 Finance Minister Paul Martin is expelled from cabinet.

4 The House of Commons passes Bill C-15B, according to which those convicted of intentional cruelty to animals could face a maximum sentence of five years in prison and a $5,000 fine.

– The entire board of directors of Hydro One resigns over a dispute with the Ontario government about the compensation package for chief executive officer Eleanor Clitheroe.

– The Bank of Canada boosts its bank lending rate by 0.25 per cent to 2.75 per cent, and its overnight lending rate by the same amount to 2.5 per cent.

– Statistics Canada reports that contractors took out a record high value of residential building permits in April, as municipalities issued $2.6 billion in housing permits, up 10.1 per cent from March.

5 Alexa McDonough announces her resignation as leader of the New Democratic Party of Canada.

11 Conservative premier Ernie Eves names former New Democratic Premier Bob Rae to the board of directors of Ontario's Hydro One.

– Immigration Minister Denis Coderre introduces the Immigration and Refugee Protection Act, which contains new regulations for potential immigrants designed to improve Canada's security and expand the country's pool of skilled labour.

– Inco Ltd. and the government of Newfoundland and Labrador ink a $2.9 billion deal to develop the Voisey's Bay mineral deposits.
– Prime Minister Jean Chrétien introduces ethics guidelines that include provisions to stop cabinet ministers from promoting the private interests of their constituents, and to force cabinet ministers running for the Liberal Party leadership to reveal the names of personal and corporate donors to their campaigns.
12 The Ontario government decides not to fully privatize Hydro One.
– Ontario Environment Minister Chris Stockwell reveals that the drinking water in sixty-seven Ontario communities has been improperly tested by MDS Laboratory Services in London, Ontario.
13 The Quebec National Assembly unanimously asks the monarchy to admit responsibility for the deportation of the Acadians in the 1750s and 1760s.
14 The Synod of the Anglican Diocese of New Westminster, led by Bishop Michael Ingham, votes 215 to 129 to become the first Anglican diocese in the world to bless homosexual unions.
– Indian Affairs Minister Robert Nault tables a bill to alter the Indian Act, which would make bands more accountable for the money they spend, give the Canadian Human Rights Commission power to hear complaints about First Nations, and accelerate the land claims process.
16 *Ottawa Citizen* publisher Russell Mills is fired over an editorial criticizing Jean Chrétien, which he did not submit for approval to CanWest Global Communications Corp., the newspaper's parent company.
17 Action démocratique du Québec, led by Mario Dumont, wins three of four provincial by-elections in Quebec. This is seen as a major breakthrough for the fledgling party.
– MP Bill Blaikie announces his candidacy for the leadership of the federal New Democratic Party.
19 Ottawa announces a federal–provincial farm aid program, later revealed to be valued at $5.2 billion, designed to provide relief to drought-stricken western

farmers. Saskatchewan, Manitoba, and Quebec later refuse to sign the deal.

– A Statistics Canada survey finds that in 1999 working Canadian women earned 80 per cent of what male workers earned. This was partly explained by the concentration of women in low-paying jobs such as those in the service sector.

21 Statistics Canada reports that in the first quarter of 2002 corporate operating profits rose by 9 per cent over the previous quarter, to $34.7 billion. This represents the first quarterly gain in more than a year.

25 Journalist Pamela Wallin is appointed Canada's consul general in New York City.

– Liberal Party strategist and former MP David Smith is appointed to the Senate.

– Quebec Appeal Court Judge Michel Robert is appointed Quebec chief justice.

26 City of Toronto outside workers go on strike. Garbage collection in the city stops.

– The U.S. Securities and Exchange Commission lays fraud charges against WorldCom.

28 The Immigration and Refugee Protection Act becomes law.

JULY

2 The tourist industry rebounds somewhat in the first quarter of 2002, according to Statistics Canada, posting an increase of 0.7 per cent over the previous quarter.

3 British Columbia's referendum on Native land claims gives 85–95 per cent support to Liberal Premier Gordon Campbell's eight negotiating positions.

– Public Works Minister Ralph Goodale backs out of deals with nine advertising firms because of allegations of impropriety in the awarding of federal advertising contracts.

– Statistics Canada reports that the Canadian fertility rate hit a record low in 1999 of 1.52 children per woman. The downward trend was strongest among women who were between the ages of 20 and 29.

5 A forest fire forces the evacuation of 550 Cree residents from the region of Nemiscau in northern Quebec.

8 Former WorldCom chief executive officer Bernard Ebbers refuses to testify at a U.S. congressional hearing.

9 The Church of England Synod votes 269 to 83 to allow divorced individuals to remarry in exceptional circumstances at the discretion of parish priests. This paves the way for Prince Charles, the heir to the throne, to marry divorcée Camilla Parker Bowles if he so desires.

11 Cabinet ministers Allan Rock, John Manley, and Sheila Copps all comply with Jean Chrétien's new regulations and reveal donations to their leadership campaigns. Front-runner Paul Martin is under no obligation to do so and does not.

– The Ontario legislature passes back-to-work legislation bringing Toronto's sixteen-day outside workers' strike to an end. The strike saw garbage pile up across the city.

– Statistics Canada reports that 1.2 million Canadian couples lived in a common-law relationship in 2001, up 20 per cent from 1995. The proportion of married couples, in contrast, increased by only 3 per cent (from 6.2 to 6.4 million).

– British Columbia–based Telus Corp. announces that it will lay off 6,000 workers in B.C. and Alberta.

12 Canadian Press reports that Justice Minister Martin Cauchon is considering decriminalizing simple possession of marijuana.

16 The Bank of Canada raises its overnight lending rate by 0.25 per cent to 2.75 per cent. Statistics Canada releases a second round of data from the 2001 Census, showing an aging Canadian population.

17 Federal and provincial regulators announce the creation of the Canadian Public Accountability Board to regulate and discipline auditors.

– Statistics Canada reports that in 2001 police across the country investigated 55,000 more criminal incidents than in 2000. This represents a 1 per cent increase over the previous year, the first increase in a decade.

19 Chief executive officer Eleanor Clitheroe is fired from her position with Ontario's Hydro One.
20 Approximately 800 soldiers in Kandahar, from the Princess Patricia's Canadian Light Infantry, finish their tour of duty and begin to return to Canada via Guam.
21 WorldCom files for bankruptcy.
22 Judge Jean-Guy Boilard resigns from the trial of seventeen Hell's Angels bikers in Quebec.
– Toronto city councillor Jack Layton announces his candidacy for the leadership of the federal New Democratic Party.
23 Prime Minister Jean Chrétien, Ontario premier Ernie Eves, and Toronto mayor Mel Lastman greet Pope John Paul II at Pearson International Airport. The Pope is arriving for Catholic World Youth Day.
– Solicitor General Lawrence MacAulay bans Al-Qaeda and six other affiliated groups from operating in Canada.
24 Canada is ranked as the third most desirable place to live according to the UN's quality-of-life index.
– British Columbia announces the sale of its 224 provincially owned liquor stores.
25 Statistics Canada reports that in 2001 49 per cent (more than 5.8 million) of Canada's 12 million households had at least one member who used the Internet from home on a regular basis. This marked a 23 per cent increase over 2000.
26 The World Trade Organization issues a preliminary ruling against the United States on eight of nine points concerning the duties that Washington applied in spring 2002 on Canadian softwood lumber imports.
– Michel Chrétien, adopted son of Prime Minister Jean Chrétien, is charged with sexual assault in Yellowknife.
27 Omar Khadr, a 15-year-old Canadian, is taken prisoner near Khost, Afghanistan, by U.S. troops, after he allegedly killed Sergeant Christopher James Speer.
28 Catholic World Youth Day is held in Toronto.
– Twenty-three Cubans defect to Canada during Catholic World Youth Day.
29 Justice Minister Martin Cauchon announces that the

government will appeal a court ruling recognizing gay marriage.

31 MP Lorne Nystrom announces his candidacy for the leadership of the federal New Democratic Party.

AUGUST

7 Quebec Superior Court Justice Pierre Béliveau orders a new trial in the high-profile prosecution of seventeen Hell's Angels bikers in Quebec.

– Prime Minister Jean Chrétien shuffles his cabinet in a move seen as strengthening the position of his loyalists.

8 Health Canada announces that a Saskatchewan man became the first Canadian to die from Creutzfeldt-Jakob (mad cow) disease earlier in the summer. Seventy-one people were potentially exposed to the disease at a Saskatoon hospital.

– The National Parole Board launches an investigation into how Robert Moyes secured day parole in 1993 while serving a life sentence. Moyes was charged on 7 August 2002 with seven counts of first-degree murder for killings committed while he was on parole in 1995 and 1996.

– Quebec Court of Appeal judge Marie Deschamps is announced as the replacement for retired Supreme Court justice Claire L'Heureux-Dubé.

14 Former Ontario Hydro One chief executive officer Eleanor Clitheroe launches a lawsuit against the utility.

21 Prime Minister Jean Chrétien announces that he will not seek a fourth mandate.

– Statistics Canada announces that for the 2002–3 academic year undergraduate students will pay an average of 4.1 per cent more in university fees than they did in 2001–2. Students will pay an average of $3,733 in tuition. The increase exceeds the expected level of inflation.

22 Statistics Canada reports that retail sales in the second quarter of 2002 were 0.8 per cent higher than in the first quarter. Retail sales were 5.3 per cent above 2001 levels.

26 John Robin Sharpe is arrested for indecent assault and gross indecency for incidents that allegedly occurred between 1979 and 1982.

– The Canadian Biotechnology Advisory Committee finds that existing genetically modified food is safe and does not require mandatory labelling.

27 Nortel Networks Corp. announces that it will lay off 7,000 employees.

– Michel Chrétien is charged with a second count of sexual assault.

– A Statistics Canada survey finds that Native people who live off reserves are in poorer health, on average, than non-Natives.

29 Former British Columbia premier Glen Clark is found not guilty of breach of trust and accepting a benefit.

– Statistics Canada reveals that corporate profits rose 10.7 per cent in the second quarter of 2002, reaching $38.8 billion.

30 The Canadian economy posts a growth rate of 4.3 per cent in the second quarter of 2002, according to Statistics Canada. Gross domestic product advanced 1.1 per cent over the previous quarter.

SEPTEMBER

4 A 600-page report by the Senate Special Committee on Illegal Drugs urges the legalization of marijuana.

– Quebec's minister of intergovernmental affairs Jean-Pierre Charbonneau, of the Parti Québecois, announces that the government will hold a referendum on national sovereignty in 2004 if it is re-elected.

5 Statistics Canada reports that in July the value of building permits reached more than $4 billion, an unprecedented high. This was a 3 per cent increase from the figure for June.

9 A speech by former Israeli prime minister Benjamin Netanyahu at Concordia University is cancelled following violent protests.

13 U.S. airmen Major Harry Schmidt and Major William Umbach are charged with four counts of manslaughter

after the report of a joint U.S.–Canadian board investigating the deaths of four Canadian soldiers in Afghanistan in April.

16 The first session of the thirty-seventh Canadian Parliament closes.

17 Ottawa issues an advisory to Canadians born in Middle Eastern countries to be careful travelling to the United States.

– The Royal Canadian Mounted Police seize several hard drives and seven boxes of documents from the offices of Groupaction Marketing.

18 Howard Wilson, ethics counsellor to the prime minister, announces he will not seek reappointment after new legislation making the job fixed at five-year terms is passed in the fall.

19 Four more murder charges are laid against Robert Pickton, bringing the total to eleven.

– Two Statistics Canada surveys show that new immigrants are generally healthier than the Canadian-born population. The gap narrows as the immigrants' time in Canada increases.

23 Kenneth Deane resigns from the Ontario Provincial Police.

25 Statistics Canada reports that spousal homicides increased in 2001 for the first time in six years, jumping from sixty-eight in 2000 to eighty-six in 2001. The general homicide rate, however, remained stable for the third consecutive year, at 1.78 murders per 100,000 people, with 554 in total, and homicides committed by youths reached a thirty-year low.

26 Canadian Maher Arar is arrested at John F. Kennedy Airport in New York.

– Thirty-five business groups form a coalition to fight ratification of the Kyoto Protocol.

27 Bombardier Inc. announces that it will lay off 2,000 employees from its aerospace division.

– Statistics Canada reports that tourism revenues rose by 0.5 per cent in the second quarter of 2002.

30 The second session of the thirty-seventh Canadian Parliament opens.

– In the Speech from the Throne Prime Minister Jean

Chrétien announces the creation of ten new national parks and five new national marine conservation areas.

OCTOBER

2 Robert Pickton is charged with four more counts of murder, raising the total to fifteen.
4 Queen Elizabeth II begins her golden jubilee visit to Canada in Nunavut.
– Deputy Prime Minister John Manley calls for Canada to cut its ties to the monarchy.
8 Ontario's Workplace Safety and Insurance Board gives workers' compensation to Heather Crowe, a former waitress diagnosed with terminal lung cancer contracted as a result of exposure to second-hand smoke in her workplace.
– Maher Arar is deported from the United States to Syria.
– Auditor General Sheila Fraser issues her 2002 status report, in which she states that all provinces are violating the Canada Health Act, and that the federal government does not monitor how its federal–provincial transfer funds for health care are spent.
11 Michel Jalbert of Pohénégamook, Quebec, is arrested at a gas station fifteen metres across the border for not reporting to U.S. Customs. Jalbert and other locals have been filling up at the station for years.
15 Queen Elizabeth II's visit to Canada ends in Quebec.
– Foreign Minister Bill Graham files an official protest with the U.S. administration over the deportation of Canadian Maher Arar to Syria.
18 A Statistics Canada survey finds that over one-third of Canadian children aged 2 to 11 years were overweight in 1998–9, half of whom could be considered obese.
22 Statistics Canada releases the third round of its 2001 Census data on marital status and related topics, revealing, among other things, that 34,200 same-sex common-law couples (representing 0.5 per cent of Canadian couples), were counted; 2001 was the first time this datum was recorded.

23 Alliance leader Stephen Harper suggests in Parliament that disgraced Liberal cabinet members' "mug shots" should be posted in the country's police stations. He then makes a remark about New Democrat Svend Robinson that can be interpreted as homophobic.

– Maher Arar meets with a Canadian consul in a Syrian prison.

25 A Senate committee recommends infusing $5 billion extra per year into the health care system.

– Following a *Toronto Star* exposé, Toronto police chief Julian Fantino announces an independent review of the service's race relations, under former Ontario chief justice Charles Dubin.

28 U.S. officials transfer Omar Khadr from Afghanistan to the U.S. naval base at Guantanamo Bay, Cuba. He is the first Canadian citizen known to be held at the controversial prison.

30 Calgary-based Talisman Energy Inc., facing considerable pressure, sells its interest in Sudan's largest oil development.

– Finance Minister John Manley releases a budget forecast predicting surpluses through 2007–8 and announces that Canada's economy grew by 5 per cent in the first half of the year. He expects the year's growth to be 3.5 per cent.

– Statistics Canada reveals that after-tax income for families of two or more increased by 12 per cent between 1995 and 2000, to $54,725. Single-parent families headed by women saw their average income reach $29,081, up 8.4 per cent from 1999, but far lower than the $39,983 average of single-parent families headed by men.

– Statistics Canada reports that there were, on average, 31,500 inmates in a Canadian federal or provincial jail or prison in 1999–2000.

31 Thirteen Alberta farmers begin their prison sentences, ranging from a few weeks to six months, for refusing to pay their fines for defying the Canadian Wheat Board in 1996 and crossing the border to sell their grain in the United States.

– The Supreme Court of Canada strikes down a provision in a 1993 law preventing federal prisoners from voting in federal elections.

– Finance Minister John Manley announces $5.8 billion in spending supplements for the 2002 budget.

NOVEMBER

5 Fifty-six Liberal MPs vote with the Opposition to strip the prime minister of the right to appoint committee chairs in the House of Commons. The new rules also mean that the vice-chairs will no longer automatically come from the official Opposition.

6 Former Ontario chief justice Charles Dubin pulls out of heading the Toronto Police Service's inquiry into race relations, after Chief Julian Fantino says he will conduct his own inquiry. Black community leaders, meanwhile, refuse to talk to either Dubin or Fantino.

– Statistics Canada reports that builders took out $3.7 billion in building permits in September, down 6.9 per cent from August.

7 U.S. Attorney General John Ashcroft announces that Canadian citizens will not be exempt from rules whereby all those born in Arab countries that the United States defines as linked to terrorism will be photographed and fingerprinted upon their entry into the United States.

11 The government appoints Parliament's first poet laureate, George Bowering.

19 British Columbia's Conflict Commissioner, in a report from earlier in the year that is made public, finds that former New Democratic British Columbia Premier Glen Clark violated conflict-of-interest guidelines.

20 The Royal Canadian Mounted Police lay thirty-three charges against four individuals, Armour Pharmaceutical Co., and the Canadian Red Cross Society in conjunction with the tainted-blood scandal that caused thousands of Canadians to become infected with HIV and hepatitis C in the 1980s.

– Prime Minister Jean Chrétien's director of communications, Françoise Ducros, is overheard by journalists calling U.S. President George W. Bush a "moron" at the North Atlantic Treaty Organization meetings in Prague.

– Information released from the 2001 Census of Agriculture indicates that the number of Canadian farm operators fell by 10 per cent from 1996. Only 12 per cent of operators were under age 35, compared with nearly 20 per cent of self-employed workers in the wider workforce. This represented a 35 per cent decrease since 1991.

21 Bulgaria, Romania, Slovakia, Slovenia, Estonia, Latvia, and Lithuania are invited to join the North Atlantic Treaty Organization.

26 Françoise Ducros leaves her position in the Prime Minister's Office and takes a job in the public service.

27 Defence Minister John McCallum calls for $1 billion to be added to the Canadian Forces' budget.

– Health Canada announces it will purchase ten million doses of smallpox vaccine.

– The Toronto-Dominion Bank reports an annual loss for the first time in its history, while the Canadian Imperial Bank of Commerce also reports a loss for the quarter.

28 The Royal Commission on the Future of Health Care in Canada, headed by Roy Romanow, issues its findings calling for an infusion of $15 billion into the system.

29 Statistics Canada reports that real gross domestic product grew by 0.8 per cent in the third quarter.

DECEMBER

2 Former New Democratic British Columbia premier Mike Harcourt falls and suffers a serious spinal injury.

3 Auditor General Sheila Fraser issues a damning indictment of the federal government's mishandling of the national gun registry, which has cost nearly $1 billion.

– Information released from the 2001 Census shows that one in seven Canadians, an estimated 3.4 million people, reported some level of disability in 2001.

5 Defence Minister John McCallum issues a call for new bids to replace Canada's aging fleet of Sea King heli-

copters. He now plans to issue the contract to one manufacturer rather than splitting the tender.

– The Supreme Court of Canada rules that higher life forms, such as genetically engineered mice, cannot be patented.

– Statistics Canada reports that builders equalled July's record in October, obtaining $4 billion in permits, a 6.9 per cent increase over September.

9 In two federal by-elections in Quebec, the Bloc Québécois narrowly defeats the Liberals. The ridings are considered Bloc strongholds.

– A parliamentary committee recommends the establishment of safe injection sites to stop the spread of disease among intravenous drug users.

– Justice Minister Martin Cauchon says the government might decriminalize marijuana use in 2003.

10 The House of Commons votes 195 to 77 to ratify the Kyoto Protocol.

– Information released from the 2001 Census shows that Canada is becoming more multilingual. Over 100 languages were listed as respondents' "mother tongues."

11 Statistics Canada reports that household spending rose 3.4 per cent from $55,830 in 2000 to $57,730 in 2001.

12 A Senate panel recommends that Canada's big banks be allowed to merge, and advises open competition in the domestic banking industry.

– The special parliamentary committee on the non-medical use of drugs recommends that that the possession and cultivation of up to thirty grams of marijuana should be treated as a regulatory and not a criminal offence.

13 Saskatchewan Native elder, former leader of the Assembly of First Nations, and member of the Order of Canada David Ahenakew makes anti-Semitic remarks at a Federation of Saskatchewan Indian Nations Conference.

14 The first thirty families from Davis Inlet, the site of chronic addiction problems among the community's Innu youth, move to their new home of Natuashish in a government relocation scheme.

16 Prime Minister Jean Chrétien signs the ratification documents for Canada to join the Kyoto Protocol.

17 David Ahenakew apologizes for his anti-Semitic comments on 13 December amid calls for him to be charged with inciting hatred.

19 Canada and the European Union sign a pledge to increase bilateral trade and investment.

– The Supreme Court of Canada rules that common-law spouses do not have an automatic right to a 50–50 division of assets in the event of separation.

CANADIAN ANNUAL REVIEW OF POLITICS
AND PUBLIC AFFAIRS 2002

EDITOR'S INTRODUCTION – THE YEAR IN REVIEW

To no one's surprise 2002 was dominated by the issues that had captivated the world's attention at the end of 2001: the attacks on the United States and the subsequent 'war on terrorism' declared by the Bush administration. Canada had chosen to stand 'shoulder to shoulder' with its southern neighbour in response to those attacks, and in 2002 the meaning of that commitment became clear as Canada entered into full-scale combat operations in Afghanistan, suffered its first casualties, and ended the year torn over whether to follow the United States should it choose to take its war to Iraq. On the home front, a battle of an altogether different magnitude reached a turning point, with the seeming resolution of the long-running struggle between the prime minister and his minister of finance – although by year's end it was by no means clear who had actually won.

When Canada first joined the U.S. fight in Afghanistan, it sent a small number of special forces. On 7 January Defence Minister Art Eggleton announced that Canada would be significantly increasing its contribution with a battle group, comprising the 3rd Battalion, Princess Patricia's Canadian Light Infantry and elements of Lord Strathcona's Horse. The group was based at Khandahar in the south of Afghanistan, attached to a U.S. force organized around the 101st Airborne Division. As the Canadian Commander, Lieutenant Colonel Pat Stogran, put it, 'our mandate is for the full spectrum of operations ... so we are going to be involved in just about everything.' Stogran's words proved tragically prophetic, for not only did Canada become involved in offensive combat operations with our U.S. allies, but four of our soldiers were killed by those allies in a 'friendly fire' incident on 17 April.

Sergeant Marc Léger, Corporal Ainsworth Dyer, Private Richard Green, and Private Nathan Smith were part of a live fire exercise in the middle of the night when U.S. F-16 aircraft flying overhead saw the muzzle flashes from the exercise. The first pilot, Major Harry Schmidt, and his wingman, Major William Umbach, were unaware of the Canadian exercise, and interpreted the fire as an attack on them. In response, Schmidt launched a 220 kilogram laser-guided bomb, killing the four Canadians and wounding eight others. The deaths captivated the country, leading to both mourning and a sense of outrage that the lives we were asking our soldiers to risk could be lost so senselessly at the hands of our allies. In the United States, investigations into the incident resulted in a series of charges against the two U.S. airmen, as it was determined that there had been a 'failure of airmanship and technique' and a 'failure of leadership.' The charges were first to be heard in early 2003 with a hearing to determine whether to proceed to a full court martial.

The question of fighting with the United States took on ever-greater urgency as the year came towards a close. In an address marking the first anniversary of the attacks on New York City and Washington, U.S. president George W. Bush escalated his long-standing rhetorical attacks on the regime of Saddam Hussein in Iraq. Joined by his closest ally, British prime minister Tony Blair, Bush spent much of the autumn making a case for war against Iraq because of its supposed possession of weapons of mass destruction. The Canadian government was decidedly ambivalent about this iteration of the U.S. global policy, with Prime Minister Jean Chrétien insisting that proof of Iraqi WMD would be needed, together with a UN Security Council mandate for Canada's participation in any action against Iraq. This was met with calls from the Canadian Alliance Party to support our U.S. allies and from the New Democratic Party to announce clearly that we would have no part of it. At the same time, the United States provided Canada with a sense of what sort of commitment it would be looking for, if the conflict with Iraq became military.

Throughout the year, with the prospect of another hot war in Iraq and the fight against Al-Qaeda and their erstwhile Taliban hosts continuing in Afghanistan, the war on terror demanded significant changes to the domestic security structure of Canada, changes that were the subject of intense debate over the course of the year. Soon after the events of 11 September 2001 the federal government had introduced omnibus anti-terror legislations Bill C-42, which had been greeted with howls of outrage at some of its more draconian provisions. In response, the government withdrew the bill and replaced it early in 2002 with Bill C-55, which reduced the scope of some of the more egregious elements of its predecessor. Civil libertarians, however, were still deeply concerned, and Bill C-55 was allowed to die on the order paper. With the new session of Parliament in the autumn, the government tried a third time, with Bill C-17, which retained some of the elements of the previous two, but again reduced the threats to civil liberties represented by Bills C-42 and C-55.

The dangers to hard-won rights that the global war on terror posed were thrown into stark relief at the time that the federal government was reworking its bill for the second time. An Ottawa software engineer, Maher Arar, was detained by the United States while in transit at John F. Kennedy Airport, in New York, on his return to Canada from a family holiday in North Africa. Arar is a Canadian citizen who came to Canada from his native Syria as a 16-year-old. Despite his Canadian citizenship and residency, and without informing the Canadian government as is its international obligation, the United States deported Arar to Syria. By year's end Canadian consular officials had been informed of his whereabouts, but Arar was still being held in Syrian jails, and there were strong reports that he was being tortured.

Human rights played a significant role in the foreign affairs of Canada in 2002 in addition to the shameful episode of Maher Arar's capture and deportation. In 2001 a Canadian working in Saudi Arabia, William Sampson, was sentenced to death along with three colleagues by the Saudi regime. Throughout the year Canadian officials worked gingerly to remove the threat of execution for a crime it seems likely Sampson and his fellow convicts had nothing to do with, but, as with Arar, the end of 2002 still found William Sampson in prison, and in his case still with his execution imminent. On a more positive note, 2002 saw the entry into force of the Rome Statute creating the International Criminal Court, well ahead of the expected schedule of 2008. Canada had had a significant role in negotiating the statute, and so it was fitting that the entry into force fell on Canada Day.

Another significant human rights story threatened to derail the prime minister's plans for the G8 summit, which was held in Kananaskis, Alberta, in June. Chrétien had planned to use the summit to build momentum for his New Partnership for African Development. But the re-election of Robert Mugabe as president of Zimbabwe, in an election that seemed to flout international norms, led to calls for Zimbabwe's expulsion from the Commonwealth. Such dramatic action could well have undermined the NEPAD, and so Canada worked for a compromise package of sanctions, which was adopted on 19 March. This cleared the way for Chrétien to tour Africa in April touting the NEPAD prior to the G8 meeting.

Once the world leaders gathered in Kananaskis, Chrétien's hoped-for African program was overtaken by the agenda of U.S. president George

W. Bush, in particular Bush's desire to discuss another peace plan for the Middle East. What is more, while the leaders of the world's richest countries could not agree on the $6 billion a year necessary to support the NEPAD, they were able to agree on a $20 billion Global Partnership Program to aid in the security of the former Soviet Union's nuclear, chemical, and biological arsenals. It was security of another kind, however, that had led the leaders to be taken to the remote Alberta resort, as it was felt that there would be less likelihood there of either a terrorist attack or the sort of protests that had marred, in the leaders' view, other summits in support of globalization in recent years. Despite the accidental publication of detailed plans of the resort the year before, the summit meeting went off without being the target of any terrorism at all.

The team overseeing this global agenda changed in 2002, with the ministers of both defence and foreign affairs replaced. In the year's first cabinet shuffle, but by no means its last, Bill Graham succeeded John Manley in the Pearson Building. The appointment of Graham, a backbencher who had for several years chaired the House of Commons Foreign Affairs Committee, was met with some consternation in the Opposition ranks for his lack of ministerial experience. The job had come available because of the continued rapid rise of John Manley, who was promoted out of the Foreign Affairs portfolio. The same cannot be said of John McCallum's appointment as defence minister at the end of May. He replaced Art Eggleton, who had begun the year clinging precariously to his job in the face of charges of lying and incompetence. By late May even the prime minister could no longer defend his defence minister when it was made public that he had paid his girlfriend $36,500 to produce a fourteen-page report on post-traumatic stress disorder in the military, despite two other ongoing investigations of the issue elsewhere in the federal government. As important as replacing the defence and foreign ministers is, these two shuffles merely set the stage for the most significant ministerial sacking of recent memory, which took place in June.

In an era when the Opposition parties were divided among themselves, the only real struggle over the future government in Ottawa was within the ruling Liberal Party. Even before the collapse of the Progressive Conservatives, in the 1993 election, that struggle focused on the Liberal leader, Jean Chrétien, and the man he had defeated for the party's leadership, Paul Martin. Throughout the decade that followed the 1993 election, the two waged an often strangely public battle for the future of their Party. Martin's supporters periodically raised the stakes in this battle in an attempt to force Chrétien from office and pave the way for their man's ascendance. In 2002 this battle came to a head as never before. In June the prime minister announced that members of cabinet would henceforth have to refrain from fundraising for a party leadership contest until there was such a contest – which would only happen when he decided to resign. Martin mused about leaving cabinet as a result, and Chrétien took that as his cue to rid cabinet of his leading rival. The finance minister, who had overseen the fiscal program that Liberals touted as their greatest success, was removed – the prime minister said by mutual consent. But this was a story that Paul Martin refused to support, and the Canadian public refused to believe.

On the face of it, it would seem that the prime minister's move against Martin backfired quite spectacularly. Martin came out of it smelling the better to the electorate, and two months later, on 21 August, Chrétien was finally forced to announce his resignation. However, Jean Chrétien once again proved himself the most wily of political operators, for although announced that he would leave the prime minister's office – and indeed politics – he would not do so for another eighteen months. This was an unprecedented denouement to a prime ministership, and was designed to wrong-foot the Martinite opposition. Chrétien's strategy was that his announcement would end the constant internal fighting, as he had already announced he would leave, but the long delay would give other candidates for the party's leadership a chance to establish themselves over Paul Martin, now out of government.

As the year ended, it looked as if being out of government might not harm Paul Martin after all. The Liberals had come to power in 1993 in large measure on a campaign against Conservative sleaze, but throughout 2002 the Liberal government faced continuing pressure on its own ethical behaviour. The January cabinet shuffle that brought Bill Graham in as foreign minister also gave him his newest diplomat, as Alfonso Gagliano was removed from public works, under pressure of the revelations about the use of sponsorship money in Quebec, and given the plum posting of ambassador to Denmark. Such blatant patronage did nothing to quell the debate over ethics in government, and neither did the auditor general's report on the sponsorship scandal, in May, which said that the government broke 'just about every rule in the book,' although it did not apportion blame. In light of the report, the House of Commons and the RCMP launched separate investigations into the affair. Both were ongoing by year's end, and it was not at all clear whether it would be more beneficial politically to be inside or outside the government.

The year also saw an apparent breakthrough in the long-standing and extraordinarily troubling disappearances of women in Vancouver. Since the 1980s women, mostly sex-workers addicted to various narcotics and many from Canada's First Nations, had been vanishing from the streets of Vancouver. Early in 2002 police searching a pig farm in Port Coquitlam discovered evidence of some of the missing women, and so charged one of the farm's owners, Robert Pickton, with murder. Over the course of the year the number of charges grew, and by year's end Pickton was facing fifteen counts. These charges, however, raised further questions about why the police had taken so long to take the problem seriously. Only in 1998 was a task force constituted to look into the disappearances.

Both at home and abroad, 2002 was rather less eventful than the previous year – for which most Canadians could be extremely grateful. The events of September 2001, however, marked the year's politics and public affairs in most arenas. As the year drew to a close, a number of the consequences of the attacks that had been seen throughout the year remained unresolved. Bill C-17 had not been passed, Maher Arar languished in a Syrian jail, and the war drums were beating loudly around Iraq. It seemed clear that 2003 would also be dominated by the fallout from that September morning, although how this would happen seemed much less certain by the end of 2002 than it had a year earlier.

ROBERT EVERETT

Parliament and politics

'I will not run again,' said Jean Chrétien on 21 August 2002. With those words a beleaguered prime minister conceded, at last, that his day was over. A rival faction within the Liberal Party of Canada had toiled, fervently and now successfully, to discomfort the prime minister and in doing so hasten the day when the new favourite, Paul Martin, could take his place. Chrétien was determined to leave on his own terms, at a time of his choosing. With his announcement, the agonizingly slow process of succession that had begun in earnest during Chrétien's second mandate (1997–2000) suddenly accelerated. Or did it? There was a catch. Although Chrétien had yielded, he insisted that he would not leave for many months or, as he said, not later than February 2004. The denouement was unprecedented in its length, but explicable in its motivation. Chrétien timed his send-off in a way that might yet foil his arch-adversary. Martin had already been ousted from cabinet in June. The languid pace could make it possible for another candidate – perhaps especially the ever-ascending John Manley, who accumulated portfolio responsibilities at a dizzying rate during the year, and who had been installed as finance minister after Martin's defrocking – to rise up and spoil the carefully designed endgame that was to culminate in a Martin-led government.

They were scarcely polar opposites. Yet, to an extent, Chrétien and Martin represented, respectively, the left and right wings of the Liberal Party. In many ways, the pitched battle for the heart and soul of the Liberal Party symbolized the year 2002 in Canadian politics. Leadership races were also concluded or under way in all of the other parliamentary parties (with the notable exception of the Bloc Québécois). The other parties also tested the ideological boundaries of their electoral appeal in the course of switching leaders. The Canadian Alliance found a new leader, Stephen Harper, who was, simultaneously, less beholden to the religious right than his predecessor Stockwell Day and more wedded to neoliberal orthodoxy than it would seem Canadian public opinion would normally tolerate. Alexa McDonough resigned as leader of the federal New Democrats, forcing her party to revisit its perpetually tormenting ideological and strategic dilemmas. Former prime minister Joe Clark, revered but unrewarded, decided to end his second term as leader of the Progressive Conservative Party of Canada just weeks before Chrétien's departure. The leadership void in Clark's party would be filled by someone who was either wholly committed to the Tory revitalization project or who, unlike Clark, was willing to move rapidly towards a reunion of the right.

Perceptible differences between the political parties were stark on matters of substance as well as leadership. The widening of the war against terror waged by the United States and a shifting axis of allies obliged Canadians, and their major political parties, to wonder. In the wake of the 11 September 2001 attacks in New York City and Washington, DC, there was muted quibbling when Canadian troops made their way to Afghanistan after the Taliban regime had been routed. The idea of participating in a mission to unseat the Baathist government in Iraq was far less appealing to parliamentarians. The nation was also shocked and wary after so-called friendly fire from U.S. aircraft resulted in the death and injury of Canadian ground forces in Afghanistan. On the domestic scene, a major report on health care delivered by Roy Romanow inspired much debate. The government's insistence on ratification of the Kyoto agreement to curb emissions of carbon dioxide also brought views on the environment into sharp relief. As had been true throughout the Liberal renaissance since 1993, the legislative agenda was rather thin in 2002. Yet when members of Parliament did have a chance to debate, the issues were often grave and compelling.

In some respects the year 2002 will be known for the scandals that engulfed the Liberal Party of Canada. A decade after it was first elected, the Chrétien government stumbled through a series of controversies. Ethical issues rained down on the Liberals, and a number of cabinet ministers were cut adrift. Martin's abrupt dismissal staggered the party and the government. No longer in cabinet, Martin expounded on the need to pay down a 'democracy deficit' by granting more power to backbenchers while restraining an imperious cabinet. It may have been a principled statement, but it was also interpreted as a thinly veiled attack on Chrétien's authoritarian streak. Auditor General Sheila Fraser's probes into the management of government information programs, together with Opposition harangues, identified potentially wounding examples of malfeasance. In all of this were the seeds of discontent that might, one day, smother the Liberals under Chrétien, Martin, or another candidate not as well identified with an administration seen by some to be drained and divided.

National institutions

Speech from the Throne

After Parliament was prorogued in the spring, the autumn legislative session opened on 30 September with the traditional Speech from the Throne. In a relatively crisp address of seventeen minutes, Governor General Adrienne Clarkson outlined the government's priorities for the second session of Canada's thirty-seventh Parliament. The document, entitled 'The Canada We Want,' suggested nothing if not an activist agenda. By all accounts the government of Jean Chrétien was set to embark on its most ambitious period since the Liberals returned to power in 1993. This dismayed those on the right, who decried the federal government's 'tax and spend' attitude, and heartened, as always, those in various quarters who placed their trust in Ottawa to advance sundry causes (environmentalists being especially buoyed). But was this so? NDP leader Alexa McDonough went so far as to bring a blue plastic recycling bin into the House of Commons to express her doubts about the government's commitment to the initiatives contained in the speech – many of them dating back nearly a decade.

The major promises contained in the speech, as summarized by the *Toronto Star* on 1 October, were as follows:

- A reduction in child poverty
- The implementation of heath care reforms, especially those proposed in the Romanow Report, due in November
- Balanced budgets (by which it was understood to mean surpluses) for the foreseeable future
- Tougher ethical standards for senior elected officials and civil servants
- A closing of the gaps, with respect to a variety of measures, between Aboriginals and other Canadians
- Substantial gains in education and innovation across the board
- A better deal for Canada's increasingly important urban centres
- Protection for endangered species
- Increased assistance to developing nations, together with less discriminatory trade practices

- 'Smart regulation' (streamlining and confidence-building in the private sector).

House of Commons by-elections

Ten members of the House of Commons resigned their positions in 2002, and nine of them had been replaced in by-elections by year's end. Four once-prominent Liberals gave up their seats on 14 January. Ronald Duhamel, MP for Saint Boniface, Manitoba, resigned and was called to the Senate the following day. Herb Gray, MP for Windsor West, Ontario, resigned after a long, diverse, and generally respected legislative career; his reward was the chair of the Canadian section of the International Joint Commission with the United States. Alfonso Gagliano resigned his seat in the Commons to take up a new job, as ambassador to Denmark. Prime Minister Chrétien was almost certainly mistaken if he had hoped to quell the controversy surrounding the MP from St-Léonard–St-Michel, Quebec, by packing him off to Europe. The diplomatic appointment only fuelled Opposition criticism – Gagliano had been under fire for many reasons, including his involvement in the administration of the federal government's sponsorship programs and his alleged ties to unsavoury individuals. Most surprising was the sudden vanishing of Brian Tobin, a fairly recent cabinet recruit who resigned as the member of Parliament for Bonavista-Trinity-Conception, Newfoundland and Labrador on 14 January. For the record, Tobin left to spend more time with his family. Pundits doubted this explanation. They were convinced that Tobin's decision reflected disappointment over policy debates within cabinet (where he had served as industry minister since leaving the premiership of Newfoundland and Labrador in October 2000) and despair at the prospect of defeating Paul Martin for the leadership of the federal Liberals. More predictable was the 31 January resignation of Reform Party founder and one-time Leader of the Opposition Preston Manning. As he had previously announced that he would, the Calgary Southwest MP left public life to take up fellowships at two conservative think tanks, the Fraser Institute and the Canada West Foundation. Although his plans had been disclosed in March 2001, members of the House of Commons gave Manning a heartfelt send-off.

On 25 March Prime Minister Chrétien created two more vacancies in the Commons when he appointed a pair of Liberal MPs to the Senate. Summoned to the upper chamber were Raymond Lavigne, MP for Verdun–St-Henri–St-Paul–Pointe St-Charles, Quebec, and George Baker,

MP for Gander–Grand Falls, Newfoundland and Labrador. A member of Parliament for twenty-eight years, Baker had also served, for just over a year, as minister of veterans affairs (in 1999–2000). He was dropped from cabinet to make way for the return of Tobin – a move that, at the time, was reported to have been a blow to the morale of other long-tenure backbenchers with cabinet aspirations.

These seven vacancies were filled on a single day, amounting to a mini-election on 17 May. The outcome was disappointing to the Liberals, who managed to hold four of the six ridings they contested but lost two seats that had been in their fold for decades. The most predictable result was recorded in Calgary Southwest, where new Canadian Alliance leader Stephen Harper was safely installed against token opposition (among the major parties only the NDP fielded a candidate). Liberal, and former Newfoundland and Labrador provincial politician, John Efford was elected in Bonavista-Trinity-Conception; Massimo Pacetti won a seat for the Liberals in Gagliano's old bulwark of St-Léonard–St-Michel; Liza Frulla was elected in the perennial Liberal stronghold of Verdun–St-Henri–St-Paul–Pointe-St-Charles; and Liberal Raymond Simard was elected in Saint Boniface.

Neither of the Liberal setbacks was overwhelming, but both stung. In Windsor West, where Herb Gray had served for forty years, NDP candidate Brian Masse upended Richard Pollock. Masse was something of a star candidate in a region of southwestern Ontario that was often friendly to the NDP, but the Liberals had coveted an extension of their domain. In Newfoundland and Labrador, Tory candidate Rex Barnes eked out a win over a former acting premier, Beaton Tulk, in Gander–Grand Falls.

Two Bloc Québécois backbenchers resigned within days of one another to run for the Parti Québécois at the provincial level. Stephan Tremblay, member of Parliament for Lac-St-Jean–Saguenay, announced his departure on 7 May. Michel Bellehumerur, MP for Berthier-Montcalm, followed on 18 May. By-elections took place on for 9 December, and in both cases Bloc candidates held on to the seats. Roger Gaudet was victorious in Berthier-Montcalm, while Sebastien Gagnon reclaimed Lac-St Jean–Saguenay; Liberal candidates finished second in both of those races.

The final resignation of the year came on 11 October when John Richardson, Liberal incumbent from Perth-Middlesex, Ontario, announced that he would be stepping down as MP. Richardson had been absent for long stretches because of health problems. A by-election was planned for early 2003.

Exit Mr Martin

The tempestuous rivalry between Finance Minister Paul Martin and Prime Minister Jean Chrétien came to a stormy head in early June. On an ordinary Sunday afternoon the extraordinary saga ended with Martin's departure from cabinet. Although the prime minister tried to portray the exit as a mutual decision, Martin insisted that he was caught off-guard by the announcement. The two adversaries could not even agree on their estrangement.

The feud came to a head over Chrétien's insistence that cabinet ministers refrain from involvement in organizing or fundraising activities until he, the prime minister, stepped down, and a leadership race was officially under way. In the face of this ultimatum, Martin announced that he was giving serious thought to leaving cabinet. This was the final push. Chrétien notified his finance minister that he wanted him to sign a joint statement agreeing to his departure. Martin declined to do so.

Universally, the daily print media reproduced copies of the correspondence exchanged by the feuding pair. In a letter to Martin expressing 'sadness' over the split, Chrétien wrote that, 'you and I have worked extremely well together, ever since we took office in November 1993, on all matters relating to government policy. We have always been in full agreement on economic and fiscal policy. But, unfortunately, matters unrelated to governing have gotten in the way of our working together on government policy. As such, we both understand, with real regret, that it is in the best interest of the government and the country that you step down from the cabinet.' In the course of a lengthy reply, Martin said that 'for a long time the natural tensions between my views and those of the prime minister were well within the manageable, even healthy, range that is customary in a sound, working relationship. In fact, we were always able to resolve disagreements working issue by issue. Unfortunately in recent months, and certainly during the last few days, the working relationship between myself and the prime minister had deteriorated. It was therefore threatening to impede our focus on the very important choices that confront us as a nation.' Martin took the opportunity to confirm that he would stay on as an MP, and he beseeched financial markets to remain calm despite the changing of the guard.

Chrétien was the loser in all of this. A poll, conducted by EKOS for the *Toronto Star*, Canadian Broadcasting Corporation, and *La Presse*, showed that a healthy majority of those polled faulted the prime minister for the breach. Only 7 per cent accepted his version of the story, and

60 per cent of those surveyed thought that he should step down sooner rather than later (*Toronto Star*, 8 June). Even though the Liberals were far and away the preferred party in a hypothetical election, the seeds of change sown by Martin's advocates within the party had begun to take root in the larger population.

Exit Mr Chrétien?

After nearly forty years in the House of Commons, and an almost equally long history of holding senior appointments, Jean Chrétien announced on 21 August that he was finally prepared to retire. Chrétien went on, however, to say that he would leave no later than February 2004, a full eighteen months from the day of his announcement. No prime minister had ever tried to plot out such a protracted interregnum. If his internal rivals had their way, he would be gone long before those seventy-eight weeks had expired.

First elected to the House of Commons in April 1963, Jean Chrétien could look back on a career brimming with achievements made all the more noteworthy by virtue of having been accomplished by a 'little guy from Shawinigan.' It was not an unblemished record. Early on he had earned the trust of prime ministers Lester Pearson and Pierre Trudeau, but later, as finance minister and leadership aspirant, he tangled openly with Prime Minister John Turner and with Liberal Party factions that were more receptive to constitutional change than he was. Polls revealed that he was a much-respected prime minister in most parts of Canada, yet he was an often-reviled and even parodied figure in his home province of Quebec. His progressive rhetoric was not always redeemed in policy measures. Media commentaries, naturally, reflected this range of opinion. Chrétien's departure was seen as graceful and high-minded by some, and as combative and destructive by others.

Jean Chrétien did not fully reveal the calculations that had informed the timing of his decision, but pinpointing them was not particularly difficult. It was proving harder to keep his caucus in line, and the 2 June ouster of Finance Minister Paul Martin, his presumed successor, was poorly received within the party and across the country. A postponed but mandatory leadership review was scheduled for February 2003. According to most pundits, Chrétien would be humiliated by the result. If the review was cancelled – which it was – it would be easier to preserve his legacy. In his 21 August speech, the prime minister acknowledged that personal and partisan in-fighting had distracted the party and cabinet to the point where the capacity to govern was impaired. For these reasons, he had to go. For the same reasons, it seemed better for the party for him to withdraw sooner rather than later. With regard to the timetable, *Globe and Mail* columnist Jeffrey Simpson, analysing a nearly pathological desire to block Paul Martin, argued that Chrétien's overriding goal was to prevent an automatic transition. 'The Chrétien strategy,' wrote Simpson, 'has always been that the longer he occupied 24 Sussex Drive, the poorer Mr Martin's chances would be of occupying it. As long as the opposition parties, in their tragicomical ineptitude, posed no electoral threat, the prime minister could stay on and on so that Mr Martin would get that much older, and the party would be inclined to replace Mr Chrétien eventually with someone younger than the prime minister' (22 August).

On the positive side, eighteen months of relative peace could provide an opportunity for the prime minister to bring some long-standing initiatives to fruition. For example, it might prove possible for Chrétien to redeem his long and sincere interest in bettering the lives of Aboriginal peoples. Chrétien was also said to be keen to oversee real reform to the health care system and to enshrine new codes of conduct for cabinet ministers and members of Parliament. Opposition MPs were of a mind to think that the prime minister's final days would be ragged and unproductive, with the affairs of state ignored at the expense of Liberal Party machinations.

Serial cabinet shuffles

On 14 January Industry Minister Brian Tobin resigned. Insisting that he would never again return to public life, Tobin (who had returned to the House of Commons in 2000 after a stint as premier of Newfoundland) left behind his battered leadership hopes and a reputation diminished by thwarted initiatives. Meanwhile, Alfonso Gagliano, a close ally of the prime minister, had become embroiled in a withering controversy over the management of Canada's advertising and sponsorship programs. As the Opposition parties relentlessly probed the public works minister's relationships with Quebec-based firms contracted under the program, his continuation in cabinet became increasingly doubtful. Herb Gray, the deputy prime minister, resigned after nearly forty years the House of Commons, to take up an appointed post with the U.S.–Canada International Joint Commission as head of its Canadian sector.

Against this backdrop, on 15 January, Prime Minister Chrétien engineered the biggest cabinet shuffle since the Liberals came to power in 1993. Tobin, Gagliano, and Gray were heavyweights in the party.

Among the lesser known ministers dropped from cabinet were Manitoba's Ronald Duhamel, minister of veterans affairs; Hedy Fry, from British Columbia, who had been secretary of state for multiculturalism and women's affairs but was criticized for remarks that she had made about 'cross burnings' – which had not in fact accurred – in her province; Maria Minna, a Toronto-area MP who had served as secretary of state for international development until questions about ethics (including votes cast in a municipal election and contracts awarded to friends) tarnished her reputation; Gilbert Normand, the secretary of state for science and MP for the Quebec riding of Bellechasse-Etchemins-Montmagny-L'Islet; and James Peterson, another Toronto MP, dropped from the international financial institutions portfolio. Within this group only Duhamel executed a safe exit strategy: he was awarded an appointment to the Senate.

The cabinet, including second-tier ministers of state, expanded to a near-record total of thirty-nine members. Only Brian Mulroney's forty-member cabinet, which the Liberals of the day criticized for being bloated, was bigger. With more than 177 members from which to choose, the prime minister was in a position to promote ten Liberal backbenchers to the front ranks. Consequently, Chrétien's theme in introducing the revamped line-up was one of renewal.

The shuffle was also effected in the context of the race to succeed the prime minister. In the eyes of punters, the biggest winner was John Manley. His new role as deputy prime minister gave him a more prominent perch from which to challenge Finance Minister Paul Martin for the party's leadership. Manley was also asked to chair the cabinet's Security Committee and to work with the Americans, including newly installed Homeland Security Secretary Tom Ridge, on post-9/11 border issues. Also in his portfolio was responsibility for infrastructure and for Crown corporations. The management of federal Crown corporations had been condemned by both the auditor general and the ethics counsellor, and Manley had the delicate task of restoring confidence in the process by which senior officials were appointed and day-to-day affairs were carried out. If there was one drawback for Manley, it turned on the burden of hoisting such a heavy load in so many crucial and closely watched areas.

With Tobin out of the leadership race, Sheila Copps (who was left at Canadian Heritage) and Allan Rock, happily if laterally moved to industry from the daunting health portfolio, remained in cabinet. Both continued to harbour leadership aspirations, despite Martin's prodigious momentum and Manley's enhanced stature. In moving to health,

Full Ministries of Cabinet – Prior to Shuffle and as of 15 January 2002

Portfolio	Minister prior to Shuffle	Minister after Shuffle
Prime Minister	Jean Chrétien	Jean Chrétien
President of the Treasury Board	Lucienne Robillard	Lucienne Robillard
President of the Privy Council (Intergovernmental Affairs)	Stéphane Dion	Stéphane Dion
Finance	Paul Martin	Paul Martin
Deputy Prime Minister	Herb Gray (Resigned)	John Manley
Canadian Heritage	Sheila Copps	Sheila Copps
Government Leader in the Senate	Sharon Carstairs	Sharon Carstairs
Infrastructure / Crown Corporations	n/a	John Manley
Justice and Attorney General	Anne McLellan	Martin Cauchon
Health	Allan Rock	Anne McLellan
International Trade	Pierre Pettigrew	Pierre Pettigrew
Industry	Brian Tobin (Resigned)	Allan Rock
Agriculture and Agri-Food	Lyle Vanclief	Lyle Vanclief
Solicitor General	Lawrence MacAulay	Lawrence MacAulay
Immigration	Elinor Caplan	Denis Coderre
Human Resources Development	Jane Stewart	Jane Stewart
Natural Resources	Ralph Goodale	Herb Dhaliwal
National Revenue	Martin Cauchon	Elinor Caplan
Fisheries and Oceans	Herb Dhaliwal	Robert Thibault
Leader of the Government in the House	Don Boudria	Ralph Goodale
Public Works and Government Services	Alfonso Gagliano (Resigned)	Don Boudria
Labour	Claudette Bradshaw	Claudette Bradshaw
Transport	David Collenette	David Collenette
National Defence	Art Eggleton	Art Eggleton
Foreign Affairs	John Manley	Bill Graham
Indian Affairs and Northern Development	Robert Nault	Robert Nault
Western Economic Diversification	Brian Tobin (Resigned)	Allan Rock
Atlantic Canada Opportunities Agency	Brian Tobin (Resigned)	Allan Rock
Atlantic Regional Development	Robert Thibault	Gerry Byrne
Veterans Affairs	Ronald Duhamel (Resigned)	Rey Pagtakan
International Cooperation	Marina Minna (Demoted)	Susan Whelan

Ministries of State and Incumbents – Prior to Shuffle and as of 15 January 2002

Portfolio	Minister prior to Shuffle	Minister after Shuffle
Multiculturalism and Women	Hedy Fry (Demoted)	Claudette Bradshaw
Asia-Pacific	Rey Pagtakan	David Kilgour
Canadian Wheat Board	Ralph Goodale	Ralph Goodale
La Francophonie	Ronald Duhamel	Denis Paradis
Latin America and Africa	David Kilgour	Denis Paradis
Science, Research, and Development	Gilbert Normand	Maurizio Bevilaqua
Amateur Sport	Denis Coderre	Paul De Villiers
Central and Eastern Europe / Middle East	n/a	Gar Knutson
La Francophonie	Ronald Duhamel	Denis Paradis
International Financial Institutions	James Peterson (Demoted)	John McCallum
Economic Development Agency (Quebec)	n/a	Claude Drouin
Western Economic Diversification	Ronald Duhamel (Resigned)	Stephen Owen

Alberta's Anne McLellan, another rising star, had a mandate to work with the provinces on reforms to the national medicare system. Bill Graham of Toronto earned a swift promotion to foreign minister, and Saskatchewan's Ralph Goodale edged closer to the innermost circle with his elevation to house leader.

The shuffle was greeted with mixed reactions. Opposition parties were unmoved by the attempt to portray the changes as rejuvenating. They were also appalled by the parting gift handed to Gagliano. An editorial in the *Globe and Mail* captured the mood in Ottawa when it pointed to the relief felt in many quarters that the prime minister had 'finally accepted what most Canadians noticed long ago ... his cabinet was well overdue for a house cleaning' and ended the tempered view that 'perhaps a refreshed cabinet ... can help breathe a little life into a stale regime' (16 January).

The second shake-out came on 26 May. One minister, Art Eggleton, was dropped from cabinet altogether over allegations that he had authorized a $36,500 contract for an intimate friend, Maggie Maier, to prepare a brief report on stress and other health concerns of military personnel. The former defence minister had also been subjected to scrutiny by a parliamentary committee over charges that he had misled the House of Commons about the activities of Canadian Forces operating in Afghanistan. He tried to hang on to the bitter end with the support of

Prime Minster Chrétien, but when Ethics Counsellor Howard Wilson concluded that cabinet guidelines had been violated, his fate was sealed. Don Boudria fared rather better than Eggleton in the shuffle. He, too, had come in for criticism from the Opposition after accepting the hospitality of an individual caught up in the spreading sponsorship scandal (see below). His stint at the public works ministry was terminated, but Boudria was allowed to return to the post of government house leader despite the fact that Chrétien insisted that this was the first instance of a change resulting from a genuine conflict of interest by one of his ministers. Into the maelstrom surrounding public works stepped Ralph Goodale. Over at the Department of National Defence, John McCallum was summoned from the ranks of minister of state to head another troubled department. Maurizio Bevilaqua was promoted to minister of state for international financial institutions, while Jean Augustine was recruited from the backbenches to take over responsibility from Claudette Bradshaw, as a minister of state for multiculturalism and the status of women.

John Manley was relieved of parts of his overly taxing duties on 3 August. Industry Minister Allan Rock took over responsibility for the government's $2.6 billion infrastructure programs (including $600 million set aside for Canada–U.S. border controls). Rock was also named chair of the cabinet's Social Policy Committee. Transport Minister David Collenette inherited responsibility for five Crown corporations, while Public Works Minister Ralph Goodale was given the job of acting as the chief negotiator in the government's dispute with Aboriginal peoples and churches over compensation for victims of abuse in residential schools. The moves seemed innocuous enough on the surface. Canadian Alliance house leader John Reynolds, however, situated them in the context of the ongoing Liberal leadership race when he complained that Rock and Collenette, both Chrétien loyalists, would be able to use their positions to help cultivate support for the prime minister (*Toronto Star*, 8 August).

The final change in cabinet occurred on 23 October when Solicitor General Lawrence MacAulay was forced to resign after a disapproving report from Ethics Counsellor Howard Wilson. The contretemps over MacAulay's deportment began with multiple accusations that he had improperly helped family and friends. Although Wilson cleared him of more recent allegations, in looking back to 1999 he had discovered that MacAulay had violated ethical stipulations when he steered business towards Holland College. The ethics counsellor concluded that contracts for the training of corrections officers at the college were inappropriate, given that the school was headed by MacAulay's brother. Insisting on his innocence, MacAulay penned a resignation letter that warned of lawsuits against Canadian Alliance leader Stephen Harper, Progressive Conservative Peter Mackay, and the *Globe and Mail* for their role in besmirching his reputation. His replacement as solicitor general was fellow Prince Edward Island MP Wayne Easter.

Government sponsorship scandal

In 1995 the people of Quebec narrowly rejected a referendum initiative to negotiate the province's sovereignty. The uncomfortably slim margin of victory for the federalist side set in motion a train of events leading to a reference to the Supreme Court of Canada on the constitutional framework for sovereignty negotiations and legislation, approved in 2000, setting out the ground rules for the conduct of such referenda. The federal government also took another tack in the struggle. Part of this involved directing funds to various programs intended to enhance the federal presence in Quebec. This gave birth to an ostensibly nationwide program of advertising and promoting cultural and sporting events that was aimed, disproportionately, at Quebec.

In the year 2000 Public Works Minister Alfonso Gagliano came under fire over the awarding of sponsorship contracts to a company, called Groupaction, that subcontracted business to another firm employing the minister's son. Gagliano was cleared by Ethics Counsellor Howard Wilson, on 23 May 2001, in connection with this relationship, but the case resulted in heightened awareness of the overall program and its operations. Groupaction was one of a number of marketing and public relations firms doing business with the federal government that had made significant contributions to the Liberal Party of Canada. On its own, the company had donated some $70,000 to the party over a five-year period. Gagliano became the distracting centre of a swirling storm – and a growing liability to the government despite this temporary reprieve.

Gagliano was finally dropped from cabinet in the shuffle announced on 15 January. He was rewarded for his loyalty to Chrétien with the ambassadorship to Denmark, but his removal from the scene did little to stifle criticism. Gagliano's successor, former Liberal house leader Don Boudria, was forced to admit that his ministry was unable to locate a Groupaction report worth $650,000 that should have been delivered in February 1999. The report did turn up on 19 March 2002; however, it was virtually identical to another document, priced at $575,000, that was submitted in October 1999. Boudria cast blame on his predecessor for the mess. With the Opposition in full throat, Boudria asked Canada's Auditor General Sheila Fraser to look into the Groupaction contracts and granted her a range of options – from recommending internal remedies to calling in the Royal Canadian Mounted Police.

The auditor general's report was released to much fanfare on 8 May. The news media had predicted that the findings would be harsh, and they were not wrong. The audit concluded that the federal government had violated 'just about every rule in the book' in its handling of the $40 million annual program and that it had strayed into a 'completely unacceptable way for government to do business' (*Toronto Star*, 9 May). A close examination of the paper trails for three particular contracts with Groupaction for reports on sponsorship initiatives (valued at $500,000, $550,000, and $575,000) revealed the following details:

- The need for the reports themselves was unclear, and it was especially difficult to fathom why the third report was required, since it was virtually identical to the first two.
- Tthe government did not receive all that it had contracted for, and key elements were never delivered.
- After extensive searching, no one was able to find the second report.
- Payments were made for verbal advice for which there was no tendering process and no contractual stipulations.
- Officials had violated parliamentary legislation and explicit guidelines for the verification of work.

It was a scathing indictment. But who was to blame? Had bureaucrats lapsed into habitual laxity? Was there a culture of favouritism in the Department of Public Works and Government Services? Or, as opposition critics implied, did all this denote rampant patronage? Conclusive answers were in short supply. The auditor general did what she felt was required in the face of these troubling riddles: she rang the RCMP and recommended an investigation. This move was endorsed from afar by Prime Minister Chrétien, who, while visiting Spain on government business, asserted that the Mounties could be counted on to do a thorough and impartial job. The Opposition disagreed. In calling for an independent inquiry, members of the other political parties cited the need to discern whether the patterns detected by the auditor general could be traced to isolated acts or to systematic, politically directed abuses. Members of Parliament also expressed fears that a police probe would allow the government to evade difficult questions (as Tonia Mac-

Charles wrote in the *Toronto Star* on 9 May). To complicate matters, the RCMP had been the recipient of $1.5 million under the sponsorship program.

Meanwhile Boudria himself came under fire when it was revealed that he had been treated to a weekend ski holiday at the home of Claude Boulay, a senior executive with the firm of Groupe Everest, another company doing significant business with the federal government that had run afoul of investigators. Boudria's excuses were brushed aside by the Opposition, especially when it was learned that an $800 cheque for the excursion had mysteriously gone uncashed. Under the circumstances it was no surprise that Boudria was sent packing to his former job of house leader (where he professed himself happy to be home) in a 26 May cabinet shuffle that also claimed Defence Minister Art Eggleton. Ralph Goodale was asked to take over the public works portfolio and inherit the mess. In one of his first acts the new minister revealed that the RCMP had taken possession of department files relating to the sponsorship program. This came after an internal audit of 721 files (later praised by Sheila Fraser as one of the most intensive audits ever conducted by the federal government).

During the early summer the House of Commons Public Accounts Committee took evidence from senior bureaucrats as it surveyed the dimensions of the scandal. The spotlight fell on two civil servants involved in the program, Chuck Guité and Pierre Tremblay. Guité, since retired, was the program's chief administrative officer at its inception. Tremblay, a one-time chief of staff in Gagliano's office, who had moved to the Canadian Food Inspection Agency, succeeded Guité. They were among a group of five individuals called before the committee. Although the hearings were held in camera, Tory MP Peter Mackay openly called Tremblay's testimony 'unprofessional, unbelievable, illegal.' Catching himself, he added, 'Well, we'll leave that [allegations of indictable conduct] to the RCMP' (*Globe and Mail*, 10 July). Members of the committee were also unimpressed by Guité. He refused to answer questions about the involvement of politicians but justified bending rules because of a war against 'separatists.' Mackay's blunt assessment was that the witness was 'unrepentant, evasive and completely defiant' (*Ottawa Citizen*, 10 July).

When it reconvened in the autumn, the committee's hearings were overshadowed by other investigations. For example, it was revealed, on 3 December, that the government had conducted a second audit of the program. According to Public Works Minister Ralph Goodale the second review merely confirmed the findings of the first, and he could not release the results, even under a formal access-to-information request, because of ongoing police probes (Groupaction's offices had been raided on 17 September as part of the ongoing investigation). The chair of the committee, Canadian Alliance MP John Williams, complained that Parliament appeared to be taking a back seat to the RCMP in the matter and that the government was stonewalling (*Ottawa Citizen*, 4 December).

This was clearly not the sort of legacy that Jean Chrétien wanted to leave behind. Whenever he was challenged, the prime minister insisted that the sponsorship program was always worth every penny if it contributed to Canadian unity. With the outcome of RCMP and parliamentary proceedings still pending, it was not clear what price the prime minister and his government would ultimately pay.

Ethics, free votes, and secret ballots

Internecine strife within the Liberal Party had many repercussions. In a major address on the topic of Canada's democracy deficit, delivered at York University's Osgoode Hall Law School, on 21 October, Paul Martin advocated for greater independence and more substantial input from ordinary members of Parliament. Even he could not guess at how quickly his ideas would translate into action. Sensing an opportunity, the Canadian Alliance put forward a motion, on 5 November, to have committee chairs elected by secret ballot. Chrétien and his supporters argued against the measure, citing principles such as the need to ensure regional and gender equity through a process of appointment. This was followed by protracted exertions by Chrétien and his top officials to find a compromise that would maintain caucus unity on the question. These efforts failed. When the measure came to a vote, fifty-six Liberals joined the opposition to secure an impressive majority in favour of secret selection. In the event, Paul Martin was the first Liberal to rise in the tally of supporters. Cabinet opposed the measure en masse (with the exception of Stephen Owen, who abstained). Liberal rebels denied that their actions represented a slight to the prime minister, and Chrétien downplayed the result. But both contingents of the Liberal caucus were cognizant of the possible consequences for the prime minister's longevity and his government's manoeuvrability. Syndicated columnist Chantal Hébert wrote that the 'unprecedented prime ministerial loss of face had been a decade in the making,' given Chrétien's tendency to allow his 'personal political needs ... to take precedence over those of the government.' As a result, the end of Chrétien's tenure could be marked by further humiliations in the face of pent-up frustration, and his only salvation might be that backbenchers were not 'politically suicidal enough to precipitate a snap election' (*Toronto Star*, 6 November). The party's leadership took no chances on another Opposition motion brought forward the same day, 5 November, condemning government military policy, aimed at testing the wedge. The issue was declared to be one of confidence in the government, meaning that passage could have led to an election. Liberal backbenchers fell in line on this occasion, but it appeared to be a mere skirmish in a battle of wills and wits.

The Senate

The Chrétien government made a total of seven appointments to the upper chamber of Parliament during the year. Once again, all of the new senators joined as members of the Liberal caucus. The new crop of appointees included four former MPs: Manitoba's Ron Duhamel, who was summoned on 15 January; George Baker, a long-time Newfoundland and Labrador MP, who was called on 26 March; Raymond Lavigne of Quebec, who was named in tandem with Baker; and lawyer, past MP, and party strategist David Smith of Ontario, named on 25 June.

Duhamel died suddenly on 30 September and was succeeded, on 12 December, by Maria Chaput, a prominent Manitoba businesswoman. Also named on 12 December was a Greek-born educator and businesswoman, Pana Merchant from Saskatchewan. The Chrétien government summoned Pierrette Ringuette, a former university professor, to fill a vacancy from Quebec.

Supreme Court

Madame Justice Claire L'Heureux-Dubé, who had served on the Supreme Court since 1987, retired on 1 July. Her replacement was another Quebec judge, Marie Deschamps. Justice Deschamps was appointed to the country's highest court from the Quebec Court of Appeal, where she had served for nearly a decade and had applied her expertise in the field of commercial law. The appointment was made by the government on 7 August.

Auditor General

Auditor General Sheila Fraser had an especially busy year in 2002, issuing a series of reports and adopting new approaches to her work. Major reports were submitted to the House of Commons in April, October, and December, and the findings of a special investigation into the government's sponsorship programs was released in May.

The 16 April report was highly critical of the way in which the Treasury Board had exercised the government's discretionary spending authority. Although this was supposed to cover small payouts, it had been invoked to cover relatively large expenditures, such as the tens of millions of dollars granted to airlines suffering revenue jolts following the events of 11 September 2001. The report restated concerns about the government's control over the billions of dollars that it had invested in various foundations for research and culture. It also described an emerging problem for the military associated with the inability to recruit and retain the kinds of specialists needed for engineering projects, advanced research, and the delivery of health care.

On 8 October Fraser followed up on previous recommendations in taking a selective look at high-cost, high-risk programs. The report focused on the integrity of the social insurance number, the national health surveillance system, federal support of health care delivery, management of a NATO flight training program in Canada, and the Small Business Financing Program.

The auditor general's main report was released on 3 December. The most notorious revelation revolved around a critique of the federal gun registry (or Canada Firearms Program). The justice department was roundly condemned for having permitted enormous cost overruns in setting up the computerized registry of gun owners and then hiding this fact from Parliament. When it was approved in 1995 (against the vehement opposition of conservatives), the program was expected to cost about $117 million, with all but $2 million recouped from remittances. The auditor general reported that escalating costs had driven the estimate to over $1 billion by the time of its full implementation in 2004–5. Parliament had not been given the information needed for revised costings and had not been provided with anything like a compelling rationale for the changes made over time. The government had significantly reduced its estimates of both the number of gun owners in Canada, and the number of firearms that they held. Although fees had been adjusted upwards in compensation, the government was unable to cover the mounting costs associated with tweaking technology that was inappropriate, archaic, and unadaptable. Moreover, the police could not verify the accuracy of the millions of records sent to the database, and entries were sometimes wildly erroneous. At the end of the day, said the auditor general, the issue was not the policy itself or the mismanagement of the project but rather the 'inexcusable' fact that Parliament was kept in the dark.

Other major findings of the report, as summarized in the 4 December edition of the *Ottawa Citizen*, were as follows:

- First Nations were submitting so many reports to the government that they were diverted from attending to important matters, and the information exchanged was of little benefit to either party.
- The government badly needed better strategic planning for the purchase and leasing of land and facilities for its many and growing departmental tenants, especially in the Ottawa capital region.
- Canada's planned contribution of nearly $1.4 billion towards the international space station could be squandered because of financial problems encountered by partners of the Canada Space Agency and technological hurdles, and the agency itself appeared to be overextended and had not developed a realistic plan to invest its limited resources.
- Government revenues had been depleted by nearly $1 billion thanks to a porous tax system that allowed multinational corporations operating in Canada to attribute earnings to offshore subsidiaries.
- The Customs and Revenue Agency needed the kind of additional support necessary to ensure that Canadian residents and businesses were properly taxed on foreign transactions.
- Although Canada's coastal lighthouses were fully automated, it was costing millions of dollars to maintain staff above minimum requirements on the grounds of nostalgic 'heritage objectives.'
- The Canadian Coast Guard needed to better ensure that national standards were set and maintained across its five regions.

In general, Fraser was not satisfied with the progress made to improve financial management (a lament that echoed her predecessors). She also shared the oft-stated concerns of other auditors general over the government's bulging surplus of Employment Insurance premiums. The EI surplus had been used inappropriately to reduce government deficits, and the impact of higher rates on individuals, employers, and the economy had not been properly analysed. Fraser drew raves, once again, for the substance of her reports and for the style in which they were presented. Writing in the *Ottawa Citizen*, Susan Riley praised her 'cool, lucid and fact-based approach' to sensitive issues (4 December).

A question of ethics

One of the themes resounding on Parliament Hill throughout the year 2002 was ethics. The issue was fuelled by concerns about the conduct of cabinet ministers (four were demoted or expelled from cabinet altogether in 2002 for various transgressions), as well as controversies surrounding the financing of Liberal leadership campaigns. All of this was a reminder that the Liberals owed their ascent to power in 1993, at least in part, to voters' distaste for the lapses of the Progressive Conservative government led by Brian Mulroney and on a promise to restore ethics to politics. The events of the year forced Chrétien's hand, and he eventually unveiled a package of reforms in the autumn.

The first batch of recommendations was announced on 23 June. In an eight-point plan, the government proposed to institute changes such as greater independence for the ethics counsellor, who, henceforth, would only be appointed after consultation with Opposition parties and could only be removed with the consent of the House of Commons and the Senate. The ethics counsellor would also file an annual report to Parliament. Even so, the incumbent would report to the prime minister (an organizational model that rankled the Opposition parties). A wider mandate meant that the ethics counsellor could investigate any complaint brought by a parliamentarian rather than focus solely on referrals from the prime minister. The ensemble of changes also included a new handbook for cabinet ministers on their legal and ethical responsibilities, new rules governing the relationship between cabinet ministers and Crown corporations, and a set of strictures placed on the personal political activities (especially fundraising for leadership campaigns) of cabinet ministers.

The issue returned in the autumn when, on 23 October, House Leader Don Boudria presented draft legislation and a new bill to the House of Commons. The revisions clarified the role of the ethics counsellor and the length of his or her term (five years). The code of conduct would be extended to members of the Senate but not to the spouses of MPs and senators. Boudria introduced amendments to the Lobbyists' Registration Act, in Bill C-15. The primary objective of the legislation was to make this sort of activity more transparent. If approved, the bill would redefine and expand the definition of lobbying. It would also make it easier to prosecute those who failed to declare their roles (paid and unpaid) on behalf of clients seeking a benefit from government. For the moment, the government sidestepped two rather more contestable initiatives: one to limit campaign contributions by individuals and corporations, and the other to put ceilings on donations and establish clear disclosure rules for those contesting the leadership of political parties.

Canada, Afghanistan, and Iraq

The Afghanistan mission

Canada was quick to endorse the U.S.-led initiative to topple the Taliban regime of Afghanistan and hunt down the leadership of Al-Qaeda. Working out the precise nature of Canada's involvement took far more time. With limited resources at its disposal, and a growing tradition of peacekeeping rather than offensive engagement at stake, the Canadian military was finally assigned the role of following into Afghanistan after the main offensive.

On 16 January advance teams arrived in the city of Kandahar. Their task was to pave the way for a long-term presence in the city and its environs, with a mandate that ranged from seeking out belligerents to assisting with nation-building. Canadian Forces contingents were self-contained in most respects but ultimately reported to the U.S. Army's 101st Airborne Division in the area. By early February approximately 750 Canadian soldiers, all of them ground troops, had established their presence in Kandahar. The deployment was essentially complete by March.

Canada's involvement in Afghanistan took some unusual twists as it unfolded. On 28 January Prime Minister Jean Chrétien dismissed as 'purely hypothetical' a question directed to him about how Canadian soldiers would deal with any detainees. Would detainees be turned over to Americans, for example, and routed to prison camps such as the facility in Guantanamo Bay, Cuba, where normal legal rights had been suspended? As it turned out, the question was not purely speculative. Six days before the prime minister's retort, that is, on 22 January, the *Globe and Mail* ran a photograph on its front page of a suspect being whisked away from an aircraft by unidentified captors. The troops wore oddly camouflaged uniforms, but in other respects the picture was unremarkable. Three days later Defence Minister Art Eggleton was informed that the custodians in the photograph were Canadians. Indeed, the minister had been briefed on 21 January about the Canadian military's capturing prisoners in Afghanistan and transferring custody to U.S. authorities. Yet he shared this news with cabinet only on 29 January. It was not until then that the government confirmed that the military's Joint Task Force 2 had been operating in Afghanistan since late 2001, and that members of the unit had been featured in the now-infamous photograph.

Eggleton was buffeted by questions in the House of Commons. Why had the government not revealed the extent of Canada's involvement? Why had he been so slow to inform his prime minister and cabinet colleagues of the true import of the newspaper photograph? Why was the prime minister allowed to mislead Canadians? Could the government guarantee that anyone turned over to the Americans would have access to appropriate legal protections? These questions buffaloed Eggleton. Speaker Peter Milliken ruled that conflicting versions of the events had come up in debate, and on 30 January the matter was turned over to the Standing Committee on Procedures and House Affairs. On 7 February the committee (at least the majority composed of Liberal MPs) concluded that the minister had definitely erred, but had not intended to obfuscate. Since he had not misled the House of Commons, Eggleton was not in contempt.

'Friendly fire' or fratricide? Death at dawn

On 17 April Canadian troops were conducting night exercises outside of Kandahar. In the dark skies above two U.S. aircraft, piloted by Major Harry Schmidt and Major William Umbach, on assignment from an Illinois Air National Guard unit, were nearing the end of a routine patrol. From on high the Americans sighted traces of gunfire. The pilots were advised by flight controllers that the activity was attributable to 'friendlies.' For some reason – confusion, adrenalin, fatigue, or bravado – the fighters turned to strike. A few moments later, four Canadian soldiers lay dying and eight others were injured as a result of bursts of lethal air-to-ground munitions. The incident received scant attention in the United States. In Canada, these few transformative moments led to grief among the loved ones of the dead and injured, and to anguished national introspection.

The first order of business was to determine the cause of the 'friendly fire' attack. At the end of two month-long parallel inquiries, Canadian and U.S. investigators released their findings on 28 June. The Canadian report used the stronger term 'fratricide' to describe the tragedy. Canadian troops were absolved of any blame for what transpired on 17 April. Sole responsibility was assigned to the U.S. pilots. The U.S. report faulted the pilots for deviating from rules of engagement and firing protocols, but it was also critical of a fatal breakdown in communications, starting with a failure to properly inform surveillance authorities of the exercise under way early that morning. The U.S. report recommended disciplinary hearings for the individuals involved in the incident, along with remedies for the communications shortcomings that it documented. Canadian military leaders stressed the need to improve coordination the field, but some, notably General Raymond Henault, noted that cooperation on the inquiries had strengthened Canadian – U.S. relations despite the avoidable loss of life.

The families of the Canadian victims were among those who pressed for the U.S. authorities to prosecute the pilots. An indictment was brought down against the two on 13 September. Major Schmidt was charged with four counts of involuntary manslaughter and eight of assault. Major Umbach faced the same number of indictments for aiding and abetting in manslaughter and assault. Both would be subject to a wide range of penalties if convicted and, many Canadians hoped, to an appropriate degree of justice.

Canada and the coalition against Iraq

Capitalizing on widespread solidarity following the events of 11 September 2001, the U.S. government encountered little difficulty in building an international force to invade Afghanistan or, equally importantly, silencing those who might otherwise protest U.S. interventionism. After offering predictably tame resistance against a mighty onslaught, the Taliban were ousted from power – or at least pushed out of the Afghan capital of Kabul into remote redoubts. Many of the leaders of Al-Qaeda and the Taliban had escaped the net or had met uncertain fates. Even so, the Americans began turning towards the Baathist government in Iraq, one of the three 'axis of evil' countries that President George W. Bush warned of in a speech made not long after 9/11. The Americans argued that the Iraqis, who were supposed to be actively developing so-called weapons of mass destruction in defiance of international sanctions and detection programs, represented another major outpost of global terrorism. To many, Washington's bellicose stance towards Iraq made little sense in the context of the fight against terror. The secularist Baathists appeared to have little in common with Al-Qaeda, and the government of Saddam Hussein, while undoubtedly repressive and defiant, posed little threat after years of crippling economic sanctions and inspections by UN teams looking for evidence of nuclear and chemical weapons. If it came to a military action against Baghdad, it was more likely to be motivated by simple revenge or thirst for oil rather than any real fear that Saddam Hussein's regime was part of an international terrorist network.

It was against this backdrop that Canada was forced to choose whether to participate in a possible military action against Iraq. As the year 2002 wound down the Americans sought to tighten the vice around Iraq in the court of world opinion by pointing to evidence of weapons violations. Although some countries supported Washington, and shared the view that the world would be safer without Saddam Hussein, others chipped away at the logic of invading Iraq.

Citizen opinion divided over whether to participate in an invasion of Iraq, but tended against military intervention without a UN mandate. As a consequence, Ottawa was non-committal. On 5 September Prime Minister Chrétien confessed that he had his 'reservations' about Canadian involvement in a confrontation with Iraq. Mindful of gaps in evidence about weapons of mass destruction, the prime minister held out for a more compelling dossier. He also warned Washington (and its increasingly reliable British partner) that it should try to forge a coalition under the auspices of the United Nations. Meeting with President Bush in Detroit on 9 September to review the implementation of a joint 'smart border' action plan, Chrétien reiterated the need to convince the United Nations and the world before Canada would sign on. The House of Commons was also divided. New Democrats and members of the Bloc Québécois remained steadfastly against an invasion of Iraq. The Canadian Alliance argued that Canada should do all that it could to help the Americans.

In a symbolic sidebar story, one of the casualties of the debate was the prime minister's director of communications, Françoise Ducros. On 21 November, at a North Atlantic Treaty Organization meeting in Prague, President Bush read a speech in which he argued that NATO allies should ramp up their military spending. At a reception later that day Ducros expressed her opinion that the U.S. president was a moron, in an offhand remark that was overheard by the press and almost immediately splashed across the media. The prime minister's reaction was mixed. On the one hand, he insisted that President Bush was not a moron but a friend; on the other, he stood by his press secretary and refused to accept her resignation. Finally, on 26 November, Ducros insisted on leaving and the prime minister relented. The incident, although trivial and overblown, underscored just how serious relations between Canada and the United States had grown.

National parties

The Liberals and the on-again race to succeed Jean Chrétien

With the expulsion of Paul Martin from cabinet and the pending 'retirement' of Jean Chrétien, the Liberal Party entered into a new phase in its transition. Up until these events Chrétien had tried unsuccessfully to reign in his cabinet colleagues, who were obviously campaigning for a job – his job – that was not yet vacant. He scolded when they squabbled, he admonished when they strayed, and in the spring, he tried a dose of discipline that led to Martin's departure. At last, on 22 October, Chrétien gave the go-ahead for cabinet ministers to resume the fundraising activities that he had suspended. He was confident that it would be possible for ministers to discharge their responsibilities while campaigning. If not, they would be excused. Martin, of course, was free to campaign openly once he was out of cabinet. Party rules on spending limits and donor disclosures had still not been finalized, even though money raised by prospective candidates had almost certainly reached the multimillion-dollar level. With a convention unlikely until late in 2003, the fundraising frenzy was bound to continue.

Canadian Alliance

The priorities for the Canadian Alliance (the new name for the rebranded Reform Party, coined in 2001) were to hold a successful leadership convention and begin the process of healing a deeply fractured party. Stockwell Day's leadership had proven to be disappointing, then embarassing, and finally disastrous. A number of party stalwarts had fled into the arms of the Progressive Conservatives in reaction to a spate of gaffes by Day. The whipsawed leader was forced into an unscheduled leadership campaign. The last time he ran for the senior post in the Alliance, Day was a fresh face. At the leadership convention of 2002, Day was a scarred and vulnerable supplicant.

Stockwell Day was supremely confident that Canadians were in his corner, despite, or perhaps because of, all of his travails. He had good reason to believe that Alliance members, at least, would affirm his leadership. He enjoyed support among many core party constituencies (notably Christian fundamentalists) and the endorsement of many members of Parliament. However, two caucus mates had entered the leadership race, and each was capable of siphoning off some support. This could work to the advantage of an already formidable candidate, former MP Stephen Harper. When the Reform Party was born, Harper, then a young graduate student, was at the side of party founder Preston Manning. After serving in Parliament in the heady days of Reform, Harper joined the National Citizens Coalition, a right-wing advocacy group, in 1997, after a falling out with Manning. In other respects Harper's libertarian streak kept him at odds with party faithful who were social conservatives, and his diffidence towards populist touches such as referenda and recall, so cherished by Day, went against the ideological grain of the Reform charter. Harper was authentically fluent in French and calmly cerebral, in contrast to Day.

The other two aspirants in the field of four were Diane Ablonczy and Grant Hill, two MPs in the all-Albertan slate of candidates. In the end no one had the traction to halt the ascent of Harper. The first ballot gave him the support of fully 55 per cent of the 88,000 members who voted, a surprising and crushing margin. Day finished in second place, with 37.5 per cent of the votes cast. Ablonczy edged Hill for third place, but they each garnered less than 4 per cent of the votes.

The jubilation of the crowning moment was restrained by the realization that the party faced an uphill struggle. The hard fall taken by Day left his supporters downhearted. Convention goers were aware that Harper had some personal liabilities. He had once famously advised Alberta premier Ralph Klein to 'build a firewall' around his prosperous province against intrusions such as the Canada Pension Plan, the RCMP, and medicare. In a post-convention editorial, the *Globe and Mail* argued that, in switching from Day to Harper, the party had merely traded old problems for new ones, the new leader's ideological purity could make it difficult to make the kinds of accommodations necessary to broaden the Alliance's appeal, and he was seen to be a 'principled man who seems prepared to let the Alliance become the NDP of the right – influential, without a hope of rising to power nationally – rather than bend to circumstance' (21 March). In the *National Post*, columnist Robert Fulford, commenting on a desultory convention that resulted in a tepid endorsement, said of Stephen Harper that he was 'certainly a man who can be relied upon (as Day could not) to put policy ahead of temporary advantage' but observed that 'there are times when listening to him or reading one of his bloodless speeches, when one wonders whether he should be in politics at all' (21 March).

Harper wanted to claim a seat in the House of Commons as soon as possible in order to assume the role of Leader of the Opposition, reveal himself to the public, and begin the task of restoring the party's credibility. There, in the vacant riding of Calgary Southwest, lay the obvious solution. One of the party's brain trust, Ezra Levant, had professed himself ready to abandon his own candidacy in favour of the new leader. However, Levant had succeeded so well in capturing the constituency association and had invested so much money in the process that he grew reluctant to step aside. After a brief stand-off, Levant withdrew. Harper had to confront other problems as the year unfolded. During a House of Commons debate over the government's ethics proposals, the new leader made a lame joke at the expense of NDP member Svend Robinson. Robinson, openly gay, took the remark as an innuendo about his sexuality and called it 'probably a pretty thinly veiled homophobic attack' by a 'scumbag' (*Toronto Star*, 23 October). Harper was forced to apologize, causing the *Ottawa Citizen*'s Susan Riley to observe that his behaviour had 'raised old doubts about the Alliance leader's character and appeal,' given his 'almost rabid partisanship' and unforgiving nature (24 October). The furore also blunted the Alliance's advantage over the Liberals on the question of ethics and handed the Tories yet another reason for keeping their distance from a merger with a non-inclusive group.

All was not grim for Harper. The vanquishment of Day, who was rewarded with the plum caucus job of foreign affairs critic and assigned a front-row seat in the House of Commons, made it possible for party dissidents to return to the fold. Most of the seven holdout members (six returned to the fold between September and November 2001), who had either bolted from caucus or been expelled, were readmitted on 10 April. The five who rejoined in April were members of the Democratic Representative Caucus, an arrangement entered into with the Progressive Conservatives. One MP, Manitoba's Inky Mark, preferred to remain outside of the Canadian Alliance and eventually signed on with the Tories. The application of another, Saskatchewan MP Jim Pankiw, was denied. Panikiw was thus exiled to the lonely ranks of independents.

New Democrats

Alexa McDonough announced her decision to step down as leader of the New Democratic Party of Canada on 5 June. McDonough planned to stay on as a member of Parliament and signalled her intention to run in the next election. It had been a rocky reign for the MP from Halifax and former leader of the Nova Scotia wing of the NDP. Her conviction that the party should move closer to the centre – or, put another way, bring the social democrat message to proprietors of small businesses and other neglected constituencies – was deemed heretical by major union leaders and leftist colleagues in caucus. Like other leaders of the NDP, McDonough departed with her reputation for intelligence and integrity intact, but without a breakthrough in hand. In electoral terms, the NDP had spun its wheels under her watch, and militants were still divided on the question of whether or not to take a more moderate, McDonough-like approach.

Into the leadership void rushed a crowd of candidates. The first to enter the field was Manitoba MP Bill Blakie, the party's house leader. He was embraced by the mainstream progressive wing of the party. An ordained minister and experienced member of Parliament, Blakie enjoyed the support of a number of prominent members of the party, including Manitoba Premier Gary Doer. Among other contenders was Saskatchewan's Lorne Nystrom; an MP since the age of twenty-two, he had vied for the party's leadership on two previous occasions. The third caucus member to contest the NDP leadership was Joe Cromartin, MP for Windsor–St Clair. As a former attorney for the Canadian Auto Workers, Cromartin had a strong base in the Ontario labour movement. Three 'outsiders' also entered the fray. Pierre Ducasse, the youngest candidate, was the party's associate president; he also had the cachet of hailing from Quebec, where the party had been unable to lure social democrats away from the Bloc Québécois. The only woman in the race was Vancouver activist Bev Meslo, a member of the party's socialist wing. The challenger with the most intriguing resume was Toronto city councillor Jack Layton. Although he had failed in past attempts to capture a parliamentary seat, Layton was tipped as a probable front-runner, given his prominence in southern Ontario and his past presidency of the Federation of Canadian Municipalities.

Bloc Québécois

While other political parties wrestled with leadership questions, the Bloc Québécois stood fast behind Gilles Duceppe. This stoicism was understandable. The Bloc successfully defended two by-elections and managed to avoid major missteps. The party was generally ignored by the mainstream English-language and Aboriginal-language media outside of Quebec, but it earned grudging kudos for its principled stands against an invasion of Iraq and in favour of the Kyoto Protocol. While the other political parties dealt with devilish leadership issues, Duceppe carried on without interruption. Some of those who favoured sovereignty for Quebec were impatient with the Bloc's approach, but Duceppe and his colleagues seldom wavered from the view that Quebec's interests were paramount no matter the issue.

Progressive Conservatives

For the Tories, the year was marked by ongoing tribulations. Optimistic members talked of opportunities, but it was hard to find a silver lining in the dark clouds hanging over the Progressive Conservative Party of Canada. Plagued by debts and languishing in the polls, the party remained in the shadow of the Canadian Alliance on the right. The goal of uniting the right had not been completely taken off the shelf, but the Tories were clearly a junior partner in any plausible scenario. When Stephen Harper was confirmed as leader, the core band of former Alliance members who had worked with the Tories in the Democratic Representative Caucus was enticed back. This left the Progressive Conservatives perilously close to losing official party status. It also ended an experiment aimed at demonstrating that the right could develop common positions without merging.

Shortly after Harper took the helm of the Alliance, he and Joe Clark reviewed together the status of their on-again, off-again dalliance. On 10 April the two leaders held a ninety-minute discussion to explore options. Clark presented a three-pronged strategy calling for greater cooperation in Parliament, joint policy development, and strategic electoral preparations (such as agreements to run a single candidate in certain ridings). All of this fell short of a merger, of course. Harper was unmoved. Sensing some vulnerability on the part of the Tories and coming off a personal triumph, Harper rejected Clark's proposals. Instead, he suggested that it was time to move quickly and decisively towards a much more coherent arrangement, one that he would be willing to present to his caucus in a matter of days. Clark demurred for the obvious reason that a speedy union would have been tantamount to being absorbed into the larger, more vibrant Alliance. The talks fell apart.

It seemed that Clark was willing to stay on as leader of the Progressive Conservatives, or so he said on 15 April. This left the bigger question of whether his leadership was tenable. He was as aware as the pollsters were that he was trusted and respected. He also knew that his capacity to attract votes was limited. After months of reflection, the former prime minister announced his decision to quit politics on 6 August. He planned to leave the leadership post following a 2003 convention to choose his successor. Because of his stature, other politicians were generous in their praise of someone who had led his party twice (from 1976 to 1983, when he was ousted by Brian Mulroney, and again from 1998 on) and had served as prime minister in a short-lived minority government from 1979 to 1980. The Alliance's Stephen Harper was among those who commented on the end of an era. In his remarks, however, Harper added the thought that Clark's withdrawal was a blessing that could pave the way to a merger. The next day Conservative MP Scott Brison responded by saying that Harper's comments were graceless and gratuitous. It was another signal that the process of amalgamation, even if it succeeded, would not be without rancour.

For the Tories, the immediate chore of selecting a new leader focused on the Maritime Provinces, home to ten of the party's thirteen MPs and incubator for its rising stars. Foremost among the prospective contenders was New Brunswick premier Bernard Lord. A profile in the *Toronto Star* of 8 August was typical in extolling the virtues of a youthful politician unencumbered by political baggage. Lord was described as being 'fluently bilingual, a proven campaigner [despite his age] ... and charismatic in a low key, reassuring way.' He was also not interested. On 23 October the premier ended speculation by announcing that he would remain in New Brunswick for the time being. Another possible candidate, Ontario corporate executive and consummate backroom strategist, John Tory, also chose to steer clear of the contest. The mantle of favourite instantly fell to MP Peter Mackay. The son of a former Tory cabinet minister, Mackay was first elected in the Nova Scotia riding of Pictou – Antigonish – Guysborough at the tender age of thirty-one (curiously, he was born on the same date as Lord). It took him some time to decide, but when he did Mackay became the front-runner. Among the challengers was David Orchard, a Saskatchewan farmer and anti–free trade activist, who had fared surprisingly well in the 1998 contest that confirmed Clark.

National economy

Economic indicators

In a year of modest economic recovery from the slackness of 2001, Canada continued to fare well compared with other industrial nations. The federal budget continued to yield surpluses while many countries wrestled with deficits and debts. The gross domestic product grew by 3.3 per cent (up from 1.9 per cent in the twelve previous months). As a result, unemployment rates began to fall in the final quarter on the way to a yearly average of 7.7 per cent. Although this performance paled against the average of 7.2 per cent in 2002, the economy did produce an impressive 560,000 new jobs, most of them full-time. An upward trend in the overall workforce participation rate continued and peaked at 66.9 per cent, the highest that it had been in more than a decade. Gains were distributed unevenly. The three prairie provinces had the lowest jobless rates, while the four Atlantic provinces lagged behind.

Inflation pressures eased again, and this closely monitored index

Canadian Voters' Preferences (%) – Environics Research Polls, 2002

Party	January	March	July	August	October
Liberals	45	46	40	44	43
Canadian Alliance	14	14	13	18	19
Bloc Québécois (Quebec only)	8	9	9	9	8
New Democrats	13	13	16	13	13
Progressive Conservatives	18	16	15	20	15
Other	2	2	2	2	2

dropped to 2.2 per cent, after cresting at 2.6 per cent in 2001. Despite relatively favourable underlying trends, the Canadian dollar sagged to 63.68 cents against the U.S. dollar, down nearly a full penny from the year before. Stock prices on the Toronto Stock Exchange were also off by nearly 1,000 points. There were other worrying portents in the final quarter of 2002: the value of goods and services in the vital export sector fell by 2.1 per cent (imports declined by 0.3 per cent during the same three-month period).

Financial and economic update

Finance Minister Paul Martin delivered a belated budget in December 2001. Because of his ouster from cabinet in June, he was never able to deliver another budget. Indeed, there was no budget in all of 2002, a first in modern political history. The new finance minister, John Manley, delivered a traditional autumn update on 30 October during an appearance before the House of Commons Committee on Finance. At a special gathering near the Port of Halifax, the committee heard messages that were decidedly, and in some ways surprisingly, mixed.

Manley was pleased to cite the legacy of Paul Martin in his remarks. He was at pains to trumpet Martin-era successes such as five successive years of budget surpluses, the elimination of $46 billion in debt, and a reduction in the ratio of debt to gross domestic product from 71 per cent to 49 per cent. The good news did not stop there. Thanks to a growth spurt approaching 5 per cent during the year, the Canadian economy was on track to increase by 3.4 per cent for the calendar year 2002. Growth was expected to remain strong, at 3.5 per cent, in 2003. These forecasts meant that Canada was on pace to continue to lead all major industrial nations. Canada was springing like a 'northern tiger,' zooming ahead, after the fashion of Asian economies in the 1980s and 1990s.

This rosy outlook was offset by more sobering factors, however. The budgetary surplus for fiscal 2002–3 was expected to fall precipitously to just $1 billion. This compared with $8.9 billion in 2001-2. In part this drop-off was due to the restoration of contingency funding (a $3 billion portion set aside in reserves plus an allocation for so-called prudence) that had been suspended because of the economic downturn attributable to the events of 11 September 2001. The surplus was expected to rebound in 2003–4, to approximately $3.1 billion. Over a six-year period, the total surplus was pegged at $71 billion, with $39.5 billion available for further debt reduction, spending, or tax cuts after deduction for reserves and prudence. This figure was subject to downward revision if global and national trend lines dipped. Manley was thus crediting his government while warning that spending options were limited and potentially constrained. He reminded the committee that the government's stated and firm commitments to health care and the military precluded any significant new spending notwithstanding the testimony and pleas of other witnesses that it would hear in the run-up to the 2003 budget.

Manley argued, not altogether persuasively, in favour of caution. Opposition critics did not bite. The finance minister was criticized for attempting to pull off an all-too-familiar Liberal trick, that of deliberately underestimating the size of surpluses in order to dampen demand for new spending. Simon Tuck of the *Globe and Mail* quoted Sherry Cooper, chief economist with the Bank of Montreal / Nesbitt Burns, who asserted that Manley was intentionally 'low balling the surplus' to 'keep a lid on government spending initiatives from his Liberal Party compatriots' and noted that at least one Liberal committee member, former cabinet minister Maria Minna, was sceptical of Manley's dour projections (31 October). In a similar but even stronger vein, the *Toronto Star* editorialized the day after his presentation that Manley appeared to be laying the groundwork for cuts to social programs in order to fund emerging needs such as military spending or health care and was, as a result, striding in the footsteps of his tight-fisted predecessor. An article by Les Whittington in the *Toronto Star* caught the distemper of NDP leader Alexa McDonough, who contended that Manley's fixation on dubious vicissitudes meant that 'there's not even an acknowledgment in this financial statement ... that we do have a growing social deficit, that we do have a growing gap between rich and poor' (31 October).

At any rate, Manley was certain that the government would not have to resort to tax increases or be forced to renege on rate cuts promised by

Martin. At the same time, deficits were to be avoided and cushioned by reserves. Therefore if, as was likely, the surplus for 2002–3 was greater than advertised, debt reduction would be the main beneficiary, with tax cuts a more remote possibility. Left-wing critics were of the view that investment (or reinvestment) in spending was vitiated. To this, cabinet colleagues including the prime minister responded that recent promises to boost health care funding were sacrosanct and that more help to the provinces was on the way. To the right wing, Manley was no more persuadable or reliable than his predecessor when it came to cutting taxes.

Trade issues

Yet again the vexed issue of trade in softwood lumber dominated bilateral relations with the United States in 2002. The two countries had sparred for the better part of a decade over the export of Canadian softwood lumber (so vital to the construction industry). U.S. interests complained that products from British Columbia were pegged at artificially low prices by virtue of favourable 'stumpage fees' (paid by extractors for access to forests) and other policies. A temporary agreement reached in the year 2000 was due to expire early in 2002. With a deadline looming, negotiators from the two sides worked towards a renewed and more lasting arrangement,

A deal proved elusive. Early in the year there were ominous warnings that the talks had gone off the rails. Ottawa worked with British Columbia and other provinces to forge an alliance with key players to develop a unified front. The Canadian parties were keenly motivated. Painful experience had shown that any additional levies on domestic lumber shipments would result in mass lay-offs, diminished investment, and cascading economic instability. Part of the strategy that they adopted involved cultivating U.S. enterprises in the home-building sector and politicians who were worried about the economic implications of higher prices or scarcity of supply in their districts. On 28 February International Trade Minister Pierre Pettigrew met with U.S. enthusiasts in order to raise the issue in the U.S. Congress. Pettigrew had already warned, on 26 February, that Canada would use every mechanism available – including provisions of the North American Free Trade Agreement and the World Trade Organization's treaties – to challenge any U.S. move if talks broke down.

Notwithstanding unity at home and pockets of sympathy south of the border, Canada's prospects were poor. U.S. opponents were entrenched, and only a last-minute reversal would prevent some form of punitive action once the deadline passed on 21 March. It was no surprise when, on 22 March, the United States imposed new duties on Canadian softwood importers. The scale of the counteraction , however, was astonishing. Beginning 8 May imports would be hit with duties of 29 per cent. This figure was composed of a 19.34 per cent countervailing duty and an anti-dumping penalty of 9.6 per cent. The total was down from a levy of 32 per cent imposed in 2001, but it was sufficiently large for Pettigrew to call it 'obscene' (*Globe and Mail*, 23 March).

Who was to blame for the impasse and imposition? To those in the United States who favoured strong measures against Canada, the situation was wholly the result of a system designed to undermine U.S. loggers and mill operators on the West Coast (eastern Canada had been generally excluded from punishments meted out during the protracted dispute). The Canadian Alliance offered the rather arch theory that the Liberal government's tacit enthusiasm for the candidacy of Democratic presidential contender Al Gore in the 2000 U.S. elections had antagonized the Bush administration. To others in Canada, the problem was U.S. protectionism in the face of a demonstrably superior supply regime in British Columbia.

Whatever the cause, the consequences were severe. While Canada pursued various dispute resolution options, the federal government worked with British Columbia to develop a program to assist those dislocated by U.S. sanctions. On 9 October Natural Resources Minister Herb Dhaliwal, himself a British Columbian, announced an aid package of $246 million. Of this total, some $110 million would be invested in a 'community adjustment fund.' Another $71 million was earmarked for direct help to displaced workers, while $40 million was to go to fighting a ravaging infestation by the pine beetle. Dhaliwal described the ensemble as unfinished business owing to a fluid situation that might require further intervention to soften the blow to the industry, workers, and communities. In the meantime, the federal government worked on the diplomatic and legal fronts.

Policy areas

Health care and the Romanow Report

The Royal Commission on the Future of Health Care in Canada submitted its much-anticipated report on 28 November, the Romanow Report. Former New Democratic premier Roy Romanow of Saskatchewan, the birthplace of public medicare in Canada, was single-handedly responsible for the 365-page report and its contents. After extensive consultations across Canada, and a review of myriad studies, Romanow tabled forty-seven recommendations on how to 'strengthen and modernize medicare, and how to place it on a more sustainable footing for the future,' (*Toronto Star*, 29 November).

Few commissions in Canadian history have been subjected to so much scrutiny. In the years leading up to the commission, public opinion polls had found – consistently and unequivocally – that health care was the main priority for Canadians. The public health care system had suffered budget cuts, even as the population was aging and unforeseen crises had arisen. Despite ballyhooed agreements between the federal and provincial governments, dealings between the two had been characterized by discord, disappointment, suspicion, and impatience. The modest charge to Romanow was simply to change all of this by proposing remedies that would be acceptable constitutionally, politically, practically, and financially. Fortunately for him, he earned praise for even trying.

In a sense, the solution was simple. The provincial governments (who are assigned responsibility for health care under Canada's Constitution) needed more money and, envious of federal surpluses since the late 1990s, wanted Ottawa to increase the amount that it transferred to the provinces. The federal government argued that any increments should be accompanied by greater accountability and equity. Romanow struggled to find a middle way. To the bedrock principles of medicare he proposed to add accountability. This was a victory of sorts for the federal government. Prime Minister Chrétien was pleased that accountability was to be a foundation of the framework imagined by the commissioner. Yet Romanow also recommended a significant infusion of cash by the federal government, with the accent on up-front money to restore and then retool the system. The cost over three years would be $15 billion. Writing in the *Toronto Star*, Tim Harper and Vanessa Lu identified five core areas where new money would be spent to 'kick start' the changes in the first two years of the proposed plan:

- $1.5 billion to shorten waiting times for diagnostic services, including magnetic resonance imaging and computed tomography scans
- $1 billion for individuals spending more than $1,500 annually on prescription drugs in a catastrophic medicine package
- $2 billion for post-hospital, palliative, and mental health care
- $2.5 billion for the replacement of hospital emergency treatment by visits to physicians

- $1.5 billion for the care of people in rural and remote communities.

In addition to these special envelopes it was recommended that the federal government move towards paying 25 per cent of provincial health care costs (reckoned at an extra $6.5 billion in 2005). Distilled to its essence, the spending regime recommended by Romanow called for predictable emoluments over a prescribed period of time. By earmarking these specific projects, however, the commission invited dissent, and the recommendations were rejected by many salient political actors. The Canadian Alliance and the Bloc Québécois quickly criticized the report as a planned intrusion on provincial powers. They were joined in this by the Progressive Conservative governments of Alberta and Ontario. Alberta's premier Ralph Klein said he would turn down any money that came attached to conditions and was not based on provincially defined priorities. Ontario's Ernie Eves complained of being short-changed, given his province's size and relative needs. Supporters of Romanow included the Liberals and NDP at the federal level, and the smaller, poorer, or traditionally progressive provinces that had historically welcomed equitable national programs and that could least afford to say no. Journalists also found ample numbers of caregivers, patients, and ordinary citizens who lauded Romanow's affirmation of the right to public health care.

The commission disdained fundamental changes. The text of the report reinforced the consensus view that Romanow had taken a cautious, incremental stance, saying that he had 'challenged those advocating for radical solutions to reforming health care – user fees, medical savings accounts, de-listing services, greater privatization, a parallel private system – to come forward with evidence that these approaches would improve and strengthen our health care system. *The evidence has not been forthcoming*. I have also carefully explored, 'the experiences of other jurisdictions with co-payment models and public-private partnerships and have found these lacking' (*Toronto Star*, 29 November; emphasis in original report). It was this very quality of stolidity that some commentators saw as a virtue. Syndicated columnist Thomas Walkom argued that the formula was doable, affordable, and sensible and that Romanow had rightly gauged 'that no matter what agreements are written on paper, the provinces will go only so far and the federal government will be loath to push them farther' (*Toronto Star*, 29 November). It was a perfectly Canadian scenario for success or, in the words of a *Toronto Star* editorial, a 'realistic road map' (29 November).

Since the commission had been created by the federal government, the response of Prime Minister Chrétien was important. Speaking on behalf of the government the prime minister expressed appreciation to Romanow and indicated that Ottawa would be able to find most, if not all, the funding advocated by him. Chrétien was grateful for Romanow's advice, but acknowledged that the report would only form the basis for talks with the provinces. When asked if Ottawa would require a form of nationwide compliance in return for additional funds, the prime minister exclaimed: 'No way, I don't want to run the hospitals!' Even so, the federal government would not wholly give up the notion that dedicated transfers to the provinces should be subject to transparent accounting.

Environment and the Kyoto Protocol

One of Prime Minister Chrétien's legacy projects was tied to parliamentary ratification of the Kyoto Protocol on global warming. Ratification meant reducing the emission of greenhouse gases. Despite the U.S. government's refusal to sign onto to the global agreement, and in the face of considerable opposition at home, the Liberals insisted that they would seek – and win – approval for a plan to implement goals set for Canada under the Kyoto framework. In this they were aided by support from the New Democrats and the Bloc Québécois, environmental organizations, and some of the provinces. Pressure was also applied by the scientific community in Canada and around the world.

The path towards formal endorsement was nonetheless imposing. Home-grown opponents included oil-rich Alberta and oil-dependent Ontario. These provinces, under the stewardship of right-wing governments hostile to regulation, were joined by major industries relying on conventional energy supplies. Alberta was at the forefront of these forces, and Premier Ralph Klein personified antagonism to the Protocol. Federal Environment Minister David Anderson released a discussion paper on 16 May that raised the stakes in a debate that raged into the autumn. The federal government announced a tactical delay in the release of its implementation plans on 21 October as part of a strategy to engineer a consensus by year's end. With the backing of other provinces, Alberta insisted that the Protocol should be subject to negotiations at a full first ministers' conference, given the impact of the plan on a variety of provincial jurisdictions. In Ottawa, Alliance leader Stephen Harper was vocal in his opposition to the government's intentions. He had seen nothing that amounted to a real plan and was fearful of the economic consequences of cutting back on carbon dioxide emissions. Environmentalists, too, were sceptical of the government's commitments, but continued to embrace ratification as a necessary step towards cutting back on harmful emissions.

A revised 'Climate Change Plan' in support for Kyoto was finally released on 21 November. Broadly speaking the goal was to reduce carbon dioxide emissions by 24 megatonnes annually by the year 2012. In personal terms this translated into a 20 per cent cut in fuel consumption by every Canadian. The government estimated the impact on gross domestic product at 0.4 per cent. The plan was woven around five themes:

- Transportation, where a goal of 25 per cent greater efficiency would be achieved through the production of alternative fuels, stimulation of demand for safer energy, and greater reliance on public transit
- Housing, commercial facilities, and institutional buildings, where various measures would be enacted to promote fuel efficiency
- Large industrial emitters (no targets were set per se, but Ottawa would work with the provinces to reduce reliance on Kyoto-targeted fuels)
- Small and medium-sized enterprises and 'fugitive' emissions (from flaring and venting at production sites), which would be the subject of voluntary controls and government subsidies
- International emissions, which would be reduced by efficiency measures.

The issue of containing cross-border emissions was acutely controversial. The Kyoto framework provided for a global system of credits that could be exchanged by countries. By virtue of its vast forests and tundra, Canada was defined as a 'carbon sink.' Efforts by the government to earn more credits had been partially successful in 2001. Ongoing attempts to sweeten this bargain had been rebuffed, most recently at the G8 summit, which concluded in Banff, Alberta, on 14 April. It was then that European countries rejected the argument that Canada should enjoy greater relief on the grounds that it was an exporter of cleaner fuel such as natural gas. Under the final climate change plan, the Canadian government would purchase up to 10 megatonnes of foreign credits to cushion the impact on domestic suppliers and users, a clear but modest gain for the foes of Kyoto. In response to other criticisms, the government said it would consider additional monetary subsidies if the costs to industry rose above the projected range of $5 to $10 per tonne.

The plan was brought to a vote on 10 December. In the end the government prevailed 195-77, with the help of the NDP and Bloc Québécois. The Canadian Alliance and Progressive Conservatives remained implacable and continued to condemn a plan that they saw as fantastical and extravagant.

Amendments to the Indian Act

Although it had provided the framework for relations between the federal government and Canada's aboriginal peoples, the Indian Act had been virtually unchanged in 126 years. On 14 June Minister of Indian Affairs and Northern Development Robert Nault introduced legislation that would overhaul the act. Given this long stagnation, the changes might have been seen as bold and innovative (as the government had hoped), but the move was far from universally popular.

The legislation proffered by Nault was the First Nations Governance Act, or Bill 61. Its contents were informed by consultations conducted in 2000 and 2001. The government was quick to emphasize that the initiative would not undo existing treaties or stymie negotiations over self-government. Rather, the bill contemplated higher standards for local band councils in terms of elections and day-to-day administration. Native bands would be required to set fixed terms for elected leaders and to adhere to stricter electoral rules. Financial affairs would be made more transparent and subject to third-party audits. The amendments also included repeal of the Indian Act's exclusion from the Human Rights Act.

Some Aboriginal constituencies endorsed the proposals. The Congress of Aboriginal Peoples, a small and primarily urban-centred organization, welcomed the changes. Larger and more inclusive groups did not. On a Canadian Broadcasting Corporation news segment, Assembly of First Nations Chief Matthew Coon Come denounced the Indian Act as a deeply flawed and ultimately 'racist document' that should not be a foundation for evolving policy (14 June). Critics also faulted the government for failing to recognize traditional means of designating leaders and trampling on rights to self-determination. Bill 61 survived first reading but lapsed on the order paper when Parliament was prorogued on 19 June. Notwithstanding the harsh reception, the government stood by the bill's principles and was expected to reintroduce the legislation. Nault did so on 9 October, when the First Nations Governance Act re-emerged as Bill C-7.

Drought on the Prairies

Experts tended to agree that climate change stemming from global warming would have profound implications for Canadian agriculture. If so, the year 2002 brought an unwanted foretaste of such consequences. The spring was dry on the Prairies, and crops struggled. On 11 June the spell was broken by a deluge of destructive floods. Early in the growing season the harvest seemed all but doomed. These climatic jolts added to the misery of farmers who were grappling with past droughts and floods, low yields, pestilence, global competition, and frantic subsidization of U.S. and European agribusinesses. As they had done in the past several years, farmers and provincial governments looked to Ottawa for help. On 20 June the federal government outlined a proposal for long-term relief. The offer was $5.2 billion over six years, but there were strings attached. Provinces would be expected to contribute 40 per cent of the amount. Three provinces – Manitoba, Saskatchewan, and Quebec – said that they could not afford the bail-out. This left the federal plan up in the air, even though Ottawa reiterated that it would lend a hand to farmers.

The situation was exacerbated as the drought resumed. On 29 June devastating fires ignited in Saskatchewan and Alberta. Two weeks later the Department of Agriculture and Agri-Food in Ottawa advised growers to diversify crops and even abandon some. Wealthy Alberta provided $342 million to its agriculture sector on 17 July, an act of generosity that other provinces could not match. Yet, even with this largesse, Alberta farmers could not cope with the drought of 2002. Cattle raisers were particularly affected. On 8 August the first shipments of hay donated by farmers in the eastern half of the country arrived in the west. They continued for several weeks, leading up to a grim Thanksgiving.

In the midst of the drought Statistics Canada released a discouraging report. By all estimates the crop of 2002 would be the worst in many years, with reductions of 40 to 60 per cent in yields from wheat, canola, and barley. On 6 September the Canadian Wheat Board took the unusual step of dropping out of the world market, given the sparse harvest. By year's end no consensus had formed around the long-term future of Prairie farming. The west had survived droughts before, and a characteristic streak of independence had not been deterred by a run of bad fortune. If the drought continued, however, it might be necessary for governments to take a harder look at the causes and consequences of the situation.

Passings

On 19 December former Governor General Ray Hnatyshyhn died at the age of 68. Hnatysyhn, who served as justice minister under Prime Minister Brian Mulroney, succumbed to cancer. He was acclaimed for many virtues and was remembered fondly for opening the grounds of Rideau Hall to the public and otherwise bringing a populist touch to the office of governor general of Canada.

CHRISOPHER SPEARIN[1]

Foreign affairs and defence

Canada continued to come to grips with the changed contours in world politics in the wake of both the attacks of 11 September 2001 and the advent of President George W. Bush's 'America first' unilateralism. With its 'you're either with us or against us' mentality, the Bush administration made it plain to the world that, for Washington, it would not be business as usual. As a result, former prime minister Pierre Trudeau's assessment of Canada–U.S. relations as like 'a mouse in bed with an elephant' seemed as applicable as ever: 'No matter how friendly ... one is affected by every twitch and grunt.' Thus, U.S. policy changes placed pressures on Canadian firms who found the markets for their products drying up south of the border. These changes posed challenges to Prime Minister Jean Chrétien's favoured style of multilateral engagement on the international stage. These changes tired an already overcommitted and underfunded military that had seen its operational tempo increase, rather than decrease, since the end of the Cold War. Finally, these changes taxed new people in key ministerial positions in the Department of Foreign Affairs and International Trade and the Department of National Defence. Although Finance Minister Paul Martin's abrupt departure from cabinet was a big news story in 2002, the arrival of fresh, and untested, ministerial faces to DFAIT and DND in the midst of international flux was something for analysts and policymakers alike to watch in 2002.

Foreign affairs

Ministerial change – Department of Foreign Affairs and International Trade

Following the federal cabinet shuffle on 15 January, Bill Graham was named Canada's foreign affairs minister. John Manley, Graham's prede-

1 The author would like to thank Donald Spearin for his assistance in the preparation of this chapter.

cessor, became the deputy prime minister. Although there were several cabinet changes, Graham's appointment attracted the most criticism from the Opposition parties, for several reasons. First, because this was Graham's first-ever cabinet appointment, the Opposition parties charged that he lacked the necessary experience for such a prominent position. The words of Progressive Conservative leader Joe Clark, himself a former minister of external affairs, were not flattering: 'He's the most junior minister in the history of Canada to serve as foreign minister. He has no strength in Cabinet. He has no strength in caucus. He has no strength in the country' (*National Post*, 17 January). Graham fired back, citing his training as an international lawyer and his chairing for six years of the House of Commons Foreign Affairs Committee. Other prominent liberals made the observation that Joe Clark had not even held a cabinet post before becoming prime minister. Graham was also defended by Prime Minister Jean Chrétien, who contended that Graham was an ideal choice for the post: 'He can teach to all these guys in the Opposition a lot of things on foreign affairs' (*Charlottetown Guardian*, 17 January).

The second criticism, also related to Graham's perceived junior status, was that his selection was representative, according to Joe Clark, of the government's 'trivialization of international affairs' (*Calgary Herald*, 17 January). For Clark, the choice of Graham illustrated the downgrading of DFAIT in government circles. Not only was Prime Minister Chrétien known for his general activism on the international stage, but the responsibility for handling key issues pertaining to Canada–U.S. relations, especially regarding the border, were to be handled by Deputy Prime Minister Manley. Moreover, Graham's appointment came in the wake of cuts to DFAIT's budget and the government's appointment of Alfonso Gagliano, the scandal-plagued former public works minister, as Canada's ambassador to Denmark. As emphasized by Bill Casey, the Progressive Conservative foreign affairs critic, 'I'm sure Mr Gagliano did not pass the foreign service exams' (*Ottawa Citizen*, 17 January). Graham asserted that, for his part, he would not play second fiddle to his cabinet colleagues, but that it was crucial to recognize that the policy process was a cooperative endeavour: 'Foreign affairs in this country is teamwork. Cabinet is a collaborative effort, and obviously I'll be working most closely with the prime minister and Mr Manley ... I think I'll be able to bring my own perspective because I've had a great deal of experience in this area' (*Ottawa Citizen*, 17 January).

Third, and in contradistinction to the assertion of a lack of influence, other Opposition members of Parliament wanted to know in what direction Graham would take Canadian foreign policy. For New Democratic Party leader, Alexa McDonough, Manley had treated Canada as 'a 51st state' (*Calgary Herald*, 17 January). During Manley's time as foreign affairs minister, he was known to have championed closer economic integration with the United States and campaigned for greater security cooperation with Washington. Graham defended the government's increasing closeness with the United States, especially in the wake of the 11 September 2001 terrorist attacks: 'Canada–United States relations are without a doubt the most important thing in terms of Canada, in terms of our economic prosperity, in terms of our geography' (*Toronto Star*, 17 January). However, Graham also espoused Canada's multilateralist credentials and reiterated his desire for an independent Canadian voice in international affairs: 'I am inspired by [Prime Minister] Pearson because Mr Pearson was able to show the world that there are Canadian values and Canadian aspirations that have a global value. And that is the goal of our foreign policy' (*Toronto Star*, 17 January).

Trade disputes

Softwood lumber

Canada's ongoing dispute with the United States regarding softwood lumber continued throughout 2002 with no end in sight. The dispute was sparked in March 2001 following the expiry of the 1996 bilateral Softwood Lumber Agreement and the subsequent imposition in the autumn of 2001 of provisional or preliminary countervailing duties (19.3 per cent) and anti-dumping duties (12.6 per cent) against Canadian softwood producers. As a result of these strictures, Canadian timber producers had to post bonds equal to the preliminary duties. At issue were charges by U.S. producers that provincial governments provided subsidies through low stumpage fees and that Canadian producers sold their wood in the United States at below-market prices. Thus, to protect U.S. producers, the U.S. Commerce Department indicated on 22 March 2002 that, effective 8 May, the United States would implement formal and final tariffs and charges averaging approximately 29 per cent. This move by Washington threatened to devastate the Canadian softwood lumber industry, the single largest component of Canada–U.S. trade and worth about $10 billion to Canada annually. For instance, even with just the preliminary duties, the B.C. Lumber Trade Council estimated that 15,000 logging and sawmill jobs had been lost and that the formal duties would push this number to 30,000.[2]

In light of the high stakes, the federal government in 2002 continued with its multiprong strategy, initiated in 2001, of being open to negotiations and active in both legal forums and advocacy endeavours. With respect to the North American Free Trade Agreement, the government on 26–27 February filed notices of intent for a NAFTA review concerning the U.S. countervailing and anti-dumping determinations. Ottawa launched a formal NAFTA challenge on 22 March. Similarly, at the World Trade Organization, Canada pursued redress through examinations of the methods behind the preliminary and final determinations of Canadian subsidies. Here the government achieved some success. On 26 July, the WTO ruled that the preliminary U.S. duties were in violation of international trade rules. Finally, on 27 May International Trade Minister Pierre Pettigrew announced that the government would provide $20 million to raise awareness in the United States of the negative implications of the duties. These monies were divided between the Forest Products Association of Canada ($17 million) and Canada's embassy and consulates in the United States ($3 million). For Pettigrew, U.S. consumers had to be made aware of the detrimental impact of the tariffs on both sides of the border: 'In addition to hurting Canadians, punitive U.S. lumber duties also hurt American consumers, home builders and workers. We fully support our industry in its efforts to bring these damaging costs to the attention of Americans. When they realize that these duties favour the few at the expense of many, perhaps Americans will see the need to resolve the dispute in a reasonable way' (DFAIT News Release no. 58, 27 May).

Because this strategy might take years, however, the government created lumber aid packages for ailing timber producers. On 16 May Natural Resources Minister Herb Dhaliwal announced three initiatives, valued at $75 million, to ensure the competitiveness and long-term future of the Canadian softwood lumber industry. Additionally, on 9 October Dhaliwal launched a $246 million fund that would assist displaced workers and affected communities. Near the end of the year, Pettigrew also initiated a $15 million assistance package directed at

2 Victoria was particularly concerned because 85 per cent of the province's softwood lumber was for export and forestry accounted directly or indirectly for 14 per cent of all the jobs in BC – the largest contributor to the provincial economy. Softwood producers in the Maritimes, however, were not hurt as much by the American actions. They were only subject to the anti-dumping charges due to their different timber management policies.

Canada's softwood lumber industry associations. In total, however, these packages were the subject of some criticism because they fell well short of the $1 billion demanded by forestry unions.

Canadian Wheat Board

In 2002 the United States challenged in several ways the Canadian Wheat Board's conformity to international trade regulations. First, on 15 February U.S. Trade Representative Robert Zoellick responded to a complaint filed in October 2000 by the North Dakota Wheat Commission that accused the CWB of providing subsidies to Canadian wheat producers, thus placing U.S. producers at a disadvantage. In particular, the NDWC disliked the CWB's special monopoly rights and the subsidies that it provided for the shipment of wheat by rail. For Zoellick, therefore, anti-dumping and countervailing investigations were in order to learn whether tariff rate quotas were necessary. Later in the year, following the filing of petitions on 13 September by U.S. wheat producers who accused Canada of subsidizing the production of Canadian durum and hard red spring wheat, the U.S. Department of Commerce indicated on 24 October that it would launch an investigation of Canadian practices. In mid-December, armed with arguments that the CWB undermined international trading rules and adversely affected the U.S. market share internationally, Washington took the bilateral dispute to a new level by bringing it to the WTO. For Zoellick, the U.S. stance was clear: 'The Canadian Wheat Board is a monopoly, and its special benefits and privileges put American wheat farmers at a disadvantage and undermine the integrity of the international trading system' (*Calgary Herald*, 18 December).

The dispute over the CWB's policies remained unresolved at the close of the year. Under WTO guidelines, Canada was permitted thirty days to agree to negotiations before the United States could request the WTO to form a dispute-settlement panel. Canadian politicians, for their part, appeared not to be overly concerned by Washington's moves, even though annual wheat shipments to the United States from 1999 to 2001 ranged between $360 million and $460 million. Nonchalance was evident because, even before the 2002 actions, Washington had challenged the Canadian practices eight times since 1990; each previous challenge had ended in failure for the Americans. With the end of 2002 fast approaching, the minister responsible for the CWB, Ralph Goodale, expressed optimism that the Canadian position would again win out in 2003: 'We've had lots of practice. They have launched these proceedings in the past based on the same allegations, the same complaints. We have always been able to successfully defend ourselves in the past and we will once again' (*Ottawa Citizen*, 18 December).

Dairy

The World Trade Organization dealt Canadian dairy exports a blow in 2002. On 24 June a WTO panel ruled that the federal government was illegally subsidizing Canadian dairy farmers, a ruling that affected approximately $250 million in annual dairy exports. This ruling stemmed from an ongoing dispute initiated by the United States and New Zealand in 1998. At that time these two countries argued that the Canadian pricing system permitted dairy producers to sell their exports at a lower price than milk and cheese produced for the domestic market. Although Ottawa had made changes to the Canadian system since the initial complaint, these alterations apparently did not suffice and thus the United States and New Zealand renewed their charges. As a result of this ruling the WTO opened the door to these two countries applying approximately $75 million in sanctions.

Over the course of 2002 the federal government's stance on the issue gradually shifted to one of acceptance. Initially, following the June ruling, Ottawa indicated that it would appeal the decision, hoping that would hopefully lead to a successful conclusion, from a Canadian standpoint, on this long-running dispute. The appeal was forthcoming on 23 September. The optimism regarding the Canadian position was evident in the words of Minister of Agriculture and Agri-Food Lyle Vanclief: 'With our appeal, we hope to lay this dispute to rest once and for all, allowing our dairy sector to focus on creating the world-leading dairy products it is known for' (DFAIT News Release no. 107, 23 September). However, when the WTO appeal panel ruled on 20 December that the initial decision would not be overturned, Ottawa indicated that it would abide by the decision. Moreover, the government immediately started to downgrade the significance of the decision. International Trade Minister Pettigrew argued that the impact would be minimal: 'The decision was about this very specific dairy case, so I don't think we should extrapolate any significance of today's decision' (*Calgary Herald*, 21 December).[3] The year 2002 ended with consultations between the federal and provincial governments as to how the ruling was to be implemented.

3 Less than half of the exports would likely have to stop and the decision affected less than 5 per cent of total Canadian milk production.

Regional jets

The year 2002 was one both of positives and negatives for Canada's ongoing dispute with Brazil regarding the financing and subsidization of the two countries' respective regional jet producers, Bombardier and Embraer SA. The WTO ruled on 28 January, stemming from a 2001 charge made by Brazil, that three Canadian financing policies were consistent with international trade regulations: the Canada Account program, the Corporate Account program, and the Quebec government's Investissement Québec. But the WTO also ruled that the specific application of these programs in certain instances was in breach of international trade regulations. At issue was the government's decision in 2001 to match Brazilian financing deals to help sway, in particular, the purchase of aircraft by Air Wisconsin, Air Nostrum, and Comair. Canada's argument that such a matching strategy was allowable under guidelines set out by the Organization for Economic Cooperation and Development fell upon deaf ears. Nevertheless, Minister Pettigrew made it plain on 19 February that Canada would not appeal the WTO's decision: 'We are committed to a trade system based on clear rules – a priority we hope will be shared by Brazil. We disagree with certain elements of the decision, but since there are sufficient positive elements for Canada, we have decided that, on balance, it's better to let the decision stand. We want to turn the page on this trade dispute and find a mutually acceptable solution with Brazil' (DFAIT News Release no. 17, 19 February). Turning the page, however, would be a challenging task for Canadian negotiators because Brazil's hand was strengthened considerably at the end of 2002. As a result of the WTO's findings at the start of 2002, Brazil asked the World Trade Organization to grant it authorization to level economic countermeasures as high as $5.2 billion against Canada. Although the amount actually approved by the WTO on 23 December was much lower ($385 million), this decision nevertheless strengthened the Brazilian negotiating position considerably. Canadian officials, such as Minister Pettigrew, tried to downplay the significance of this WTO determination: 'The ruling is what we expected. Negotiations to find a mutually satisfactory solution have progressed substantively. I believe that both countries will benefit greatly when we will have this dispute behind us. Let's move forward and invest our energies into rebuilding our economic relationship' (DFAIT News Release no. 179, 23 December). This relationship rebuilding between the two countries was scheduled to resume in a further round of talks in March 2003.

Crime, punishment, and human rights

International Criminal Court

A long-standing goal of Canadian foreign policy regarding human rights came to fruition in 2002 with the setting up of the International Criminal Court. The ICC, based in The Hague and the first ever permanent court of its kind, has jurisdiction over genocide, crimes against humanity, and war crimes. To facilitate the court's creation, Canada signed the Rome Statute on the ICC on 18 December 1998 and subsequently was the first state in the world, in June 2000, to develop comprehensive legislation to implement ICC obligations. This led to Canada's ratification of the ICC statute on 7 July 2000. Moreover, Canada helped to draw in the support of other countries for the ICC. For instance, Philippe Kirsch, a legal expert and senior official in DFAIT, was the chair of both the ICC negotiations and the ICC preparations committees.[4] Additionally, Canada provided legal assistance to other countries to help ensure their ratification of the ICC statute. Thus, Canada could take some of the credit for the ICC statute coming into force well ahead of schedule on 1 July 2002. Although the expectation was that the statute would take ten years to come into force, sixty-six countries had ratified the ICC statute by April 2002 – only sixty were required for the creation of the court. The momentous nature of this occasion was not lost on Prime Minister Chrétien: 'This is truly a watershed moment for the cause of international justice and human decency' (*Calgary Herald*, 12 April). The next stage in the process was a week-long meeting in New York City at the start of September 2002, the objective of which was the adoption of procedures for the nomination of the judges and the prosecutor of the new court.

William Sampson

The unfortunate saga of Canadian William Sampson's incarceration in Saudi Arabia continued in 2002. Saudi officials arrested Sampson, a pharmaceutical engineer, in 2000 and accused him of being involved in bombings in November of that year that killed one Briton and injured four other foreigners. The kingdom's position was that the bombing was an escalation in a feud between Western bootleggers. Another argu-

4 In 2002, Philippe Kirsch was Canada's ambassador to Sweden.

ment, however, was that Sampson was a scapegoat for the actions of anti-Western militants in Saudi Arabia. Sampson was held in solitary confinement, and allegations were made by many that he was being tortured by his Saudi jailers. What made the case even more troubling in 2002 was that Sampson was sentenced to death by beheading.

As 2002 progressed, Sampson's fate remained no clearer. Canadian diplomats had waited a good part of the year for the Saudi Supreme Council to rule on an appeal regarding his case. No ruling was forthcoming by September. Instead, Canadian officials in October suggested that a political solution involving the intervention of the Saudi crown prince might be in the works: 'The crown prince has indicated to us that there is going to be a political solution ... A political solution, in our view, is that the death penalty is going to be removed, there will be a prison term, and during that prison term, we'll be able to negotiate Mr Sampson's exit from Saudi Arabia' (*Ottawa Citizen*, 21 October). At issue, however, was whether this process would occur speedily enough for Sampson, given reports that his mental condition was deteriorating rapidly. In this regard, many individuals, including medical officials, the Canadian ambassador to Saudi Arabia, and Government House Leader Don Boudria had tried to provide assistance to Sampson, only to be harshly rebuffed by him. The aforementioned political intervention was not forthcoming by the close of 2002. Sampson saw in the new year in his Saudi Arabian jail cell with a death sentence still hanging over him.

Diplomatic immunity

The year 2002 featured the conclusion of the drunk driving case against Andrey Knyazev, the former first secretary of the Russian embassy in Canada. In Ottawa, on 27 January 2001, he struck and killed one woman and severely injured another while driving home from an ice fishing trip. At the time, Ottawa police charged Knyazev with criminal negligence causing death, impaired driving, failing to provide a breath sample, and criminal negligence causing bodily harm. Russian officials, however, refused to waive his right to diplomatic immunity and sent him back to Moscow. But in November 2001 Knyazev was charged under the Russian Criminal Code, as a result of his actions in Ottawa. This case ended in March 2002 when a Russian judge, Elena Stashina, found that Knyazev had committed thirteen crimes under Russian law. Informing the judge's decision was the Russia–Canada legal treaty that allowed her to take into account Ontario's traffic laws. As a result of this determination, Knyazev received a stiff penalty: four years of hard labour in a penal colony (one year short of the maximum), a subsequent three-year driving ban, and responsibility to pay for the court's costs.

In the wake of the January 2001 accident, the Canadian government instituted tougher regulations regarding the drunk driving of diplomatic officials, regulations that were tested in 2002. On 23 March Hideyuki Taguri, a third secretary at the Japanese embassy, just missed five teens in Orleans, Ontario, when he crashed his car into a traffic light while driving drunk. He was charged with dangerous driving, impaired driving, and refusing to take a breathalyser test. As in the Knyazev case, Japanese officials refused to waive Taguri's right to diplomatic immunity. Under Canada's new zero tolerance policy, however, Taguri's driving privileges were suspended. Moreover, when Japanese officials sent Taguri back to Japan in April, Crown Attorney Hilary McCormack issued a bench warrant for Taguri's arrest. Should he ever return to Canada as a private citizen, Taguri would be arrested and prosecuted under Canadian law. Unlike the Knyazev case that featured Russian prosecution, Canadian officials decided not to seek justice in Japan. Carl Schwenger, a DFAIT spokesperson, rationalized Canada's decision: 'If it wasn't possible to apply the [new] policy here, had he withdrawn to Japan, and it was a serious offence, I think we would have tried to follow the precedent that was established in the Knyazev case and asked the Japanese government to please prosecute him under Japanese law' (*Ottawa Citizen*, 1 May).

Talisman Energy

The long-running dispute regarding Talisman Energy's operations in war-torn Sudan came to a close in 2002. Ever since the Alberta-based firm acquired its 25 per cent stake in Sudan's Greater Nile Petroleum Operating Company, in 1998, it had been dogged by controversy.[5] Although the firm claimed that it was improving the lives of the Sudanese and contributing to the peace processes, non-government organizations and Canadian government officials claimed that Talisman's presence supported, either directly or indirectly, the Sudanese government in a civil war that had consumed the lives of over two million people. While Canadian officials had not been able to curtail Talisman's operations because of a lack of political will and the limitations of Canada's Special Economics Measures Act, the Talisman saga, for

5 Talisman's other partners were the China National Petroleum Corporation, Petronas (Malaysia), and Sudapet (Sudan).

many, was a blight on Canada's stated desire to promote human rights. Thus, it came as some relief that on 30 October Talisman announced that it was selling its stake to India's Oil and Natural Gas Corporation for US$1.2 billion.

Although the 230,000 barrel-per-day project was highly lucrative for Talisman, it would appear that controversy regarding the endeavour took its toll. This sentiment is echoed in the words of Jim Buckee, the firm's chief executive officer: 'The project was really good and we liked the people and we felt we were doing good things in Sudan. But, as it was, every newspaper mention of Talisman was qualified under 'involved in Sudan' and we hope to move on from that instant association' (*Calgary Herald*, 31 October). Four factors likely contributed to the 2002 decision to pull out. First, although it was not passed by the U.S. Senate, in 2001 the U.S. House of Representatives voted in favour of a bill that would have prevented foreign companies operating in Sudan from being listed on U.S. stock markets. Second, the U.S. Congress did pass a bill in October 2002 that gave President Bush the right to impose economic sanctions against the Sudanese government should it be found to be obstructing peacemaking efforts. This would have detrimentally affected oil exports. Third, NGOs and church groups had begun to target Talisman shareholders in North America. Fourth, in 2001 Sudanese civilians and the Presbyterian Church of Sudan launched a lawsuit against Talisman in New York under the Alien Tort Claim Act. This act allowed foreigners to sue firms in U.S. courts over actions stemming from their operations overseas. In the end, as expressed by Talisman spokesman Dave Mann, the company hoped it could soon put its Sudan operations behind it: 'Ultimately, we will be best known for what we do well, which is being a Canadian-based company that has been extremely successful for exploring around the world' (*Calgary Herald*, 1 November).

Zimbabwe, human rights, and African development

The highly disputed presidential election in Zimbabwe on 10–11 March 2002, which saw President Robert Mugabe win over Opposition leader Morgan Tsvangirai, posed significant challenges for Canadian policy-makers. Even before the election, observers commented that the process was rigged, in light of violence that had targeted Opposition supporters. The long line-ups and irregularities on the voting days themselves added more fuel to the fire. Whereas some African leaders in the Commonwealth accepted the election's verdict, other leaders, such as British

Prime Minister Tony Blair, suggested that Zimbabwe should be expelled from the Commonwealth. Prime Minister Jean Chrétien, for his part, thought that expulsion would be counterproductive. The tension regarding this issue threatened to tear the Commonwealth apart. Eventually, on 19 March a panel of influential Commonwealth leaders – Australian Prime Minister John Howard, South African President Thabo Mbeki, and Nigerian President Olusegun Obasanjo – decided that sanctions against Zimbabwe were in order in light of 'a high level of politically motivated violence' (Canadian Broadcasting Corporation, 19 March). What the Commonwealth implemented, according to observers, was a Canadian-inspired compromise that featured Zimbabwe's suspension from the international organization for one year.

Canadian activism on this issue was likely inspired by Prime Minister Chrétien's plan to advance a new development deal for Africa at the June G8 summit, a key component of the prime minister's hoped-for legacy on the international stage. To bolster support for his proposed plan, the prime minister conducted a tour of Africa in April 2002. During this eleven-day tour, he met with more than twenty African leaders and presented them with his 'New Partnership for Africa's Development.' At the root of this proposal, a modern-day Marshall Plan for Africa, was aid and investment from the developed world in return for African advances in terms of governance, justice, and human rights. Chrétien made it clear that both developed states and Africa would have obligations under this plan: 'I'm not talking charity, I'm talking investment. The conditions are clear. If you create a proper climate, with democracy, human rights ... then money will come' (*Ottawa Citizen*, 6 April). No doubt this plan would have been stillborn at the outset had significant divides remained within the Commonwealth or had there been no international response to the election in Zimbabwe's.

G8 Summit in Kananaskis

Despite fears that protestor and/or police violence would plague the G8 summit in Kananaskis, Alberta, as it had earlier G8 meetings and other international gatherings since the late 1990s, the 26–7 June meeting was a relatively tranquil affair. This came as some relief, especially because tensions were heightened even more as this was the first G8 summit since the 11 September 2001 terrorist attacks. To protect the various delegations, the Canadian Forces deployed more than 5,000 personnel along with helicopters, fighter jets, and air-to-air refuelling tankers. As for Calgary, the presumed locale for protest, given the high level of security at the conference site, local officials also increased the police presence: 550 'visiting' police officers from jurisdictions across Canada supplemented the 450-strong Calgary police force. This contingent was expected to face-off against a group of 15,000 protestors. However, only a few thousand individuals participated in the Calgary protests. Moreover, the police contingent followed a 'soft approach' that helped to contribute to the low level of destruction and violence. In fact, in light of this success, Calgary police chief Jack Beaton received queries from interested parties, including French officials responsible for security for the 2003 G8 summit in France. Even protestors were generally pleased with how police and protestors interacted. To quote one, 'I think both sides agreed avoiding violent acts was not only more effective to gain respect from the public for our intentions, but as well to guarantee future occasions to voice our concerns with issues like globalization and the policies of the G-8' (*Edmonton Journal*, 29 June).

As for the G8 policies devised at the 2002 meeting, the results were mixed. The summit launched the U.S.-inspired Global Partnership, a US$20 billion project to make secure and destroy Russia's antiquated Soviet-era biological, chemical, and nuclear arsenal, lest elements of it fall into terrorist hands or pose environmental hazards; however, the G8 offered only US$580 million per year for three years to support a UN-initiated US$10 billion plan to combat AIDS, tuberculosis, and malaria in the developing world. Furthermore, Prime Minister Chrétien's aforementioned 'African agenda' was derailed, in part, by President Bush's desire to discuss his latest peace proposal for the Middle East and his call for the Palestinians to replace Yasser Arafat as their leader. The summit also suffered because, despite the urgings of the World Bank, G8 leaders could not agree on providing at least US$6 billion in annual aid to Africa, necessary to support the plan. If anything, the G8 leaders made only vague promises and reiterated commitments already made during previous meetings. Although G8 leaders agreed to discuss the issue further, in France in 2003, this was empty rhetoric for critics like Oxfam's Phil Twyford: 'They are offering peanuts to Africa and repackaged peanuts at that ... When it comes down to the wire they could not get their act together' (*Vancouver Province*, 30 June). As a result of this lack of assertiveness, the development of Prime Minister Chrétien's 'African legacy' was put on hold.

Kyoto Protocol

Problems continued to dog Canadian policymakers responsible for dealing with the Kyoto Protocol on international climate change. At the start of an April meeting of G8 environment ministers in Banff, Alberta, environmentalists criticized Canadian Environment Minister David Anderson's plan to downplay global warming and focus the discussions on other matters. Consider, for instance, the assertion made by Greenpeace's Joanne Dufay: 'We agree, there are many important environmental issues. But of those issues, climate change is the most important. And if Minister Anderson cannot use this opportunity of this international meeting to address [the] Kyoto issue and commit to ratification, then really you have to ask, where is this government's commitment?' (Canadian Broadcasting Corporation, 13 April). When the Kyoto Protocol was eventually raised at the meeting, other international ministers attacked Canada's call for revisions to take into account Canada's export of natural gas and electricity to the United States. For them, not only did this approach not feature the cutting of greenhouse gas emissions, it was also of little utility, given that the U.S. government had indicated that it would not ratify the Kyoto Protocol. As for Minister Anderson, he remained unconvinced by these arguments: 'I think we're going to have to have a better explanation from the critics of clean energy exports as to why they oppose measures that reduce the amount of greenhouse gases in the atmosphere' (Canadian Broadcasting Corporation, 15 April).

Despite these challenges, the federal government continually asserted that it would ratify the protocol. Not only was ratification mentioned in the Throne Speech, but also the government introduced in the House of Commons on 21 November its plan to cut 240 megatonnes of greenhouse gas emissions by 2012. Many Canadian politicians, however, such as Alberta Premier Ralph Klein, voiced their scepticism: 'Now they are starting to wonder about the protocol, what impact it will have on the economy, the validity of the scientific evidence' (Canadian Broadcasting Corporation, 4 September). In fact, in September, the Alberta government launched a $1.5 million national campaign to publicize the faults and problems of the Kyoto Protocol. Similarly, for Canadian Alliance leader Stephen Harper, the Canadian plan was still too vague and so fraught with uncertainties that he warned it could become 'another in a long list of multibillion-dollar boondoggles' (ibid., 10 December). Nevertheless, on 10 December the Parliament approved Canadian ratification of the Kyoto Protocol, a decision that the prime minister heralded as a momentous occasion: 'It's a great day for Canada, a great day for the environment and a great day for the future of our kids ... It's not for us. It's for generations to come' (ibid.). The final vote was 195 for and 77 against, with the Bloc Québécois and the New Democrats siding with the government, while the Progressive

Conservative and Canadian Alliance parties voted against ratification. Although Canada delivered to the United Nations in New York its instrument of ratification on 17 December, Ottawa also made it plain that more work remained. According to Natural Resources Minister Dhaliwal, 'ratification is an important milestone in Canada's contribution to addressing climate change. Now, we can look forward to the next challenge of the implementation phase' (DFAIT News Release no. 174, 17 December). Addressing this considerable challenge was left to 2003.

War on terror

As outlined below, Canada's participation in the war on terror continued on a variety of fronts in 2002. These activities were made all the more poignant when, in November 2002, the Arabic television network al-Jazeera aired a tape purportedly made by Osama bin Laden. On this tape the voice indicated that Canada – along with Australia, France, Germany, and the United Kingdom – would be the target of future attacks in light of its support for U.S. policies. After the broadcast, Canadian officials went to great pains to assert that attacks on Canada or Canadians were not deemed to be imminent. Moreover, as expressed by Deputy Prime Minister Manley, the tape would not change Canada's stance on the war on terror: 'Threats such as these merely strengthen our resolve' (Canadian Broadcasting Corporation, 14 November).

Nevertheless, Canadian diligence was seemingly warranted, given other concerns regarding threats either posed by or to Canadians. In January the U.S. Justice Department indicated that it was looking for two Canadians linked to Al-Qaeda. The two Tunisian-born men and holders of Canadian passports, Al Rauf bin Al Habib bin Yousef Al-Jiddi and Faker Boussora, were last known to have lived in the Montreal area. At the time, other agencies such as the U.S. Federal Bureau of Investigation, the Canadian Security and Intelligence Service, and the RCMP were working to track down these individuals. Later, in March, the Senate Standing Committee on National Security and Defence reported that Canadian port security was weak. The committee concluded that organized crime had infiltrated the docks and that 15 to 39 per cent of the employees at the ports had criminal records. For the committee, the risk was evident: 'Clearly, this lack of control creates a fertile ground for terrorist activity, including covert immigration, and potentially the covert importation and shipment of weapons and other agents of mass destruction' (cited in Canadian Broadcasting Corporation, 2 March). The implications, therefore, were that either organized crime would assist in terrorist operations or, if the ports were so permeable to crime, then terrorist organizations could take advantage of these security weaknesses, too.

The federal government was put on the defensive by U.S. border and immigration policies introduced in 2002. In October Ottawa advised Canadian citizens born in Iran, Iraq, Libya, Syria, and Sudan to avoid travel to the United States, as they would be both fingerprinted and photographed by U.S. officials. Similarly, Ottawa indicated that Canadian citizens born in Pakistan, Saudi Arabia, or Yemen might also attract attention at the border. In response to this U.S. policy, Foreign Affairs Minister Graham complained directly to U.S. Secretary of State Colin Powell: 'People only come to this country and get access as landed immigrants and Canadian citizenship if we've done thorough security checks. And that's what I'm telling my American colleague' (Canadian Broadcasting Corporation, 31 October). Graham's protests were made more urgent by the fact that the United States had already deported one Canadian to Syria. On 26 September U.S. officials at New York City's Kennedy Airport detained Maher Arar, a Syrian-born Canadian, as he returned to Canada via the United States from a vacation in Tunisia. U.S. officials deemed him to be an Al-Qaeda operative, and deported him to Syria, a country that he had not visited since his immigration to Canada in 1988. For NDP leader Alexa McDonough, the Arar case was an extreme violation of human rights: 'Maher Arar was detained, imprisoned, interrogated, and deported without the benefit of legal counsel, without consular access, without any explanation to his family. With no explanation to government. This should be a concern to every Canadian' (*Ottawa Citizen*, 17 December).

On the proactive side, as one of the continued signs of Canada's growing engagement in the war on terror, the federal government re-established diplomatic relations with Afghanistan on 25 January 2002.[6] Canada had terminated these relations in the wake of the Soviet Union's invasion of the country in 1979. Deputy Prime Minister Manley announced the renewed ties while on a nine day trip to Pakistan, India, and Afghanistan to discuss the war on terror with regional leaders. For Manley, improved relations between the two countries were a key element to ensure a stable and terror-free Afghanistan: 'The re-establishment of diplomatic ties with Afghanistan underscores Canada's support for the Interim Administration and our commitment to continue work-

6 Konrad Sigurdson, Canada's High Commissioner to Pakistan, was given concurrent accreditation to Afghanistan.

ing closely with officials in Kabul to rebuild the country and improve the lives of its citizens' (DFAIT News Release no. 6, 25 January). This re-engagement was also necessary, given the augmented Afghan-focus in Canadian development assistance. Whereas Canada provided only $144 million in aid to Afghanistan from 1990 until 11 September 2001, Canada pledged $100 million during the 21–22 January 2002 Tokyo Conference on Reconstruction in Afghanistan.

Also on the international level, Canada was at the forefront in terms of advancing international law pertaining to terrorism. On 15 February at the United Nations in New York, Canada announced its ratification of the International Convention for the Suppression of the Financing of Terrorism. This convention 'required Canada to criminalize the provision or collection of funds used or intended for use in committing terrorist acts' (noted in DFAIT News Release no. 16, 15 February). Canada's Anti-Terrorism Act ensured that Canada complied with the convention's stipulations. Similarly, on 2 December Canada became the first country to announce its ratification of the Organization of American States' Inter-American Convention Against Terrorism. According to Justice Minister and Attorney General Martin Cauchon, this ratification clearly demonstrates Canada's resolve in the war on terror: 'Today the government advances that commitment [to fight terror] by ratifying this Convention, allowing more effective collaboration with our international partners in the Americas. The Convention complements Canada's Anti-Terrorism Act, which represents a comprehensive legislative strategy against the threat of terrorism' (DFAIT News Release no. 166, 2 December). This convention calls for all OAS members to develop their own anti-terrorism laws and to be parties to all ten UN counter-terrorism instruments. Canada had signed and ratified all ten by the close of 2002.

At the domestic level, however, the government's approach was not so smooth, as it faced challenges and policy changes. In December the federal government elected to outlaw both the military and social wings of Lebanon-based Hezbollah, even though Foreign Minister Graham had contended earlier that this was not appropriate because the social arm was a legitimate charity that ran hospitals and schools. Both the Canadian Alliance and Jewish groups criticized this position. Indeed, B'nai Brith Canada launched a lawsuit to force the government to change its policy. When the policy change was made, government ministers insisted that they had not buckled to pressure. According to Solicitor General Wayne Easter, 'the decision was made, and why it takes so long to make it, is that we base that decision on criminal, security intelligence reports that we can back up factually' (Canadian Broadcasting Corporation, 13 December). With the announcement of the banning, Hezbollah joined fifteen other organizations on Canada's blacklist that included Al-Qaeda, Hamas, the Palestinian Islamic Jihad, Aum Shinri Kyo, and the Kurdistan Workers Party.

The federal government also faced problems and criticism directed at its Public Safety Act. First introduced as Bill C-42 in the autumn of 2001, the government dropped it in light of widespread opposition regarding the threat that the bill, if passed, posed to civil liberties. The Chrétien government replaced it on 29 April with Bill C-55. Like its predecessor, Bill C-55 afforded ministers the ability to suspend laws and issue decrees in the name of national security. But unlike Bill C-42's provisions, Bill C-55 called for these decisions to receive approval from cabinet within forty-five days rather than ninety days. Also, Bill C-55 gave the minister of national defence authority to declare temporary military zones, but only around military equipment located in civilian areas. Bill C-42, in contrast, allowed the minister to declare much wider zones. Largely unchanged from C-42 were the new bill's provisions for Canada's security bodies to scan air passenger manifests for terrorists or individuals with outstanding warrants for serious offences. For Transport Minister David Collenette, the changes in Bill C-55 were warranted: 'The changes proposed in this legislation are just plain common sense. It responds to the need for enhanced security while respecting the rights of Canadians' (*National Post*, 30 April).

Bill C-55, encountered a rocky time both within and outside of the House of Commons. Despite the changes, for civil libertarians and for many within the Liberal caucus itself, the proposed legislation was still draconian. As such, the government allowed Bill C-55 to die on the order paper when Parliament prorogued in September. In its place, the government introduced yet another edition, Bill C-17, at the end of October. Gone were the proposed powers regarding military zones. In their place, the defence minister could establish special access zones in the ports of Halifax, Esquimalt, and Nanoose Bay. The provisions regarding airline passengers were also watered down. Once again, Minister Collenette put a brave face to the government's stance: 'After reflection and debate in the House, the government has listened to members on this side and on the other side and has improved the legislation ... That is why we introduced Bill C-17 today, an improved bill that will guarantee our security' (*Leader Post*, 1 November). Even with these changes, however, the bill was not voted upon in the House of Commons during the remainder of 2002.

One twist that the government had to contend with in the war on terror was the Bush administration's focus on Iraq. President Bush signalled this during his 29 January State of the Union Address, when he labelled Iraq as one component of the 'Axis of Evil' (the other two being Iran and North Korea). For Bush, matters of concern were Iraq's presumed programs to build weapons of mass destruction and the links that Saddam Hussein's regime might have with terrorist organizations. These concerns were reinforced in September when the White House issued its *National Security Strategy of the United States*, which emphasized the need for pre-emptive action against terrorist threats: 'We must be prepared to stop rogue states and their terrorist clients before they are able to threaten or use weapons of mass destruction against the United States, and our allies and friends ... The greater the threat, the greater is the risk for inaction, and the more compelling the case for taking anticipatory action to defend ourselves, even if uncertainty remains as to the time and the place of the enemy's attack' (cited in *Vancouver Province*, 22 September).

Early on in the new year, therefore, the Liberal government faced pressure not only from the United States to support action against Iraq, but also from Opposition parties on how to respond to Washington's intentions. Alexa McDonough of the NDP called for Canada to disavow U.S. policies: 'I just think Canadians want to hear loud and clear just like other countries have said that they will not be part of any U.S. aggression toward Iraq, period' (Canadian Broadcasting Corporation, 19 February). The Canadian Alliance, however, wanted Canada to step up and align itself with the United States. Consider the words of Alliance MP Brian Pallister: 'I believe Canada should offer its support to the United States. The least we can do is make sure we don't hide in the sand or let our wobbly knees get in the way' (ibid.). The prime minister, for his part, cautioned the United States not to undertake any unilateral move against Iraq, but contended that everything was hypothetical, that there was no cause to believe a U.S. strike was imminent: 'You can have an academic debate if you want, but we deal with reality and reality is that it's not on the table at this time' (ibid.).

The matter was increasingly 'on the table,' however, as the year progressed. As a result, the Chrétien government started to offer the provisos that, first, there had to be clear evidence that Iraq possessed Weapons of mass destruction and, later, that any attack had to be sanctioned by the United Nations. Although expressed in a somewhat confusing way, the prime minister wanted the necessary evidence before Canada made any official commitments: 'A proof is a proof. What kind of a proof? It's a proof. A proof is a proof. And when you have a good proof, it's because it's proven' (Canadian Broadcasting Corporation, 6 September). Perhaps more eloquently, Foreign Minister Graham suggested that Iraq must be found to be not only producing weapons of mass destruction, but also to be actively threatening the West with them because 'otherwise, there are lots of countries around that have weapons of mass destruction. We can't presumably attack them all' (ibid.). Again, the opposition parties chimed in with their views. Canadian Alliance foreign affairs critic Stockwell Day suggested that Canada 'should be very seriously looking at allying ourselves with Britain and the U.S.,' while Alexa McDonough charged that 'it is a grotesque absence of leadership on the part of the prime minister to just kind of shrug and say, "Sure Bush, bring on the evidence and then count us in on a war"' (ibid.).

By the end of the year, even as the crisis heightened, the federal government had not yet officially stated whether it supported U.S. policy in Iraq. In the autumn of 2002, Iraqi officials agreed both to let UN arms inspectors return to Iraq and to provide documentation on its WMD programs. This came on the heels of Security Council Resolution 1441, passed on 8 November, which warned of serious 'consequences' if Iraq did not admit weapons inspectors. Nevertheless, whereas Iraq's subsequent moves were met with some optimism by countries like France and Germany, they were greeted with scepticism in Washington. The Canadian government's fence-sitting, therefore, caused consternation and confusion for many U.S. and Canadian officials. Although the prime minister reiterated at the end of the year that Canada would not act against Iraq without the approval of the United Nations, the Bush administration had already provided Canada with a list of military personnel and equipment that it would like Ottawa to deploy should it agree to military action against Iraq. Given that in mid-December the Bush Administration indicated that more than 100,000 U.S. soldiers would be in the region by January 2003, it was evident that the Canadian government would likely have to rule conclusively in the new year on the issue of Canadian participation in military operations against Iraq.

Indeed, Washington's stance on Iraq in the larger war on terror was already causing some embarrassment for the Chrétien government. During what she thought was a private conversation with a CBC Radio reporter during the NATO summit in Prague in November, Françoise Ducros, the prime minister's director of communications, asserted that President Bush was 'a moron.' After the comment became public, the prime minister refused to accept her resignation on 22 November, but then did accept it on 26 November in light of the growing controversy. For Canadian Alliance leader Stephen Harper, the remark was 'the insult heard around the world' (Canadian Broadcasting Corporation, 26 November). It was a topic on U.S. news programs. It was picked up by Iraq's official newspaper and used to question international support for U.S. policies. It was also apparently a topic of conversation when former Prime Minister Brian Mulroney met with President Bush in the White House in December. For Mulroney, the comment had damaged relations between the two countries: 'I can guarantee you, this is not a comment that escaped attention in Washington; let me put it to you that way' (*Windsor Star*, 14 December). Finally, Progressive Conservative leader Joe Clark accused the prime minister of making the matter worse by never issuing an apology and not immediately accepting Ducros' resignation: 'Jean Chrétien [refused] to act on a matter that has obviously caused a great embarrassment to the government and the country. She acted honourably; he has acted irresponsibly' (*Calgary Herald*, 27 November).

Another controversy on whether the government acted responsibly in the war on terror arose on the first anniversary of 9/11, and it too involved the media. At issue here was a CBC TV program, taped in July but aired on 11 September 2002, in which government officials talked about their response to the terrorist attacks. First, David Collenette and Margaret Bloodworth, the minister and deputy minister of transport respectively in September 2001, indicated that when the United States closed its airspace, they diverted hundreds of flights to smaller airports in the Atlantic Provinces, for fear that they might be carrying terrorists who might attack larger cities in Quebec and Ontario.[7] After the airing, the Opposition parties contended that this showed insensitivity towards Eastern Canadians, an accusation that was met with a stern response by Minister Collenette: 'To utter that kind of statement is ridiculous. It's nonsensical and it just does not pay any attention to the problem that we had. We had to react. We had to react quickly. We did' (*Calgary Herald*, 14 September).

Second, and perhaps even more controversial, was the prime minister's remark that poor countries 'necessarily will look upon us [the West] as being arrogant, self-satisfied, greedy and with no limits. And the 11th of September is an occasion for me to realize it even more.' He

7 Over 21,000 passengers were diverted to airports in Atlantic Canada in the wake of the terror attacks.

also commented that 'you cannot exercise your powers to the point of humiliation for the others. And that is what the Western world – not only the Americans, the Western world – has to realize, because they are human beings too, and there are long-term consequences' (*National Post*, 14 September). Government critics took this to mean that the United States bore some responsibility for the 11 September 2001 attacks. On U.S. television, Canadian Alliance leader Stephen Harper asserted that Canadians were 'shocked and outraged' by the prime minister's comments (*National Post*, 14 September). In a similar vein, Alberta Premier Ralph Klein also thought the prime minister's comments to be unwise: 'I don't agree with that at all – that the West is susceptible to these kinds of terrorist attacks because of our rich, so-called arrogant attitude ... I think these are attacks by people who have murder and mayhem on their minds. They're no better, and just as bad, as those people who in domestic society murder other people or rob banks and create terrible crimes' (*Calgary Herald*, 14 September). The Prime Minister's Office, in response, issued a statement on 12 September contending that Prime Minister Chrétien's comments had been portrayed inaccurately.

Defence policy

Canadian land forces in Afghanistan

In 2002 the Canadian Army became fully engaged in Operation Apollo, Canada's contribution to the war on terror in Afghanistan. In 2001 the government ordered aircraft, ships, and a contingent of Canada's special forces unit, Joint Task Force 2, to the region, and the 3rd Battalion of the Princess Patricia's Canadian Light Infantry, based in Edmonton, Alberta, was placed on standby. On 7 January 2002 Minister of National Defence Art Eggleton announced that the wait was over; Canada would send to Afghanistan a battlegroup made up of 3 PPCLI and elements of Lord Strathcona's Horse. The deployment represented the army's first offensive combat mission since the Korean War. The battle group commander, Lieutenant-Colonel Pat Stogran, indicated that his troops would not shy away from whatever was asked of them: 'Our mandate is for the full spectrum of operations. Canada's interested of course in eliminating the terrorist threat as well as building the nation, so we're going to be involved in just about everything' (Canadian Broadcasting Corporation, 16 January). The first wave of advance troops arrived in Afghanistan in mid-January, and the bulk of the battle group arrived at the start of February. By the beginning of March the battle group stood at 880 personnel.[8] In total, from the three services, Canada had committed approximately 3,000 members to this particular operation in the war on terror.

The battle group was based in Kandahar and was part of a U.S. Army Task Force built around the U.S. 101st Airborne Division. In conjunction with the U.S. soldiers, the Canadian troops did several forays out of the Kandahar region to confront elements of either Al-Qaeda or the Taliban. In particular, in March Canadian soldiers participated in Operation Harpoon in a mountainous region in Afghanistan called the Whale. They also, in May, participated in Operation Torii, again in the mountainous regions of the country. The goals of these operations were to search for enemy fighters, destroy their bases of operation, and find information about their plans and the terrorist network writ-large. Furthermore, Canadian snipers participated alongside their U.S. colleagues in Operation Anaconda, in March, an operation that featured the surrounding of a region 155 kilometres south of Gardez, Afghanistan, in order to prevent Al-Qaeda or Taliban fighters from escaping.

Despite the optimism suggested by Canadian military and political officials, there was some concern regarding the Canadian contingent. Some reports indicated that the Canadian snipers had to rely on equipment provided by the Americans and other allies. Other reports noted that the lack of Canadian strategic lift capabilities forced the army to rely on U.S. aircraft and prevented the timely arrival of the battle group. Finally, some found it troubling that the Canadians lacked the desert camouflage uniforms worn by other allied armies. Members of the battle group had to wear their forest green uniforms because the desert uniforms were on order and were not to arrive until the summer of 2002. Although the forest green uniforms would not pose a problem at night, there was a fear that the Canadians would stick out in daytime operations.[9]

On 21 May the federal government announced that the main part of the battle group was to return in July and that Canada would not be providing a follow-up contingent. In light of the level of participation that the battle group undertook in Afghanistan, Defence Minister Eggleton contended that 'Canadian soldiers made us all proud. They have proved

8 On 1 March 2002 the government announced that it would also send to the region a 130-strong company of the Winnipeg-based 2nd Battalion, Princess Patricia's Canadian Light Infantry.

9 The battle group had, in fact, trained, extensively but not exclusively, for night operations in Afghanistan. Note that the friendly fire incident (see below) occurred during one of these training sessions.

once again that they are among the most skilled and professional in the world. Our soldiers continue to make an important contribution to the overall coalition efforts to fight terrorism and fulfill the mandate of bringing peace and stability to Afghanistan' (DND News Release no. 02.032, 21 May). The first wave of Canadians returned to Edmonton on 29 July, after spending a week of rest and recuperation in Guam.

'Friendly fire' incident

Unfortunately, just as the Afghan operation was the army's first offensive mission since the 1950s, it also featured Canada's first losses since that time. At approximately midnight on 18 April, members of the Canadian contingent were participating in a live-fire exercise near their base at Tarnak Farm. Flying overhead at this time was two U.S. F-16s from the 183rd Fighter Wing of the Air National Guard, based in Springfield, Illinois. The pilot of the second jet, Major Harry Schmidt, was unaware that the Canadian training exercise was under way. On seeing the muzzle flashes below, he deemed that he and Major William Umbach the lead pilot, were being fired upon, and he dropped a 220 kilogram laser-guided bomb in response. The tragic result was the deaths of four Canadians: Sergeant Marc Leger, Corporal Ainsworth Dyer, Private Richard Green, and Private Nathan Smith. Eight additional Canadians were injured, six of them so seriously that they were airlifted to the U.S. Air Force medical hospital in Ramstein, Germany. Governor General Adrienne Clarkson visited with the six soldiers upon their arrival in Europe.

Both the United States and Canada reacted immediately to this 'friendly fire' incident. General Richard Myers, chairman of the U.S. Joint Chiefs of Staff, described the event as 'right up there with the worst news I've heard in my career' (Canadian Broadcasting Corporation, 19 April). Both the U.S. Pentagon and Canada's Department of National Defence launched investigations on 19 April. Canada also initiated the Tarnak Farm Board of Inquiry, headed by a former chief of defence staff, retired General Maurice Baril. Given a sixty-day mandate, the board conducted its investigations in Edmonton, the Arabian Gulf, and Afghanistan. It interacted with Canadians and Americans, and although it did not meet directly with Major Schmidt, the BOI did receive a written response to its queries.

In the end, both the U.S. investigation and the Tarnak Farm Board of Inquiry determined that the fire emanating from below did not put the F-16 at risk, and although Major Schmidt had been given permission to 'mark' the target, air traffic control had not given permission to bomb.[10] Major Schmidt dropped his bomb, nevertheless, in an act of self-defence as pilots are allowed to do. The board also found that the Canadians had made the proper notifications regarding their live-fire night-time exercise. The report asserted, therefore, that the Americans demonstrated 'failure of airmanship and technique' and a 'failure of leadership' (cited in Canadian Broadcasting Corporation, 29 June). As a result of these inquires, the U.S. Air Force in September charged Major Schmidt with four counts of involuntary manslaughter and eight counts of assault. As Major Schmidt's commander, Major Umbach was charged with aiding and abetting both manslaughter and assault. They also faced charges related to flight discipline, the improper firing of weapons, failure in leadership, and dereliction of duty. In total, each pilot faced upwards of sixty-four years in prison. In January 2003 the U.S. Air Force planned to convene an Article 32 hearing to determine whether there was sufficient evidence to proceed with a court martial of the two pilots.

In the midst of the investigations and the publicity surrounding the case, a number of events augmented the controversy surrounding the issue. In July the publication of some transcripts cast doubt on whether the pilots were acting without the appropriate authorization, which in turn raised concerns that the pilots were scapegoats. Later, in October, Governor George Ryan of Illinois opened his official residence for a fundraiser to raise money that would go towards the legal defence fund for Majors Schmidt and Umbach. In November it was revealed that, as part of the exercise, some of the Canadians were firing into the air, a fact that supported Major Schmidt's contention that he believed he was indeed at risk. Finally, in December, it was publicized that the U.S. pilots were on 'speed' or 'uppers' at the time of the bombing, a common practice for U.S. Air Force pilots to maintain their alertness during long flights, but one that was criticized by some for potentially impairing judgment.

Ministerial change – Department of National Defence

Art Eggleton's tenure as minister of national defence came to a close in 2002, after some rocky months at the start of the year. Many variables, taken together, precipitated his removal from cabinet. To begin, in January debate raged over whether Canadian military personnel would

10 Both reports were released on 28 June 2002.

hand over to the Americans any Al-Qaeda or Taliban operatives they captured in Afghanistan. The issue was controversial because prisoners held by the U.S. military were denied prisoner-of-war status. When asked, on 28 January, what Canada would do should Canadian soldiers make any captures in Afghanistan, the prime minister dismissed the question as 'purely hypothetical' (Canadian Broadcasting Corporation, 30 January). However, on 29 January, Minister Eggleton admitted that 'we have been involved in the capturing of prisoners, yes' (ibid.). In his reference to a photograph that had appeared on the front page of the *Globe and Mail* a week earlier, Eggleton noted 'underneath the picture it said: U.S. soldiers. But did you notice the fact they had forest green uniforms those three soldiers that were in that picture? Well, they were Canadian, JTF2 [Joint Task Force 2]' (ibid.). Eggleton also admitted that he did not learn of the JTF2 operation until 25 January and did not tell cabinet of the capture until 28 January. For Progressive Conservative leader Joe Clark, this revealed a breakdown in communications and a lack of leadership: 'Why in the world did he not tell? Why in the world did he not tell the prime minister? Who's in charge of this bunch of keystone cops?' (ibid.).

Things became even worse for Eggleton when he changed his story by asserting that he first learned of the operation on 21 January, not 25 January. Moreover, he argued that he had held off informing cabinet so that he could get more and clearer information on the operation. Given that Minister Eggleton seemingly misled the House of Commons on the issue, Speaker Peter Milliken decided that the matter had to be taken up by the House of Commons Committee on Procedure and House Affairs. During the course of the committee hearings in February, senior military leaders such as Vice-Admiral Greg Maddison asserted that they had briefed the minister fully on the issue on 21 January: 'The minister was briefed that we had been on a successful mission, that we had followed the appropriate rules of engagement, that none of our people was hurt, that we had captured suspected Afghani terrorists, or al-Qaida terrorists, that they had been transported safely, that they had been turned over to the Americans' (*Daily News*, 27 February). The chief of defence staff, General Ray Henault, asserted that the minister had even been briefed before the mission's launch. Even more damaging was the vice-admiral's claim that, although the minister had been briefed three times on the operation, it was only on the third time that the minister seemed to 'click' (*Toronto Star*, 28 February). For Alexa McDonough, such claims were damning: 'For Canadians, it's no longer a question of whether the defence minister lied or whether he's incompetent ... It's gone way beyond that. It's clear that the defence minister is not up to the task' (*Charlottetown Guardian*, 28 February). Despite these criticisms, the prime minister contended in the House of Commons that he had complete faith in his defence minister: 'Myself, the cabinet and the Liberal party has confidence in the abilities and the dedication of the minister of National Defence' (*Toronto Star*, 28 February).

The prime minister finally lost faith in his defence minister at the end of May when he was shuffled out of cabinet. The straw that broke the camel's back was the revelation that Maggie Maier, Eggleton's former girlfriend, was asked to produce, at a cost of $36,500, a fourteen-page report on post-traumatic stress disorder in the military. Eggleton defended his decision to order the report and pay Maier out of the ministerial budget: 'It was an expenditure of public money that produced a result and helped an issue that I've been concerned about and that is the health of our troops ... I asked her to keep it brief, concise and to the point and that's exactly what she did' (*Toronto Star*, 29 May). The report, however, appeared to be redundant because two federal bodies were producing similar reports at the same time. Moreover, the revelations were followed by front-page pictures in newspapers featuring the minister and Maier at a party. In light of the specific problems related to Eggleton, as well as other problems concerning the Liberal government's handling of other issues, the prime minister sacrificed his minister of national defence.

As Eggleton's replacement, the prime minister selected John McCallum, another Toronto-based MP. Prior to entering politics in 2000, McCallum had been professor of finance, the Dean of Arts at McGill University, and the chief economist for the Royal Bank of Canada. Before his assignment to the defence portfolio, McCallum had been the junior finance minister. McCallum claimed that, like most defence ministers over the previous twenty years, he had no military experience; he had only served as an air cadet at Trinity College School in the 1960s: 'I had quite a good time in cadets – target shooting, marching and all that ... Although I cannot claim to have enjoyed all the marching and shoe polishing' (*National Post*, 30 May). For Opposition MPs, like the Canadian Alliance's James Moore, the selection of McCallum simply revealed how low defence was on the government's list of priorities: 'His appointment just shows you how little respect the government has for the military ... [he] doesn't know anything about the military and was only recently elected' (*Toronto Star*, 1 June). Nevertheless, McCallum dismissed such criticism by claiming that he did indeed have the tools necessary to perform in the position: 'I think politics, a lot of it, is power of persuasion. You have to persuade the prime minister, cabinet colleagues and caucus colleagues of what you want to do and there are always competing demands. So I will be doing my very best to learn this dossier as fast and as thoroughly as I can and figure out what we want to do, and then try to persuade people' (*Toronto Star*, 1 June).

Assessment, status quo, and change

During 2002 both Senate and parliamentary committees released reports that commented on the sorry state of the Canadian military in light of its lack of resources, understaffing, and overcommitment. First, in its February report, *Canadian Security and Military Preparedness*, the Senate Standing Committee on National Security and Defence calculated that the military needed a personnel level of 75,000, up from the 60,000 mandated in a 1994 White Paper, to sustain the high level of contemporary operations. The committee also concluded that DND's baseline budget required an immediate increase of $4 billion and that annual budget increases must be 'realistic, purpose-driven, and adjusted for inflation.'

Later, in May, the House of Commons Standing Committee on National Defence and Veterans Affairs issued its report, *Facing Our Responsibilities: The State of Readiness of the Canadian Forces*, which built on the issues identified by the Senate committee. The main theme of the report's twenty-five recommendations was that 'the status quo is not acceptable.' Some of the recommendations related to general budgeting such as the call that, for Canada to stay in line with its NATO counterparts, DND's budget within three years should be raised from 1.1 per cent of Canada's gross domestic product to between 1.5 and 1.6 per cent of the GDP. This would make DND's annual budget as large as $18 billion, up from approximately $12 billion. For committee chairman David Pratt, such a change was certainly appropriate: 'What we are suggesting is realistic ... And I think as well, that in relation to our NATO allies, it would allow us to hold our heads a little higher around the NATO table not being the country next to Luxembourg in terms of spending' (*National Post*, 31 May). The committee also made very specific recommendations about procurement and repair. It found that the government should approve funding for the purchase of strategic sealift capability and heavy lift airborne capability, the replacement of Canada's Tribal class destroyers and Sea King helicopters, and the upgrading of Canada's twelve frigates and eighteen Aurora long-range patrol aircraft.

In the autumn of 2002 the Senate committee issued two more reports. In a September document, entitled *Defence of North America: A Canadian Responsibility*, SCONSAD determined that, given the limitations of the Canadian military and the nature of contemporary threats, more needed to be done with respect to coordination and cooperation with the United States. For SCONSAD, joint training and joint planning would improve Canada's ability to respond to both natural and man-made disasters. Later, in November, in *For an Extra 130 bucks ... Update on Canada's Military Financial Crisis: A View from the Bottom*, SCONSAD argued that its aforementioned $4 billion annual increase to the Department of National Defence, equating to $130 per Canadian, could be conceived as a modest insurance increase to ensure the safety of Canada. More controversially, the committee concluded that the armed forces were so overtaxed that there should be a thirty-month moratorium on overseas operations in order to revitalize and rearm the military.

For the most part, the government did not take up the various recommendations. The operational pause suggested by SCONSAD was rejected. Similarly, even though all four parliamentary parties supported the House of Commons committee's recommendations, the prime minister dashed hopes that substantial increases in funding would be forthcoming: 'There are all kinds of demands on the government, and we don't have unlimited resources' (*National Post*, 31 May). As well, in November, Defence Minister McCallum told U.S. Ambassador to Canada Paul Cellucci to mind his own business when Cellucci commented that Canada needed to take steps to ensure the strength and viability of its military.

This stance taken by Ottawa in 2002, however, was at odds with the fact that even though the United States wanted Canada to stay on longer in Afghanistan, Ottawa announced the removal of the Canadian battle group in May because of the military's limitations. In July Defence Minister McCallum announced that Canada's contribution in Bosnia would fall from 1,500 to 1,200, which meant that 600 fewer soldiers would be deployed overseas annually. Although this decision to reduce Canadian troop levels was linked to a reorganization of NATO forces in Bosnia, it reinforced the fact that the army was taking an operational pause, although not a structured one – as wished for by SCONSAD.

One issue on which the government did act concerned closer coordination and cooperation with the United States. After months of negotiations and consultations with the Americans, Defence Minister McCallum and Foreign Affairs Minister Graham announced on 9 December the creation of the bi-national planning group. This group, funded at $35 million, headed by a Canadian general, and staffed with thirty officers from both countries, was to be located at North American Aerospace Defence Command headquarters in Colorado Springs, Colorado. The group's two-year objective was to plan contingencies and joint- response policies that could be initiated in the wake of a terrorist attack or natural disaster somewhere in North America. As described by Minister McCallum, 'the new Canada–U.S. Planning Group will ensure that militaries on both sides of the border are in a better position to assist one another and civilian first responders in times of crisis in either of our countries' (DND News Release no. 02.079, 9 December). Perhaps the most controversial issue concerned control and the loss of Canadian sovereignty. Both ministers went to great lengths to indicate that this was not the case and that the planning group was not linked to the U.S. Northern Command. For instance, Minister Graham argued that 'by planning together and thinking through our joint responses in the event of catastrophe, we enhance both our sovereignty and our security' (*Calgary Herald*, 10 December). The ministers also indicated that U.S. soldiers would only come into Canadian territory upon the invitation of the Canadian government, and even then, they would be under the direction of the Canadian military. Similar requirements also existed should Canadians be asked to assist in crises south of the border. Despite these assertions, Lieutenant-General Ken Pennie, the Canadian head of the group, indicated that closer integration, along the lines of NORAD, might come into being: 'Once we do this for a period of time, and figure out what the best way of co-operation is, then the planning group may come up with other ideas that may be considered binationally. Those ideas that survive may work themselves into, potentially, the NORAD agreement in 2006 when it comes up for renewal' (*National Post*, 9 December).

Procurement

Canada's 1998 decision to purchase four used diesel electric submarines from the United Kingdom, mothballed since 1994, proved to be a continuing target of criticism is 2002. Certainly, the arrangement seemed to be a good financial deal from the Canadian perspective. Canada agreed to lease the submarines over eight years for $750 million and offer the British military access to Canadian training facilities. At the end of the eight years Canada would have the option to purchase them for £1. Given that Canada was getting four submarines for arguably the cost of one, Defence Minister McCallum described the deal as 'hugely cheap' (*Daily News*, 24 October). HMCS *Victoria*, however, the first of the submarines to be received by Canada, spent the bulk of 2002 in dry dock in Halifax because of cracks found in its diesel exhaust valves. Once in dry dock, the Canadian Navy also found a dent in the ship's hull the size of a pizza pan, the result of a collision that the United Kingdom had failed to tell Canada about. Because of this dent, the Canadian Navy restricted HMCS *Victoria* to only half of its normal diving depth. DND documents also revealed in 2002 that the life-support system on the submarine did not meet the necessary air-quality specifications. Another submarine, HMCS *Corner Brook*, still in the United Kingdom on sea trials, experienced a significant flood while off Scotland in July. As a result of problems such as these, the Canadian Navy announced that none of the four 'new' submarines would be fully operational until 2004, well behind the scheduled date of 2000. Minister McCallum did his best to downplay the significance of the delay: 'I don't think that the world will be a much less dangerous place two years from now than it is today' (*Daily News*, 24 October).

Naval officials and analysts, for their part, repeatedly offered their support for the beleaguered program. The head of the Navy, Vice-Admiral Ron Buck, pointed towards the extreme complexity of making mothballed submarines once again seaworthy, a degree of complexity that was not unexpected: 'The fact is, they were basically cocooned for a period of years. Most of these [problems] are issues that are, from a naval perspective, routine business. The good news is what we are doing is making sure these submarines will be fit for service' (*Ottawa Citizen*, 30 October). Defence analysts, such as Peter Haydon, echoed the vice-admiral's assessment: 'It's an enormously complex technical project to mothball a submarine, take it out of mothballs again and then get it all running ... Not even the Brits knew what the implications of mothballing were; it was just something that's never been done before ... That was one of the accepted facts of the deal – that it was going to take some time to reactivate these beasts' (*Daily News*, 18 August). Others noted the attributes submarines brought to the Canadian fleet and Canadian defence policy: they could conduct patrols in approximately twice the area as Canadian surface vessels; they could stay out to sea four times longer than Canadian surface patrols; their costs were lower, both in terms of reduced manpower and lower fuel consumption; and their presence in the Canadian fleet was strongly approved by key allies such as the United Kingdom and the United States. When assessed in terms of the patience required and the benefits to be accrued, Vice-Admiral Buck concluded 'at the end of the day, I would tell you these submarines are not lemons' (*Ottawa Citizen*, 30 October).

Another controversial procurement decision in 2002 was the government's $101 million rush order to buy two new Challenger aircraft meant to replace the existing twenty-year-old fleet of executive aircraft consisting of an earlier version of the Challenger. The government's rationale for the March decision was to avoid further mishaps such as the one in 1999 when the engine emergency alarms sounded on the prime minister's jet while he was returning to Ottawa from Quebec City. As well, in 2001 the prime minister's jet made an emergency landing in Stockholm, Sweden, because of a drop in cabin pressure. For the prime minister, then, necessity dictated the purchase: 'Many times, I've been involved in some urgent landings with the one we have at his moment – many times' (Canadian Broadcasting Corporation, 27 November). Other ministers, such as Deputy Prime Minister Manley, suggested that the decision was warranted for the sake of advertising Canadian technological prowess (the Challenger jet was produced by Bombardier): 'I think what really needs to be underlined here is that when either the prime minister or, quite frankly, any minister travels, especially internationally, we take a lot of pride in the efforts that we make to brand Canada as an advanced technological country' (ibid., 12 April).

For others, however, the decision was far from straightforward or positive. One reason was that the purchase had not been tendered as per usual government guidelines. Also, DND had recommended in a report that the purchase not be made: 'Given that there were no identifiable problems or trends with this fleet ... it is recommended that remedial action, such as fleet modernization or replacement is not warranted at this time' (cited in Canadian Broadcasting Corporation, 27 November). Opposition parties attacked the government for its quick action on the executive jet file while the process to replace Canada's aging Sea King helicopters still languished. As for John Manley's rationale of showing off Canadian technology, Leon Benoit of the Canadian Alliance Party made the following counter-argument: 'Having a 1994 car that's still working well demonstrates that it's a good car' (ibid., 12 April). Also along these lines, Progressive Conservative leader Joe Clark suggested that the need to showcase Canadian technology applied to the Canadian military writ-large: 'When the deputy prime minister says that Canadians have an interest in the world knowing we have high-quality equipment, that applies not only to cabinet ministers swanning around the world. It also applies to the men and women in the Canadian Armed Forces, who are in harm's way in Sea Kings that have a record of not being as safe as they should be' (ibid.).

Personnel management

A number of issues related to personnel management in the military arose in 2002. One issue was that, on 30 May, Defence Minister McCallum announced a pay increase for serving personnel, effective retroactively to 1 April. Specifically, the pay hike increased by 4 per cent the salaries of non-commissioned members and by 4.5 per cent the pay for general service officers, pilots, medical officers, and dental officers. For the minister, the pay raise served a variety of goals: 'I am pleased to announce this increase as it reflects the dedication and professionalism of the men and women in our Canadian Forces. This increase will assist our efforts to recruit and retain personnel, and is consistent with this government's commitment to quality of life for Canadian Forces members and their families' (DND News Release no. 02.034, 20 May). This pay increase followed an announcement made in February by then-Minister Eggleton for the military to offer a $40,000 recruitment allowance for applicants to become engineering officers. This policy was a response to the need to recruit 600 engineering officers over five years. Similarly, in July 2002 DND started to offer additional recruitment allowances for direct entry medical officers and for direct entry dental officers ($225,000 and $25,000 respectively). These allowances were to compensate for the fact that the military had filled only 106 of its 151 medical officer positions in the rank of captain and major and only 102 of its 119 dental officer positions. Increases and allowances such as these were to emphasize to young, ambitious, and highly skilled Canadians that the military wanted to be 'an employer of choice.'

In 2002 the military ombudsman, André Martin, placed the military's approach towards operational stress injuries under the microscope. In two reports, issued in February and December, the ombudsman charged that much more work needed to be done on this issue: 'An A for effort and a D for delivery ... It is still considered a badge of dishonour for soldiers seeking out psychological treatment. It is still seen as being a weak solder, something to be ashamed of' (*Calgary Herald*, 18 December). While plans were in place, Martin noted that military culture regarding the issue had not shifted substantially. The lack of change was troubling for Martin because, since the ombudsman's office was created in 1998, he had seen increased numbers of OSI cases: 'I recognize that change will take time. The military is like a big ship. You can't just change the direction of the ship overnight. But this fact only increases the urgency of putting initiatives into place now' (*Calgary Herald*, 18 December). Moreover, his worries were compounded by estimates suggesting that approximately 20 per cent of Canadian military personnel returning from Afghanistan likely suffered from some sort of OSI. To help speed the process of cultural change, General Henault issued a missive to senior leaders to tackle the problem: 'We are working vigorously to change the culture within the Canadian Forces to eliminate the stigma that is sometimes attached to operational stress injuries, including post-traumatic stress disorder or any type of mental injury. Failure to respect our people and treat them properly will not be tolerated' (DND News Release no. 02.076, 17 December). In this vein, Minister McCallum also initiated a number of plans to treat OSI: the development of a peer support network, the establishment of an OSI steering committee, the appointment of a special adviser to the chief of defence staff on OSI, and the creation of a specific program to help those soldiers returning from operations in Afghanistan.

The controversy surrounding the military's handling of the disconcerting case of Warrant Officer Matt Stopford continued in 2002. While serving in Croatia in 1993, it was alleged that soldiers under Stopford's command poisoned him as they feared his recklessness in operations. Stopford left the military in 1998 because of ill-health. Issues of concern related to the seeming tardiness of the military's investigations, the lack of sufficient punishment for those involved, and the difficulties that Stopford encountered regarding disability benefits and his pension. At issue in 2002 was the fact that Stopford had not received a personal invitation to a December ceremony in Winnipeg that commended Canadian soldiers who served in Croatia, even though he was credited as being one of the most able soldiers during the Medak operations. The military, for its part, indicated that it did not send out personal invitations to any soldier.

On a happier note, the case of Sergeant Mike Kipling concluded in 2002. While serving in Kuwait in 1998, Kipling, concerned for his health, had refused to take a dosage of anthrax vaccine; this led to court martial proceedings. Although the military judge terminated the court martial on 5 May 2000 by agreeing that the military had violated Kipling's rights under the Canadian Charter of Rights and Freedoms, the military filed an appeal. On 11 January 2002 the Court Martial Appeal Court, a civilian-based body, found that the appeal was warranted and that a new trial should be ordered. However, as the result of an assessment on whether further judicial action was in the public's interest, the Director of Military Prosecutions announced on 11 April that the military would not pursue the case further. Kipling, although pleased that the proceedings were ended, feared that overall military policy would not change: 'I'm overjoyed for my family, but I still believe this has not proven anything or has not come to an end' (*Edmonton Journal*, 12 April). Indeed, the military revealed that although it had lost the battle, it did not plan to lose the war with respect to vaccinations and service personnel questioning orders: 'The validity of section 126 of the National Defence Act is not affected by either the CMAC decision or the decision of the DMP, and the effect of the CMAC decision confirms that it continues to be an offence under the National Defence Act for persons subject to the Code of Service Discipline to refuse to accept a vaccination without lawful excuse' (DND Press Release, 11 April).

Finally, the military's education system, a matter for scrutiny since the 1993 Somalia Affair, continued to be reorganized in 2002. In particular, the Kingston-based Canadian Defence Academy officially opened on 16 April. The academy's purpose is to coordinate the professional development and education of both commissioned and non-commissioned officers and emphasize the four pillars of 'training, education, experience, and self-development.' The CDA is charged with the responsibility to oversee the operations of the Canadian Forces College, the Royal Military College, and the newly created Canadian Forces Leadership Institute. For the chief of the defence staff, the CDA is to be a powerful mechanism to promote adaptability and to advance the skill sets of the Canadian military in the twenty-first century: 'I'm confident that the Canadian Defence Academy will be an effective tool in the leadership and professional development structures of the Canadian Forces. It will enable the Canadian Forces to better study and operate within today's complex security environment, thereby ensuring Canada's defence and security today and well into the future' (DND News Release no. 02.020, 16 April).

EMMANUEL BRUNET-JAILLY AND
WARREN MAGNUSSON

Municipal affairs

In 2002 there was increasing attention at the federal level to the plight of Canada's cities. Discussions about new powers and forms of revenue for the major municipalities became more intense. In April the Prime Minister's Caucus Task Force on Urban Issues (chaired by Toronto area MP Judy Srgo) issued its interim report, arguing for a national urban strategy. At the end of May the prime minister's main political rival, Finance Minister Paul Martin, called for a 'new deal' for cities in a major address to the Federation of Canadian Municipalities. When Martin was forced out of cabinet in June, he made the new deal an issue in his undeclared campaign for the federal Liberal leadership. Perhaps in response, the Chrétien government highlighted urban issues in the September Speech from the Throne, calling for 'new partnerships, a new urban strategy, [and] a new approach to healthy communities for the twenty-first century.' In November the Srgo Task Force elaborated its vision of 'Canada's Urban Strategy,' calling for national programs for affordable housing, transit/transportation, and sustainable infrastructure. During the year various non-governmental organizations, including important business groups like the Toronto-Dominion Bank and the Toronto Board of Trade, had been pressing for a new deal for cities. The Contrat de Ville in Montreal and the Toronto City Summit raised new possibilities for urban initiatives at all levels of government, as did the remarkable victory of Larry Campbell – model for the crusading coroner in the CBC television series, *Da Vinci's Inquest* – in the Vancouver mayoralty election. Significantly, Campbell's campaign focused on social issues that are often at the margins of municipal politics. In the meantime, Toronto City Councillor and former FCM president Jack Layton had entered the campaign to become leader of the federal NDP, promising to bring a new urban sensibility to federal politics. All this suggested that cities might indeed be coming to the fore in Canadian politics.

Cities in the marketplace

Although international surveys again showed that Canadian cities were highly competitive in terms of business costs (enjoying a 14.5 per cent advantage in relation to their U.S. rivals) and scored very well in the *World-Wide Quality of Life Survey* (Vancouver ranking 2nd and Toronto 18th among the 215 cities covered), the Toronto Board of Trade reported that the great majority of its members still believed that their city was at a disadvantage in relation to its U.S. competitors. Clearly, the low Canadian dollar was a help cost-wise, but it might not remain that low in the future. In any case, its low value reflected the fact that per capita income had been stagnating and the gap in living standards between the United States and Canada had been growing. Various business analysts had begun to focus on the specific problems of Canadian cities as a way of understanding the country's economic difficulties. Their conclusions were surprisingly similar to those of the Federation of Canadian Municipalities, which had been campaigning on this issue for some time. Important business leaders called for more autonomy for cities, and urged all levels of government to reinvest in the urban fabric. Although they insisted that the overall tax burden should not be increased, they called for measures that would provide more money for public education, public transit, and renewal of infrastructure. They wanted Canadian governments to follow the example of their U.S. and European counterparts, which had been making massive investments – often through public–private partnerships – in their major cities.

Widely circulated reports from the Toronto Board of Trade and the Toronto-Dominion Bank were indicative of the new mood in the business community. Rather than focusing on tax cuts, the Toronto Board of Trade put its emphasis on renewed public investments as the key to economic competitiveness. It argued that Toronto had been making a net contribution to federal revenues for a long time, but that its infrastructure was now 'inadequate and deteriorating,' its supply of affordable housing 'severely constrained,' the real incomes of its citizens declining, its tax base eroding, its tourism industry stagnant, and its business leaders losing confidence in the city's competitiveness. Immediate action was required, in the form of a tri-level agreement on a five-year program of investment in: transportation infrastructure to relieve congestion and improve the environment, including investment in transit capital upgrades and expansion; social infrastructure focused largely on expanding the availability of affordable rental housing; and waterfront revitalization to anchor economic growth in the downtown and limit urban sprawl. The board justified this Toronto-centred program in terms of the benefits it would provide to the national economy. It would be an interim measure, undertaken prior to more extensive reforms in arrangements for public finance and governance in the city. The board thought that the senior governments should make room for the city to collect taxes on gasoline and hotel use, and also authorize it to use tax increment financing for urban redevelopment, including low-to-moderate-income housing. That way, the City of Toronto could be more self-sufficient. This could occur in conjunction with a major effort to reform local governance in the city to make it more efficient and effective.

Similar themes emerged in two reports from the TD Bank, one of a general nature (significantly entitled, *A Choice between Investing in Canada's Cities or Disinvesting in Canada's Future*), and the other focused specifically on Toronto. In the first report, TD analysts highlighted the fact that Canada was an overwhelmingly and increasingly urban country, with an urban economic base increasingly dependent on a highly educated urban workforce. Although Canadian cities were cost-competitive (thanks to the low dollar) and the quality of life was still high, there were signs of slippage in both respects. Poverty and homelessness had increased in the 1990s, the physical infrastructure of the major cities was eroding, there were increasing shortages of social housing, there had been underinvestment in education, and cities had been allowed to sprawl in a way that made public transit less economical and contributed to environmental degradation. Europe and the United States were reinvesting in their cities, and the progress south of the border highlighted the fact that U.S. cities had access to more revenue – and had more flexibility in using it – than their Canadian counterparts. Although the TD Bank's report was sceptical about certain U.S. devices, like tax-exempt municipal bonds, it was impressed by the way that both the Americans and Europeans had opened up new revenue sources for cities and enabled them to take advantage of public–private partnerships. It condemned fiscal arrangements in Canada that left cities dependent for half their revenue on property taxes (whereas U.S. cities got just 21 per cent of their revenue from the same source). This dependence was particularly problematic at a time when the senior governments were downloading services and facilities like transit systems, airports and harbours, social housing, and even social assistance. The TD report said that cities had to be given more authority, as well as access to a wider range of revenues. The key TD proposal was to give cities the right to levy their own excise taxes (on gasoline, hotels, tobacco, etc.), to be piggybacked onto existing federal or provincial taxes. This was linked to the idea that the senior governments should surrender tax room to the municipalities, which they would cease to treat as inferior governments. The TD Bank's hope was to get more revenue to major municipalities without increasing the overall tax burden.

The second TD's report applied this analysis to the Greater Toronto Area, which it described as 'Canada's primary economic locomotive.' According to the bank, the locomotive was 'in need of repairs,' including strategic investments in education, social housing, and urban infrastructure, as well as revisions to local government arrangements to give the city more revenue of its own and more autonomy. The private sector had to get more involved. Toronto's competitiveness was on a 'shaky foundation,' since local tax rates were high, investment in research and development was limited, and there were growing obstacles to cross-border traffic. Educational cutbacks, urban sprawl, social inequity, and infrastructural erosion added to the problems. Cities had 'to do a better job of aligning property taxes, user fees, and development charges with the cost of services.' This could involve road tolls and enhanced parking fees to bring 'the cost of road use well above that of public transit.' Steps also had to be taken to promote urban density by the appropriate use of zoning and investment in transit and other facilities. There had to be experiments in alternative service delivery (involving arm's-length corporations and/or contracting out) and efforts at region-wide coordination of municipal activities. Nevertheless, municipalities in the region could not accomplish what they needed to do without more revenues. Thus, the TD repeated its proposal that municipalities be given the right to levy their own excise taxes (with the senior governments making room for them to do this).

The TD report appeared about a month before the Toronto City Summit, held on 25–26 June. The summit was a municipally sponsored but privately funded effort to bring 'more than 150 leaders in government, business, labour, academia, culture, media, and religious and community groups' together to develop a vision for the city. The assembled leaders called for a 'New Toronto Compact' to facilitate action in the priority areas of education, infrastructure, immigration, and finance. Again, there was a call for 'long-term sustainable investment ... in transportation/transit, housing and social and cultural infrastructure,' as well as for municipal 'access to longer term, new revenue streams that are stable, accountable and transparent.' A remarkable consensus seemed to be emerging, in that the 'competitiveness agenda' of the business community was coalescing with the autonomy agenda of the Federation of Canadian Municipalities and (at least to some extent) the anti-poverty agenda of various social groups.

The culture of cities

Social and cultural issues loomed large in thinking about the new place of cities in 2002. For instance, in a series of four reports, researchers associated with the Canadian Policy Research Network related questions about poverty and affordable housing to issues about the inclusion of immigrants and Aboriginals in Canadian cities. The CPRN researchers noted that the major cities had attracted most of the new immigrants, and that the majority of Canadian Aboriginals now lived in cities as well. Poverty had been increasing at a disproportionate rate in the major centres, and the incidence was highest among Aboriginals and new Canadians. Thanks to federal and provincial cutbacks, the production of affordable non-profit housing had fallen dramatically. Affordable housing was extremely scarce in the fastest-growing cities, and the quality of housing for the poor was an issue everywhere. Income supports for the sick, the disabled, and the elderly were generally inadequate. Some people lacked the education to be successful. Often, foreign qualifications were not recognized, and immigrants and Aboriginals faced discrimination in the workplace and the housing market. Among the apparent consequences of social exclusion of all types were increases in alcoholism, domestic violence, drug abuse, petty crime, and even gangsterism – problems evident enough in the population as a whole. How could cities cope with these challenges?

The CPRN researchers wrote about the need for pan-Canadian cooperation, holistic understanding, and a collective approach to urban strategy. For instance, David Hulchanski recommended a much enhanced federal housing program, including rental incentives, mortgage insurance, and rehabilitation funds for the renovation of historical housing. He called for $1 billion for new housing, $500 million for rental supplements, $125 million for social housing services, $125 million for rehabilitation, and $250 million for homelessness. Other CPRN reports made a variety of recommendations with regard to income support, settlement services, urban revitalization, child care, education, and economic development. In a way, these recommendations complemented the ones coming forward from the Toronto-Dominion Bank and other business organizations, in that they highlighted the need for social investment to accompany investment in the economic infrastructure of cities. This was a theme developed by Toronto businessman Alan Broadbent in a speech on *The Place of Cities in Canada*, published by the Caledon Institute on Social Policy. Broadbent had become a major advocate for constitutional reforms that would empower the larger municipalities and give them more access to the tax revenues generated within their own territories. He had been instrumental in the formation of the C5 group of big city mayors, and he was a leader of the Toronto City Summit Alliance. In a report for the CPRN, Neil Bradford argued that four principal frameworks for understanding urban futures had emerged, focusing respectively on economic clusters, social inclusion, community economic development, and environmental sustainability. Although differing in emphasis, each of these emergent frameworks responded to 'the gaps and instabilities of Keynesianism and neoliberalism,' took 'more seriously than either policy regime the significance of quality local places in generating prosperity and well-being for citizens and nations,' dealt with globalization and the social character of cities, and sought 'a balance between market dynamism and community stability.'[1]

Some of the public debate on urban social problems was prompted by the issue of the first reports from the 2001 Census. These reports underscored some important trends, most notably the ongoing concentration of the Canadian population in major urban areas. In 1996–2001, the population of Canada had increased by 7.6 per cent in four 'broad urban regions' (the extended Golden Horseshoe around Toronto, the Greater Montreal area, the Calgary–Edmonton corridor, and the Vancouver–Victoria area in British Columbia), compared with only 0.5 per cent in the rest of the country. Slightly more than half of all Canadians lived in these four regions. Thus, the problems of housing and social integration there could scarcely be ignored. In May the National Housing and Homelessness Network complained that only two of the provinces (Quebec and British Columbia) had signed agreements with the federal government to implement the November 2001 accord on affordable housing. Only Quebec had fully matched federal funds. 'Five provinces are planning major housing spending cuts, which means that there will be a net loss of housing funding in those provinces.'[2]

1 Neil Bradford, *Why Cities Matter: Policy Research Perspectives for Canada*, CPRN Discussion Paper No. F/23 (Ottawa: Canadian Policy Research Networks, June 2002), p. 30.

2 National Housing and Homelessness Network, 'Province-by-province update: Nine of ten fail to make the grade' (14 May 2002).

Regional governance

The wave of municipal mergers in Ontario and Quebec had changed the landscape of municipal government, but certainly had not resolved all the issues. For instance, questions remained about the government of the Greater Toronto Area. Only a minority of the people living in the area were within the bounds of the enlarged City of Toronto, and there were big issues to be resolved about regional transit, waste disposal, and urban sprawl. Mississauga, immediately west of the city, now had a population of more than 600,000, and it was arguing that it should no longer be contained within the Regional Municipality of Peel, an upper-tier authority established in the 1970s. Mississauga's powerful and influential mayor, Hazel McCallion, was appointed in February to head a Smart Growth Panel for Central Ontario – the most important of the five established by the province to advise it on the wider issues related to urban development in the province's major regions. The Central Ontario region encompassed the whole of the GTA, plus the area around the western end of Lake Ontario, including Kitchener–Waterloo, Hamilton, and Niagara. Most Ontarians live in this region. Was it the logical area for planning? When the province enlarged the City of Toronto a few years before, it had created the Greater Toronto Services Board to deal with services shared by the city and the outer suburbs, but by 2001 it had decided that the GTSB was not working and abolished it. At the same time, it resumed control over GO Transit, the commuter services company. This suggested that the province itself would be taking primary responsibility for regional planning and services in the Greater Toronto Area, as well perhaps as in the rest of the province.

The breadth of the problem of regional governance was illustrated by the seemingly endless saga of Toronto's garbage. The last major landfill site near Toronto was scheduled for closure on 1 January 2003. A proposal to send the city's garbage hundreds of kilometres north to the abandoned Adams Mine near Timiskaming had been approved in the autumn of 2000, but negotiations with the company broke down soon afterwards. The city turned instead to an established landfill site in southern Michigan, which it had been using for several years. In December 2001 Toronto City Council decided to use the latter site exclusively for the next five years. There had been serious environmental controversies over the Adams Mine site, but the Michigan site also attracted opposition from communities along the route between there and Toronto and from Michigan residents and politicians who objected to the idea of importing another country's garbage. Various people were calling for a local Toronto solution, but there was strong opposition to building an incinerator, which was the most obvious alternative to a landfill. Debates about the issue played across the province and into Michigan, with local politicians often aligning themselves with environmentalists to push the trash elsewhere. There were exceptions, however: in northern Ontario some politicians saw economic development potential in a possible landfill agreement.

In Quebec the provincial government signed a declaration of intent in June with the recently enlarged City of Montreal. The purpose was to create a new partnership contract or 'city contract' that would take effect the following January. It was to commit both parties to a joint program of action that would increase the number and quality of jobs in the city, integrate family support services at the neighbourhood level, increase the supply of housing, reduce social exclusion, energize cultural life, and enhance Montreal's international reputation.

The Government of British Columbia also was working with various interest groups on the terms of its new Community charter. The Charter was supposed to change the regulatory environment for B.C.'s local governments from a 'paternalistic' and prescriptive relation to one of consultation. Municipalities would be recognized as an order of government and spared from forced amalgamations of the kind imposed in Ontario, Quebec, and Nova Scotia. They would also be given natural person powers of the sort introduced in Alberta, as well as the right to take whatever actions they deemed fit for local well-being, subject to provincial and federal law. The province was especially interested in giving the municipalities the means to develop public–private partnerships of the sort common in U.S. cities. Proponents of municipal autonomy received a shock in late May, when the Alberta Court of Appeal struck down a Calgary by-law limiting the number of taxi plate licences in that city. This was of great national significance, because the by-law had been adopted under the provisions of the 1994 Alberta Municipal Government Act, which gave municipalities broad powers to provide for good government and make regulations for the safety, health, and welfare of the people. The Court of Appeal ruled that there had to be specific legislative authorization for municipal by-laws that abridged common law rights: municipalities could not appeal to the general powers granted them under new-style municipal acts like the one in Alberta to justify action of this sort. The Calgary City Council asked for leave to appeal to the Supreme Court of Canada on the issue, because it clearly raised an issue that would have an effect on efforts across the country to give municipalities more autonomy. Without such autonomy, reforms in the structure of regional governance would be difficult to implement.

Local democracy

There were municipal elections throughout British Columbia in November, but it was the contest for the mayoralty in Vancouver that really caught public attention. Vancouver is one of the few Canadian cities where there is something like an established local party system. The right-of-centre Non-Partisan Association has been dominant since the 1930s. Going into the November election, it controlled the mayoralty, city council, school board, and parks board, but it lost all four to the left-of-centre party, the Committee of Progessive Electors. This was seen as a rebuff to the right-wing Liberal provincial government, led by the former NPA mayor of Vancouver, Gordon Campbell. More interestingly, it was a rebuff to the NPA, which had turned its back on its own leader, Phillip Owen, the outgoing mayor. Owen had attracted national attention because of his increasing interest in finding innovative ways of dealing with drug-related problems in Vancouver's impoverished Downtown Eastside. He had become convinced of the need for safe injection sites for heroin users, but this was not an idea that appealed to his more conservative supporters. The NPA dumped him in favour of Jennifer Clarke, a more conservative figure who wanted to focus on issues of economic development and managerial efficiency. She might have won an easy victory, had it not been for the emergence of another figure, Larry Campbell, who took up the issues with which Owen had become identified. Campbell was a former RCMP officer and coroner, and the inspiration for the central character on *Da Vinci's Inquest*, the popular CBC dramatic television series. He became the unlikely standardbearer for COPE, a left-wing party that had never won more than a minority of seats on Vancouver City Council. His coat-tails proved long, as he not only won the mayoralty decisively, but also helped COPE win all but two of the seats on council, as well as control of the school board and parks board. It was an unheard-of sweep for the left in Vancouver city politics; moreover, the turnout was exceptionally high, at close to 50 per cent.

Vancouver City Council had committed itself to the 'Four Pillars Drug Strategy' of harm reduction, prevention, treatment, and enforcement in May 2001. The controversial proposal for safe injection sites was an element in the proposed approach to harm reduction. It gained surprisingly broad support, and Larry Campbell's opponents criticized him mainly for wanting to rush the plan ahead rather than consult more widely. The federal and provincial governments were prepared to back the scheme on an experimental basis, but there was much concern south of the border, where the Republican administration was pushing for a harder line on drugs. The *New York Times* covered the Vancouver election because of the issue, and after the election, John Walters, the U.S. 'drug czar' visited the city to discuss the policy with local officials. Needless to say, he was not pleased with the city's approach.

The other big local issue in Vancouver was the bid for the 2010 Winter Olympics. Campbell's opponents were strong promoters of the bid, which already had the support of the provincial government, but Campbell himself was more cautious, and promised to hold a referendum on the issue. This enabled him to skate around the controversies, which were reminiscent of the ones associated with Toronto's unsuccessful bid for the 2008 Olympics, as well as Vancouver's own experience with Expo '86.

One consequence of the changes on Vancouver City Council was that long-time Councillor George Puil, who was Chair of the Greater Vancouver Regional District, went down to defeat. Members of the GVRD Board are selected by the municipal councils within the GVRD. Puil's defeat highlighted the fact that this powerful agency is controlled by politicians elected to municipal councils, who rarely campaign on regional issues.

Nationally, Toronto City Councillor Jack Layton's bid for the New Democratic Party leadership helped focus attention on urban issues. Layton had been an unsuccessful candidate for mayor of Toronto, and had run federally as well, but his most prominent office was the presidency of the Federation of Canadian Municipalities. His presidency coincided with an intensified campaign on the part of the FCM to bring the federal government back into urban affairs. The fact that a municipal politician could make a serious bid for the leadership of a federal party may have been a sign of the shift in consciousness that the FCM was seeking.

Cities in the Confederation

In April the Prime Minister's Caucus Task Force on Urban Issues released its Interim report. The Report began on a note of warning:

> There is mounting evidence that our cities are ailing due to deteriorating infrastructure, declining air and water quality, traffic gridlock, homeless-

> ness, growing income polarization and marginalization, and budget crises. With few ways to generate revenue other than through property taxes, urban regions are finding it increasingly difficult to provide basic services and make repairs to infrastructure.[3]

The task force made a number of specific recommendations with respect to federal programs, but the main recommendation was for a national urban strategy based on 'four pillars': a new approach for urban regions, coordination and cohesiveness in federal programming, collaboration and consultation with other actors, and capacity-building and communication at the federal level. The strategy would involve:[4]

- An integrated approach to policy and program development in order to deliver a cohesive, effective urban strategy
- Examining the effect and impact of federal policies and programs on urban regions (i.e., urban lens)
- A strong urban partnership developed in collaboration with all orders of government, the community, the private sector, and citizens through bilateral, trilateral, and multilateral agreements and initiatives
- Priority initiatives that include:
- A National Affordable Housing Program
- A National Infrastructure Program
- A National Transportation Program
- An advisory body to provide ongoing consultation and advice on urban policy to the Government of Canada
- Fostering research on best practices, providing intelligence on trends and conditions, and communicating the Government of Canada's activities related to urban issues.

Much of this was in line with recommendations coming forward from municipal leaders, but key issues of municipal finance were left open. The task force promised to engage in further consultations before issuing its final report.

The C5 group of big city mayors (from Toronto, Montreal, Winnipeg, Calgary, and Vancouver) had met again in January, and scheduled another meeting for June. In the meantime, the FCM made a forceful

3 Prime Minister's Caucus Task Force on Urban Issues, *Canada's Urban Strategy: A Vision for the 21st Century,* Interim Report, April 2002, p. 2.

4 Ibid., p. 6.

presentation to the House of Commons on municipal fiscal issues. The FCM referred to a 'growing consensus' reflected in the Task Force's Interim Report, the earlier cited reports from the TD Bank, statements from the leading Chambers of Commerce, and comments from the governor of the Bank of Canada, among others. The consensus (as the FCM interpreted it) was that municipal governments were 'teetering on the brink of fiscal unsustainability.' Although they were responsible for a huge range of services 'essential to Canada's social, economic and environmental sustainability,' they received only 7 per cent of tax revenues, and whereas federal revenues had increased by 25 per cent between 1996 and 2001, municipal revenues had gone up by only 14 per cent.[5] The FCM reviewed various options for increasing municipal access to resources now controlled by the federal and provincial governments, but its preference was for a form of revenue sharing: 'FCM urges the federal government, in collaboration with provinces and territories, to allow municipal governments to share tax revenues levied by other orders of government for municipal purposes. Municipal governments would use a common tax base and existing tax collection systems, thus encouraging tax harmonization and minimizing compliance and administrative costs.'[6] The FCM also argued for more immediate action in the next budget, in particular to make the national infrastructure program permanent, extend the national affordable housing program, and establish a multimodal integrated, national transportation system, including urban transit.

The FCM was encouraged by Finance Minister Paul Martin's address to its annual conference at the end of May. He spoke forcefully about the need for a 'new deal' for cities, which would address their fiscal requirements. FCM spokesperson and past president Councillor Ron Hayter said that Martin's position was 'a signal [that] municipalities are finally being recognized as a level of government.' In June Transport Minister David Collenette declared to the media that he was trying to convince Paul Martin that a dedicated gas tax was a good idea and that the current $2 billion infrastructure fund was 'just a start.' Later, Martin promised to consult with city leaders prior to the preparation of each annual federal budget so as to strike a new deal. In his view, this proposal was a new and ambitious change that would formalize the participation of mayors and the FCM in 'concrete discussion' of the budget.

5 Federation of Canadian Municipalities, *Strengthening Communities on the Path to Fiscal Sustainability,* pp. 2–3.

6 Ibid., p. 12.

The situation became confused when Martin was forced out of cabinet, and John Manley took over as finance minister. Manley rejected the idea of sharing federal taxes with the municipalities. Quebec nationalists were suspicious of such arrangements, and the federal Liberal caucus was clearly divided on the issue. Martin himself was less than clear, although the proposed 'new deal for cities' emerged as one of the themes of his unofficial but very public campaign to supplant Jean Chrétien as Liberal leader and prime minister. Meanwhile, Winnipeg Mayor Glen Murray, a Liberal, had emerged as an increasingly prominent spokesman for the municipalities. He had been a driving force behind the C5 group.

The federal Speech from the Throne in September was intended to signal Ottawa's new interest in urban issues, an interest duly noted in the Final Report from the Caucus task force in November. The Task Force amplified its earlier recommendations, focusing especially on its three priority programs: affordable housing, transit/transportation, and sustainable insfrastructure. The hardest issues were deferred, however. Everyone was waiting for the inevitable changing of the guard upon Chrétien's departure. Would there really be a new era for cities then?

CAREY HILL

British Columbia

The year 2002 was one of change for British Columbians, as Premier Gordon Campbell and the governing Liberal Party continued to transform the province, building on efforts they had begun after their landslide election victory in 2001. Critics weighed in to express their opposition to the changes, which included rollbacks, tax cuts, and public sector job losses. Chief among these critics was the Opposition New Democratic Party. Reflecting on Campbell's first year in power, NDP leader Joy MacPhail said, 'He has changed pretty much everything, top to bottom, in this province' (*Vancouver Sun*, 16 May).

The NDP were not alone in their discontent with the governing Liberals' agenda. Although the firebombing of the school where the Liberal leader's wife worked as a vice-principal appeared to be an isolated incident of protest, the Speech from the Throne was read while protesters filled the legislature grounds and some even set up camp.

Premier Campbell cautioned of tough times ahead. A reduction in core services was to be the order of the day. While the premier fought the British Columbia Teachers Federation and other labour unions throughout the year, his attorney general, Geoff Plant, was censured by the Law Society for cuts to legal aid, and castigated by a range of groups and organizations for the Aboriginal treaty referendum that one of Canada's foremost public opinion experts labelled 'amateurish.'

A civic election was held in Vancouver and an entirely different Campbell, Larry Campbell, was elected mayor. Larry Campbell and the left-wing Committee of Progressive Electors Party (COPE) was swept to power. A primary focus of the civic election was not transportation nor economic development but the poor of the Downtown Eastside neighbourhood. In particular, the election focused on how drug addicts could be helped by the 'Four Pillars Strategy,' which included safe injection sites. Campbell promised to begin implementing the changes the day after he was elected.

While the two Campbells fought their divergent battles, the economy continued to lose ground. British Columbia was declared a 'have-not province' in 2002 and became eligible for federal equalization payments. Finance Minister Gary Farell-Collins explained that B.C.'s have-not status would be an annual occurrence for several years to come. The downturn in the forest sector and job losses, coupled with a net migration from the province, contributed to a dismal economic outlook.

Teachers' labour dispute

The labour dispute between teachers and the British Columbia Public School Employers Association escalated as the year began. Following a Labour Relations Board ruling late in 2001 that administrative duties and extracurricular work did not constitute essential services, teachers stopped participating in volunteer activities, school clubs, dances, fine arts, fundraising, trips, and graduation activities. The basketball season was put on hold. Other job actions begun the year before continued. For example, teachers did not write report cards.

In January the British Columbia Teachers Federation said it would initiate rotating strikes, a partial withdrawal of services, and even a full work stoppage, if the Labour Relations Board would allow it. The teachers demanded a 22.5 per cent wage hike over three years, while their employer offered a 7 per cent increase (*Prince George Citizen*, 9 January).

In late January the provincial government enacted legislation to end the ten-month labour dispute with the B.C. teachers. Dissatisfied teachers continued to refuse to perform many tasks in response to legislation that outlawed teachers' job action and forced B.C. teachers to accept a 7.5 per cent wage increase over three years, far short of their demands. In response to Bills 27 and 28, Jinny Sims of the British Columbia Teachers Federation said, 'Many of the things taken away, we earned under the Social Credit government. In the late '80s and early '90s, even before the NDP was elected, we had class-size limits in most of our collective agreements. We paid for these by walking picket lines and taking lower salaries' (*Vancouver Sun*, 4 February).

Alberni District Teachers Union President Leslie Wright explained that the Campbell government's actions had led the B.C. teachers to more closely align themselves with provincial and federal labour. Wright explained, 'We're much more in line with the labour movement than we've ever been before' (*Alberni Valley Times*, 12 February).

Teachers continued to oppose the Campbell government throughout the year. They participated in protests and they vocally opposed the government's move to make Grade 10 exams mandatory. As spokesperson for the BCTF Jinny Sims explained, 'What they've done is they've raised the threshold at the Grade 10 level, and my big fear is they're going to drive students out' (*Peace River Block Daily News*, 28 October).

Speech from the Throne

Soon after passage of legislation ending the teachers' dispute, the Liberal government's Throne Speech was read by Lieutenant Governor Iona Campagnolo. The Speech from the Throne, a first for Campagnolo, forewarned of the government's reduction of core services and the need for British Columbians to realize that difficult times may be ahead. The author of the thirty-four page throne speech appeared to foresee the protest that would accompany it. In apparent reference to the two hundred protesters on the legislature lawn, Campagnolo read, 'Though the storms of change may rage, and rain hard with their resistance, they will not cloud our common purpose' (*Vancouver Sun*, 13 February).

In an apparent assault on the province's labour movement, vocal opponents of the Campbell Liberals, the speech outlined forthcoming reviews of the Employment Standards Act, Workers Compensation Act, and the Labour Code. The government's plans to review labour laws led Jim Sinclair, B.C. Federation of Labour president, to react by saying, 'When they are done there won't be an eight-hour day left in this province' (*Kimberley Daily Bulletin*., 13 February).

The Speech from the Throne also included an announcement of the government's plans to cut from the provincial public service 11,700 jobs over three years. The active pursuit of public–private partnerships in the education, health, and transportation sectors was also mentioned. Changes to the Environmental Assessment Act and Waste Management Act, as well as a reform of the Forest Practices Code were outlined. Other legislative changes included amendments to the Community Care Facility Act, changes to the School Act, child protection legislation, a thaw in the tuition freeze for post-secondary education, and new legislation regarding drinking water and ground water. The lieutenant governor explained that an Aboriginal treaty referendum would be conducted by mail-in ballot in the late spring. The establishment of a Referendum Office to facilitate this process was noted. Finally, the speech underlined changes to the ease of people to get welfare, stating that British Columbia would be changed 'from a culture of welfare entitlement to a culture of employment and self-sufficiency' (*Vancouver Sun*, 13 February)

In response to the Throne Speech, Opposition NDP member Jenny Kwan said, 'When [Campbell] talks about sacrifice, who is he asking to pay the price? Women and children and the people who are most marginalized' (*Times-Colonist*, 13 February).

Camp Campbell

To protest public sector and tax cuts, protesters gathered on the lawn of the provincial legislature on 6 February just days before the reading of the Speech from the Throne and proceeded to set up camp. About fifty people made the camp their home over the twenty-two days of its existence. During the Throne Speech, the protesters were joined by hundreds of other activists and angry British Columbians. The camp remained intact until 28 February, when protesters were ordered to remove what had become known as Camp Campbell from the legislature lawn. The protesters had camped in tents; they also planted and grew a vegetable garden, and ran a kitchen. As the camp was being taken down, one protester was arrested for assaulting a camera operator (*Edmonton Journal*, 28 February), but the rest of the protesters remained calm and the police expected them to break camp on their own.

Social policy

In the area of social policy, the governing Liberals passed significant changes to welfare. On the watch of Human Resources Minister Murray Coell, cuts to welfare were projected to save $500 million over three years and remove 38,000 people from the welfare rolls. In April single parents, employable couples, and individuals aged 55 to 64 who were receiving welfare had their payments cut by $50 to $100 a month. Other changes meant that single parents had to look for work when their children reached 3 years of age in contrast with the previous age 7 years. Young adults were no longer eligible to collect benefits until they had lived away from home for two years. The shelter allowance for a family of three was cut from $610 to $555. Human Resources Minister Coell said that rental costs in the city of Vancouver were taken into account in determining these changes (*Daily Bulletin*, 30 May). As the year closed, the Liberals were re-evaluating disability policy. Leaked documents projected some 9,000 people would be removed from disability assistance in the coming year (*Times-Colonist*, 24 December).

Concerns about government's cuts

The most vocal opponents of the provincial government's cuts were arguably the Opposition New Democratic Party. Cuts to the Ministry of Human Resources were the deepest – some $571 million with cuts of about $353 million to the Ministry of Children and Family Development. Other departments also experienced cuts, and some unconnected with the NDP expressed their concerns, not least the British Columbia Ombudsman.

Concerned that accountability in government was being undermined, B.C. Ombudsman Howard Kushner said that because of budget cuts he would no longer be able to investigate complaints against certain public agencies, including local government bodies and self-regulating professions. Kushner explained, 'As an independent watchdog, my office was created to ensure that citizens are treated fairly by public agencies. These cuts mean I am no longer able to carry out my mandate in full' (*Nanaimo Daily News*, 25 January).

Agencies he said he would not be able to investigate adequately ranged from school districts to hospital and health authorities to self-regulated professions. Kushner's budget was cut by 35 per cent over a three-year period, even though he had told the government that a 10 per cent cut would not affect accountability. The number of investigators in his office was reduced from twenty-six to fifteen. The Ombudsman was not alone among those involved in government who were expressing discontent with the Liberals' cuts. The government's Standing Committee on Finance, composed of ten Liberals and one New Democrat, issued a report that recommended a reconsideration of cuts in certain areas. While the report generally recommended that the government stay the course, it expressed concern about the gap between resource-dependent rural communities and urban ones, and the need for Kindergarten to Grade 12 funding. With respect to K–12 funding, the report stated, 'We think the shortage of funds is reaching a critical stage for rural schools and schools-based programs in urban areas.' The committee also recommended that the income threshold for child care subsidies should be reconsidered for the working poor. The lone NDP committee member, Joy MacPhail, said she could not sign the report because it did not recommend where money should come from to implement the recommendations (*Times-Colonist*, 16 November).

Aboriginal treaty referendum

As promised in the Speech from the Throne, the government held the Aboriginal treaty referendum in the late spring, and the results were announced in July. In response to the results, Herb George, spokesperson for the First Nations Summit said, 'You cannot take away our rights by referendum' (*Times–Colonist*, 9 July). Similarly, Chief Stewart Phillip of the Union of British Columbia Indian Chiefs explained, 'Native rights are enshrined in the Constitution. It does not matter if B.C. holds a hundred referendums' (ibid.). Others noted that the referendum exercise merely delayed real negotiations.

Although 760,000 British Columbians voted in the referendum, or about 35 per cent of eligible voters, the referendum was not well received by the public. Many organizations, including the Anglican Church, came out against it. Some pundits suggested that the big nail in the coffin was well-respected pollster Angus Reid's assessment of the referendum as 'one of the most amateurish, one-sided attempts to gauge the public will that I have seen in my professional career' (*Vancouver Sun*, 5 April). The B.C. Federation of Labour, the David Suzuki Foundation, the NDP, and other groups representing women, seniors, and environmentalists called for a boycott. In addition to noting the costs of this exercise, Angus Reid's criticism went further asking, 'How can we take this exercise seriously when the government distorts the ballot in such a way that the answers they are looking for all involve placing an X beside the "Yes" box?' (*Vancouver Sun*, 5 April).

Questions on the referendum ballot focused on eight principles that the government expected to use in negotiations. For example, one of the questions stated, 'Private property should not be expropriated for treaty settlements.' This question received an 85 per cent 'Yes' response. Another question read, 'Parks and protected areas should be maintained for the use and benefit of all British Columbians,' and received a 95 per cent 'Yes' response. This was the question that Angus Reid pointed to as being particularly biased. The results were overwhelmingly on the 'Yes' side. The controversy surrounding the referendum led the government to accept the responses but not to say that these would serve as the basis for negotiations.

Attorney general censured

The referendum debacle was just the beginning of troubles for Attorney General Geoff Plant. His government's decision to cut legal aid and close courthouses sparked controversy and led to his censure by the Law Society. For the first time in its history, the Law Society of British Columbia, representing about 10,000 lawyers, voted non-confidence in the attorney general: 754 members voted in favour with 325 against. Their major concern was cuts to legal aid. At the same time the government had increased a special levy on the legal bills of all clients for the purposes of legal aid from 7 to 7.5 per cent, generating $91.6 million, it only planned to spend $54 million on legal aid. Michael Mulligan, the Victoria criminal lawyer who sponsored the motion explained, 'When access to justice is denied ... the Minister of Justice must be held accountable' (*National Post*, 23 May). In response to the censure, Attorney General Plant said, 'I don't think the vote changes anything in terms of my responsibilities. I'll get up tomorrow and continue to do my job as attorney-general, to be responsible for the administration of justice in British Columbia and work within limited amounts to provide the best access to justice that we can in British Columbia' (*Vancouver Sun*, 23 May).

Forestry sector

In February the provincial government was presented with a legal challenge from a coalition of unusual bedfellows: environmentalists and forestry unions. The coalition was concerned that the government was allowing the export of raw logs cut from B.C. Crown lands. The group included the Sierra Legal Defence Fund; David Suzuki Foundation; the Pulp, Paper and Woodworkers of Canada; the Communications, Energy and Paperworkers of Canada; and Woodworkers for Fair Forest Policy. The largest union of loggers, the Industrial Wood and Allied Workers, was not part of the challenge.

The petition asked the Supreme Court of British Columbia to put a stop to a 13 February order-in-council approving log exports equal to 35 per cent of the allowable cut in three northern forest districts. B.C. Forests Minister Mike de Jong said the purpose of the three-year export permit was to preserve logging jobs. According to the coalition, these exports violated the Forest Act, allowing sales only if logs were surplus to B.C. timber processing. 'It is beyond us that while there are people being laid off and there are mills closing, and there is a purported fibre shortage in B.C., at the same time the government is encouraging the export of logs from this province,' Doug Muir, a former president of the Pulp, Paper and Woodworkers, said in a news release (*Trail Times*, 21 November). For his part, the forests minister explained, 'I don't like doing it, I would prefer that all of the timber we harvest in British Columbia is processed in British Columbia' (ibid).

Softwood lumber

As the year closed, Weyerhaueser lauded the B.C. government for putting forward a possible solution to the softwood lumber dispute which was in its twentieth month. Steven Rogel, chairman, and the chief executive officer of Weyerhaeuser, explained, 'We believe [the B.C.] approach warrants further discussion between the two countries' (*Prince George Citizen*, 24 December). The solution involved two steps. A sliding-scale export tax would be substituted for U.S. duties, and legal activities would be temporarily halted to give both sides an opportunity to negotiate a long-term solution to the softwood lumber impasse.

Forests Minister de Jong wrote to the U.S. Coalition for Fair Lumber Imports chairman Rusty Wood and proposed that the current anti-dumping and other duties be replaced with a border tax until a market-based pricing system could be implemented. The sliding border tax would increase to 17.5 percent as lumber prices dropped. The proposal also included a bilateral softwood lumber council that would serve as an institution for dispute resolution. As part of the proposal, the B.C. government suggested the United States end its anti-dumping case. John Ragosta, spokesperson for the U.S. Coalition for Fair Lumber Imports, would not respond directly about the proposal, as he noted that negotiations take place bilaterally between Canada and the United States, and not with British Columbia directly. However, Ragosta said, 'Conceptually, the proposal seems to be on the right track, imposing increasing border measures as prices drop' (*Prince George Citizen*, 21 December).

In more specific terms, the proposed agreement from British Columbia involved the following aspects:

- Current duties of 27 per cent would be replaced with a sliding border tax (collected and kept in Canada) while a market-based pricing system was being developed.
- The export tax would be based on the framing lumber composite index published by Random Lengths. The price would be set monthly, calculated as the average weekly composites from the previous month.
- The export tax would be 17.5 per cent when the lumber reference price was US$290 per 1,000 board feet (MFBM) or less, reducing to zero when the price was greater than US$380.
- Western red cedar and white pine would be excluded.
- Independent remanufactures of lumber would be exempt from the export tax.
- The United States would drop its anti-dumping case. (*Prince George Citizen*, 21 December)

Equalization payments and other federal money

British Columbia's economy received boosts from the federal government throughout the year. Infrastructure money, softwood lumber funds, and equalization payments meant a windfall of over $1 billion in federal funds during 2002.

The province's status as a have-not province was confirmed by Finance Minister Gary Farell-Collins with a promise that British Columbia would continue to be a have-not province for several more years to come. British Columbia first became a have-not province in 1999–2000 but had since moved back into the 'have' column, only to revert back to its have-not status this year. Equalization payments brought an additional $500 million to British Columbia in 2002. Upon hearing that British Columbia was declared a have-not province, Gary Mauser, a Simon Fraser University business professor explained, 'Eventually it will sink in that there are two Newfoundlands, at both ends of the country' (*National Post*, 8 February). Only Alberta and Ontario remain have provinces.

Infrastructure funds included $200 million for expansion of the Vancouver Convention Centre $50 million for the Seymour Water Filtration Plant. The plant is a cost-shared project to which Vancouverites contribute $500 million, and the province and federal government each contribute $50 million for a total cost of $600 million. These funds all come as a precursor to the significant flow of federal money into British Columbia that is expected in connection with the 2010 Winter Olympics, including $450 million for a proposed rapid transit system between Richmond and Vancouver, $335 million for road upgrades at Kicking Horse Canyon with $300 million for the Sea-to-Sky Highway, and $100 million for road improvements near the Canada–U.S. border (*Province*, 6 December).

Aquaculture and fish farming

In September the B.C. government lifted the moratorium on new fish farms that the former NDP government had initiated. The decision was to allow for expansion of the fish farming industry in British Columbia. Agriculture Minister John van Dongen explained that lifting the seven-year freeze would allow the industry to grow to its potential of $1 billion in business and 12,000 jobs over ten years.

Critics, including those from the David Suzuki Foundation, noted that tourism could be affected by the expansion of fish farming, labelling the farms 'floating feed lots.' Farmed salmon is the fourth-largest agricultural product in British Columbia, after dairy products, beef, and chicken. Farmed salmon production has outpaced wild salmon. Along with his announcement lifting the moratorium, the agriculture minister also provided $5.1 million in research funds (*Vancouver Sun*, 13 September).

One month later, federal Natural Resources Minister Herb Dhaliwal announced that Ottawa would also fund research into aquaculture and provided $200,000, including a research chair for aquaculture at the University of British Columbia.

Vancouver civic election

An election in Vancouver swept the left-wing Coalition of Progressive Electors to power, with Larry Campbell as mayor. COPE won eight of ten seats on Vancouver City Council. The second-place Non-Partisan Association had been in power since 1986. After being elected, Mayor Larry Campbell explained, 'You will see a changed city. You will see a government that listens to the people and responds to them' (*Vancouver Sun*, 16 November).

Campbell's main competition was the NPA's Jennifer Clarke, a long-time Vancouver city councillor. Phillip Owen, the previous mayor and former leader of the NPA, remained silent on the election, as he had been at odds with the party in his support of harm reduction programs in the Downtown Eastside. Although Clarke during the campaign claimed to also support harm reduction, some were sceptical. She had a longer implementation time line than Larry Campbell and COPE, who promised to act to open the country's first safe-injection site for drug addicts within weeks of being elected. During a fundraiser prior to the election, Larry Campbell explained, 'Our city can be great, but our city won't be great unless we respect everyone in it – until we take the concerns of everyone seriously, until nobody in Vancouver is disposable' (*Toronto Star*, 16 November).

Campbell, formerly a policeman and coroner, is the inspiration for the CBC television series *Da Vinci's Inquest*. Clarke accused Campbell of hijacking the campaign by focusing on one issue. During the final week of the campaign, the NPA ran ads linking Campbell and COPE to the New Democratic Party. 'Don't let Larry Campbell and the COPE/NDP do to Vancouver what they did to B.C.,' the ads said. Other ads targeted COPE candidate Jim Green, who subsequently launched a lawsuit.

COPE also introduced negative radio ads referring to Jennifer Clarke's 'questionable loyalty' over the battle for the NPA nomination. COPE quickly pulled the ads and challenged NPA to do the same.

Economy

As the year closed, the predictions of economists proved accurate. British Columbia would trail the rest of the country in economic growth. Some blamed the Liberal tax cuts of the previous year. Public sector cutbacks led to job losses. Early in the year employment grew by 88,000 jobs but remained 'essentially flat' the rest of the year (*Vancouver Sun*, 4 January 2003).

British Columbia's depressed forest sector contributed significantly to the decline in the economy. Late in the year, eight of B.C.'s largest lumber producers posted third-quarter losses totalling $86 million compared with gains of $39 million the previous year.

British Columbia lost people to Alberta, and other parts of the country. For the first time in three decades, there was a net loss from the province, of 23,630 people since 1996. Census data showed that between 1996 and 2001 Alberta attracted 89,685 British Columbians.

On the positive side, Finance Minister Gary Collins suggested that housing and consumer spending remained strong despite the downturn in the forestry sector. The fourth quarter economic picture was dismal with the Business Council of British Columbia's economic index showing 0.3 per cent compared with 1.8 per cent last year. The index, comprised of measures including employment, manufacturing shipments, single-family housing starts, international tourism, non-residential building permits, retail sales, and the Canadian composite leading index, is an important economic indicator.

Business investment in British Columbia also declined, while exports dropped sharply by about 10 per cent in 2002 from 2001 – a greater drop than the national average. Jock Finlayson of the Business Council of British Columbia explained, 'Until we see investment come back and some kind of recovery on the export side we are going to continue to have what I would call a sub-par economic expansion in B.C.' (*Vancouver Sun*, 4 January 2003).

While economists predicted the poor performance of British Columbia's economy in 2002, the provincial finance minister's analysts underestimated the poor economic performance of the previous year, leaving revenues from personal and corporate income tax about $715 million short of the forecast. Equalization payments of $500 million from the federal government offset some of these losses. The real gross domestic product shrank by 0.2 per cent in 2001, making British Columbia eligible for the equalization money. The provincial budget included a record deficit of $4 billion, but Minister Collins insisted that his government was on track to balance the budget in 2004–5.

Crime

In 2002 an arrest was made in the disappearances of some fifty prostitutes from Vancouver's Downtown Eastside. Women began vanishing from Vancouver's streets in the early 1980s, but it was only in 1998, after the Vancouver police force came under considerable public criticism for its apparent inaction, that a task force was formed to investigate the problem. Finally, in early February media outlets reported that police were conducting a forensic examination of a Port Coquitlam pig farm (*Toronto Star*, 8 February). Then, on 22 February, Robert Pickton, who owned the farm with his brother David, was charged with two counts of first-degree murder; the year ended with him facing fifteen such counts. Public relief, especially on the east side, was palpable, but criticism of the police investigation continued, as twenty-five of the missing women's families issued a report to Vancouver City Council alleging that jurisdictional rivalries had 'been a plague of serial rape and murder investigations for too long' (*Globe and Mail*, 26 November).

HAROLD JANSEN

Alberta

Environmental issues are only rarely a prominent feature of Alberta politics. The significance of resource extraction industries to the province's economy has tended to marginalize environmental concerns. That was decidedly not the case in 2002, as the year in Alberta was dominated by two environmental questions. The first was a prolonged drought that devastated Alberta's agricultural communities. The second was the federal government's ratification of the Kyoto Protocol to the United Nations Framework Convention on Climate Change.

The drought

Probably no other event in the year was felt by more Albertans than the drought that paralyzed the province in 2002. Most Albertans noticed the hot, dry weather in the summer, many communities faced water rationing, and the province's agricultural industry was devastated by what many described as the worst drought since the Great Depression. The roots of the drought lay in a winter that saw far less than normal snowfall. The diminished snowpack did not replenish an already depleted aquifer and reduced the spring run-off from the Rocky Mountains. When the expected spring rains did not materialize in most of the province, the drought began in earnest. By the middle of spring, it became clear that the situation was extremely serious. For the majority of Albertans who live in cities, the drought was an inconvenience, meaning brown lawns, fire bans, the cancellation of fireworks, and water rationing. For the province's agricultural community, however, the drought was a disaster. Crops failed to germinate or grow, pastures did not develop, and farmers faced some remarkably difficult choices. Crop farmers wrote off their crops and pinned their hopes on next year. Livestock farmers and ranchers, however, had to make decisions about their animals. Livestock auctions were deluged with animals, as many farmers chose to sell off their herds, unable to feed them. Some farmers sent their animals off to other parts of Canada, literally in search of greener pastures.

The devastation in agricultural communities drew fairly swift government response. In June the federal government announced a multi-year aid program to deal with both the drought and global agricultural subsidies. Prime Minister Jean Chrétien made it clear, however, that the amount of aid to farmers was contingent on provincial cooperation. Alberta joined most of the other provinces in signing onto the plan in late June. The importance of agriculture to the provincial economy (and to the provincial government's electoral base) made this a particularly important issue for the Klein government. In mid-July provincial Agriculture Minister Shirley McLellan announced a $324 million aid plan that would be implemented very quickly.

As welcome as the government aid was, more touching was the outpouring of support from farmers in central and eastern Canada. Farmers in those parts of the country began to donate hay in a program that became known as 'Hay West.' The difficult challenge was transporting the bulky bales across the country. Both Canadian National and Canadian Pacific railways donated railcars to the effort, but it was not enough to get the hay from east to west. Finally, both the Alberta and federal governments provided funding to bale and ship the hay. At the Alberta end, the donated hay was distributed by lottery. Although the hay could only help some of the farmers, it was a welcome gesture of solidarity and compassion from central Canada.

Although the province as a whole was hit hard by the drought, some parts of Alberta had experienced above-average rain in the spring. The province's southwest corner, typically prone to droughts and reliant on irrigation, had a rainy spring, with basements flooding in parts of Lethbridge. Consequently, these parts of the province managed to grow significant hay crops and benefited from the high hay prices. This led to charges of price-gouging being levelled against southern farmers, who responded by pointing out that they had not received much of a break when they had faced drought conditions in previous years.

The bottom line on the drought was that Alberta's farms had their worst year in three decades. Production of staple crops like canola, barley, and wheat dropped in half. On the livestock side, high feed prices hurt producers, particularly hog farmers, who were also facing low prices because of global overproduction. Although market incomes were hurt, government aid programs offset many of the losses and kept farmers afloat. The spin-off effects of the drought were felt throughout Alberta's economy. Businesses that service the agricultural industry experienced significant declines. Even large corporations like Canadian National were forced to lay off staff with the decline in crop shipments. There was little, however, that most people could do other than to hope that 2003 would bring better fortunes.

Kyoto

Although the drought certainly galvanized Alberta, it was the federal government's decision to ratify the Kyoto Protocol on climate change that sparked the most significant political battle of 2002. Negotiated in 1997, the Kyoto Protocol would commit its signatories to reducing their emissions of greenhouse gases – which most scientists believe are responsible for climate change – to between 5 and 6 per cent below their levels in 1990. Since Canada's greenhouse gas production has risen by almost 15 per cent since 1990, it would take some determined effort to meet Kyoto goals by the target date of 2012.

Although Canada had signed the Protocol, as 2002 dawned, it had yet to ratify it formally. Early in the year, Prime Minister Chrétien indicated that he wanted to see Kyoto ratified in 2002. Initially, it looked as if the federal government was aiming for ratification by mid-year, but continuing negotiations with the European Union over energy credits were not going well. As summer came, these details had not yet been worked out, but the federal government continued to indicate its commitment to Kyoto.

The Kyoto Protocol sparked a strong reaction from Alberta's Conservative provincial government. As premier of a province whose economic engine was the production of fuel whose burning is responsible for the bulk of CO_2 emissions, Ralph Klein was adamant in his opposition to Kyoto. In February the premier seized the floor at a press conference at a Team Canada trade mission to Russia to indicate that although the federal government was committed to Kyoto, his and other provincial governments continued to harbour grave reservations about its implementation. While provincial Environment Minister Lorne Taylor and federal Environment Minister David Anderson traded competing projections of the impact of Kyoto on the national and provincial economy, Premier Klein focused on building a common front with other premiers in opposition to the agreement. Klein's efforts came to a head at the premiers' conference in Halifax in August. Despite his attempt to enlist other premiers to join the fight, Klein had to settle for a call for a first ministers' conference on Kyoto. For the other premiers, Kyoto was a low priority, and it quickly became clear that most premiers supported ratification. Even Klein's closest allies on the issue – Ontario's Ernie Eves and British Columbia's Gordon Campbell – did not seem to share the Alberta premier's passion for it. Increasingly, it looked like Alberta would have to fight this one alone.

At September's World Summit on Sustainable Development, in Johannesburg, South Africa, Prime Minister Chrétien announced that Ottawa would ratify the Kyoto Protocol by the end of the year. He brushed aside criticisms that the federal government had not consulted sufficiently with the provinces. With the official announcement, the battle between Alberta and Ottawa was launched. One of the central tactics of the provincial government was to draw analogies between the battle with Ottawa over Kyoto and the battle with Ottawa over the National Energy Program more than two decades earlier. The involvement of former premier Peter Lougheed in the provincial government's campaign against Kyoto certainly helped to reinforce the linkage between the two events in the eyes of the public. The province took a three-pronged approach to challenging Kyoto.

The first was a public relations campaign against the Protocol, consisting of a series of television commercials. Part of the provincial government's objective was that it was not only challenging the federal government, but it also had to convince Albertans about Kyoto. Although polling on the Protocol was extremely difficult to do, given the complexity of the issue and the lack of public understanding of the provisions of the agreement, it seemed clear that Albertans were divided on the issue. While many Albertans were concerned about the potential impact of Kyoto on the province's economy, others were genuinely concerned about the impact of global warning. Federal cabinet ministers were all too happy to point to the drought as an example of what would happen if action was not taken to reduce the production of greenhouse gases.

The second tactic was to threaten a legal challenge against the agreement. The province argued that the implementation of the Kyoto Protocol involved the regulation of natural resources, something that was in provincial jurisdiction. The potential success of such a legal challenge was questionable, as the federal role in environmental regulation had been well established by the courts. This might explain why, as of the end of 2002, no legal challenge had been launched, despite the posturing.

The third tactic was for the government to fend off criticism that it was merely protecting its friends in the oil and gas industry from addressing global warming. In October the provincial government announced its own plan for reducing the emission of greenhouse gases. The Alberta plan proposed to curb the growth of emissions, rather than to cut them outright as proposed in the Kyoto Protocol. Much of the cut in emissions would come from technologies yet to be invented such as so-called clean coal. In presenting a plan for action on global warming, the provincial government was seeking to distinguish opposition to Kyoto from opposition to addressing global warming. The Klein government presented its plan as a 'made in Canada' option. The plan, which was broadly similar to the one developed by the Bush administration in the United States, faced significant criticism from many environmental groups.

The Alberta government's strenuous opposition to Kyoto put Alberta's Liberal members of Parliament into a difficult position. At the end of September federal health minister and Edmonton West MP Anne McLellan complained publicly that the federal government did not have a comprehensive plan for implementing the Kyoto commitments. McLellan continued to demand that Alberta be treated fairly in the implementation of the Protocol. She expressed her misgivings even after her vote in favour of it. Edmonton Southeast MP David Kilgour also voted in support of Kyoto but not before indicating that he would resign should the implementation of the Protocol hurt Alberta.

In the end, Alberta's opposition did nothing to prevent the ratification of Kyoto in Parliament in December. Strong national support for Kyoto ensured that it would pass, despite the opposition of the Alberta government. Details of the implementation of the agreement, however, remained murky, and the true effect of Kyoto on the Canadian and Alberta economy remaines to be seen. This was not the final word on the Kyoto Protocol.

The Mazankowski Report

Although environmental issues had an uncharacteristic year in the spotlight in Alberta, 2002 also saw debates in the more traditional areas of health care and education. In January the Premier's Advisory Council on Health issued a long-awaited report on restructuring Alberta's health care system. The report – commonly known as the 'Mazankowski Report,' after the committee's chair, former federal finance minister and deputy prime minister Don Mazankowski – was rumored to recommend a sweeping overhaul of Alberta's health care system.

The Alberta Liberals managed to steal some of Mazankowski's thunder by accusing the former federal finance minister of a conflict of interest. The issue centred on Mazankowski's seat on the board of the Great West Insurance Company. Among its many operations, Great West provides supplementary health care insurance. By authoring a report that could be interpreted as increasing the scope for private health care, the Liberals argued that Mazankowski might be aiding private insurance companies like Great West. Although not much ultimately came out of the Liberal charges, the party enjoyed a splash of media coverage and managed to disrupt the carefully orchestrated release of the long-awaited report.

The details of the report were far less revolutionary than most of the rhetoric surrounding it. The report recommended a new emphasis on general health and wellness and proposed action in areas such as nutrition, health education, and reducing tobacco use. The Advisory Council on Health also proposed reducing waiting times and a ninety-day guarantee of access to certain medical services. It also recommended a strong emphasis on research and technology, through continued investment in medical research and electronic health records. More controversially, the report recommended that the government 'diversify the revenue stream.' Most of the details of this part of the proposal were vague, but the council recommended an increase in health care premiums to cover 20 per cent of health care services. Even more controversial were the report's recommendations regarding comprehensiveness and competition. The council proposed establishing a panel of experts to review what was and was not covered by the health care system. Given the overall emphasis of the report on the long-term financial sustainability of the health care system, it seemed clear that this panel would look at removing services from the system. The council called for a blend of health care providers, including the public, private, and not-for-profit sectors. To that end, the council proposed that regional health authorities be allowed to sign contracts with a variety of health care providers (including, presumably, private sector providers).

The government did not appear to be in a hurry to implement the report's recommendations. Many of the more controversial elements of it – such as 'de-listing' services and the possible expansion of private sector delivery of services – were put off for further studies. Most of the government's actions were on the revenue side, including increasing taxes on cigarettes and significant hikes in health care premiums. Action to ban smoking in all public places in Alberta was shelved after opposition surfaced from within the Conservative caucus. Action to amalgamate regional health authorities appeared to stall as the year progressed. In the end, the Mazankowski Report did not amount to much in substantive action or reform of the health care system.

Teachers on strike

As the Mazankowski Report proved to be less radical than many had expected, the public agenda quickly moved from health care to education. The focus on education was prompted by a strike by the province's teachers. Alberta's teachers were seeking double-digit pay increases after generous settlements had been reached with the province's doctors and nurses in the previous year. In addition, teachers were complaining about working conditions, especially increasing class sizes. In a bid to avert the strike, Learning minister Lyle Oberg offered that the government would fund the unfunded liability in the teachers' pension plan. What made this situation difficult to resolve is that teachers had to negotiate separately with each school board. Some school boards – most notably Edmonton Catholic – had reached settlements with their teachers, but most had not. By early February talks had largely broken down, and teachers began to go on strike.

The strike involved teachers from school boards across the province. In total, more than 21,000 Alberta teachers went on strike and more than 340,000 students were left without classes. Even as parents scrambled to make other arrangements for their children, public opinion in the province was divided. Despite the considerable inconvenience for students and their parents, there was a strong current of support for teacher demands. Ten days into the strike, the provincial government began to contemplate ordering the teachers back to work. The cabinet seemed reluctant to take this step and decided against it. Two days later, however, the government reversed course and declared a public emergency, ordering the teachers back to work. As part of the order, the province gave school boards and teachers until 15 March to reach settlements. If they failed to do so, an arbitrator would impose settlements on each of the school boards.

The return of the teachers to work faced a bump on the road when an Edmonton judge ruled the back-to-work order invalid. The spectre of further job actions by teachers was averted when a meeting between Premier Klein and Larry Booi, head of the Alberta Teachers Association, produced a compromise. The province and the teachers agreed to turn their differences over to an arbitration process. This apparent hope for labour peace was dashed when it became clear that the arbitration process would only address salaries and not the issue of class sizes. Furthermore, the arbitrator would not be allowed to impose a settlement that would cause a school board to go into a deficit position. In legislating the arbitration process, the province outlawed any strikes by teachers. In response, teachers embarked on a work-to-rule campaign, withdrawing their services in coaching and other extracurricular activities. The ATA later agreed to allow a return of teachers to their extracurricular volunteering, including coaching school teams, after the province loosened the terms of reference for the arbitration, particularly the rules governing the financial ability of school boards to pay teachers more, and agreed to cover the unfunded liability in the pension plan for a year.

When the decisions of the arbitrator came down, teachers received substantial pay raises. Teachers for the Calgary Board of Education received a 14 per cent increase over two years, for example. The ability of school boards to pay these large increases when many of them were in a precarious financial position to begin with was questionable. Predictably, the school boards began to line up at the provincial government's door, demanding more funding to deal with the pay increase. The continued battle over funding, combined with the province's June announcement of a commission to examine the state of the province's education system, guaranteed that education would continue to be an important public issue.

Eyes on Alberta: The G8 Summit in Kananaskis

Alberta enjoyed a brief moment in the international spotlight when it played host to the 2002 G8 summit. As the first summit of major world leaders after the terrorist attacks on New York City and Washington on 11 September 2001, security was a paramount concern. Consequently, Prime Minister Chrétien announced that the summit would be held in the scenic Kananaskis region of Alberta, just east of Banff. Besides its scenic appeal, Kananaskis was an ideal summit location from a security point of view, because it is surrounded by mountains and accessible by only one highway.

The major implications for Alberta were security and the expected influx of protesters. The security issue was quickly dealt with when Ottawa announced that it would pick up the tab for the tight security needed around the summit site. The issue of protesters was more difficult. Because of the remote nature of the Kananaskis site, protesters had a difficult time protesting near the summit. Instead, protesters primarily congregated in nearby Calgary.

Compared with the previous years' large and often violent confrontations in places like Seattle and Quebec City, the protests in Calgary seemed almost sedate. Although some of the credit for this had to go to the protesters, who generally avoided provoking clashes with the police, most of the praise went to the Calgary Police Department. The police were lauded for the good relationships they developed with protesters through simple acts like distributing bottled water and by ignoring minor provocations. In the end, protesters had their opportunity to organize and protest, but the Kananaskis summit would be remembered for what it did (or did not) accomplish, and not for violent scenes on the streets of Calgary.

The legislature

Alberta's 2002 legislature session was a scant forty-seven days long, divided as usual into two sittings: a longer one in the spring and a shorter one in the fall. The Legislative Assembly opened on 26 February with the Speech from the Throne delivered by Lieutenant Governor Lois Hole. Given the immediate context of the Mazankowski Report and the teachers strike, the speech focused heavily on health care and education. However, the Speech from the Throne was long on generalities and short on concrete commitments.

As usual, the budget was the centrepiece of the sitting. Following several years of budgets with rosy revenue forecasts, healthy spending increases, and bulging surpluses, the 2002–3 budget was positively austere. After the previous year's overly optimistic forecasts for oil and gas revenue, provincial treasurer Pat Nelson opted for more cautious projections. As expected, the province hiked health care insurance premiums, taxes on tobacco and alcohol, and a variety of user fees. This revenue grab essentially clawed back most of the preceding year's tax cuts. On the expenditure side, the government essentially stayed the course, with little in new money, even for priority areas like health care and education.

The previous couple of years had continued to demonstrate the volatility in the province's revenues. The dependence on resource revenue has always been a difficult factor in Alberta's budgeting process, but the government's image as careful fiscal managers had taken a real beating. The government commissioned a Financial Management Commission to search for ways to break the cycle of boom-and-bust budgeting. In July the commission issued its report. Its key recommendation was that all non-renewable resource revenue should go into the Heritage and

Savings Trust Fund. The government would be allowed to draw from the fund $3.5 billion or the average of the previous three years in resource revenue, whichever was lower. The idea was to smooth out the flow of resource revenue. Public concern over political meddling with the Heritage Fund, however, forced the government to create a separate sustainability fund for resource revenue, which would otherwise function in the same way. The government hoped that the new format would avoid a repeat of the previous years' embarrassments.

One of the more controversial elements of the 2002–3 budget was the decision to eliminate Community Lottery Boards. These boards dispensed a portion of the province's revenues from lotteries, video lottery terminals, and casinos. Typically, these would fund community projects. The decision to scrap the boards was a cost-savings measure, but it faced determined opposition from within the Conservative caucus, particularly from MLAs from rural areas, where the lottery boards were an important source of funding for non-profit groups. The government remained steadfast, however.

On the legislative front, the spring sitting was dominated early by debate over Bill 12, the legislation that suspended teachers' right to strike and implemented the arbitration process to settle the labour dispute. The province also introduced legislation that allowed for certain benefits to accrue to partners in adult 'interdependent' relationships. The legislation, which covered committed relationships between adults, whether they were between people of the same or different sexes, sexual or non-sexual, was ultimately passed in the fall sitting. This was the provincial government's way of dealing with the question of the legal recognition of same-sex relationships. Although the fall sitting was overshadowed by the battle with the federal government over the Kyoto Protocol, the provincial government's climate change strategy was never introduced into the legislature. It was expected to be introduced in 2003.

The release of data from the 2001 Census triggered the beginning of the redistribution of seats in the legislature. The rapid growth in the Calgary–Edmonton corridor in the preceding five years had exacerbated the problem of rural overrepresentation. Given the Conservatives' electoral support in rural areas, the government approached the process of redistribution with a certain amount of trepidation. Bob Clark, the province's ethics commissioner, was appointed to chair the boundary commission. The fall saw the release of the preliminary report. The major change proposed was to eliminate one of Edmonton's seats in the Legislative Assembly. This proposal fired up Edmonton's coterie of

Conservative MLAs, providing them with an opportunity to demonstrate to the capital's voters the benefits of having elected a large number of government MLAs in last year's provincial election. The final outcome of the boundaries battle would be seen in 2003.

Bob Clark generated more headlines when he announced his intention to resign as the province's ethics commissioner on 1 April 2003. Clark's resignation marked the end of a distinguished career in public service, serving as a member of the Legislative Assembly for six terms, as a cabinet minister for five years, and as Leader of the Opposition for four years.

Political parties

With the challenges of implementing the Mazankowski Report, dealing with the teachers' strike, and fighting the Kyoto Protocol, the provincial Conservative Party had its hands full in 2002. The party was certainly aided in its task by the weakened state of the two main Opposition parties. Neither the Liberals nor the New Democrats could do much to weaken the Conservatives' iron grip on the province.

That said, the looming tenth anniversary of Premier Ralph Klein's ascension to the premiership occasioned some speculation about how much longer Klein was interested in serving as the province's premier. The clumsy handling of the teachers' strike and the elimination of the community Lottery Boards had led to some grumbling among members of the Conservative caucus, which only served to fuel the speculation further. Unlike the situation in the federal Liberal Party, though, there was no clear successor waiting in the wings, agitating for the removal of Klein. A number of current and former cabinet ministers – including former Treasurer Jim Dinning, Health and Wellness Minister Gary Mar, Learning Minister Lyle Oberg, and Economic Development Minister Mark Norris – were seen as potential successors, but no one was campaigning openly for the job. The premier embarked on a series of strategy meetings with cabinet ministers, which seemed to send a clear message that he expected to be around for a while longer.

The provincial Liberals did not face the same kinds of questions over leadership, but this may have been because no one was particularly interested in the job. Party leader Ken Nicol spent much of the year grappling with the problem of the party's significant $1 million debt left over from the previous election. Much of Nicol's effort was focused on cutting party expenses, fundraising through a series of leader's dinners, and assembling some kind of war chest with which to fight the next election. The Liberals were also beginning to recruit candidates for the next provincial election, a difficult task after the drubbing the party took in 2001. The erosion of the Liberals' Edmonton base and the loss of the party's only seat in Calgary raised doubts about the party's electoral viability. This made it difficult to attract quality candidates. Nicol's quiet and non-combative leadership style was certainly competent, but did not appear to be catching fire with voters. Nicol was also hampered by the provincial government's obsession with the Kyoto Protocol. The Liberals were in a difficult position: to oppose the Conservatives in a battle between Alberta and Ottawa would appear disloyal, but to support the government would doom the party to irrelevance.

The New Democratic Party was not hampered by the same problems. It had a clear position in support of Kyoto and a relatively more manageable debt load from the previous election. The emphasis on health care and education was a gift to a party seen as strong on social policy. When the Mazankowski Report did not appear to generate much in substantive or controversial health care reform, however, the NDP lost a potentially useful issue. Furthermore, the furore over the teachers' strike was relatively short-lived. With only two MLAs, the NDP was limited in its impact.

By-elections are idiosyncratic events, but it is difficult to resist the temptation to read much into them. An 8 April provincial by-election in Wainwright provided an opportunity to gauge how the parties were faring. The by-election was made necessary after the resignation of Conservative MLA Robert Fischer. Provincial Ethics Commissioner Bob Clark had ruled that Fischer had committed a serious breach of ethics laws concerning a land deal. Doug Griffiths held the seat for the Conservatives, and in winning, the twenty-nine year-old became the youngest MLA. That the Conservatives held the seat was not surprising – Wainwright had elected a Conservative in each of the last eight provincial elections – but the results revealed a certain amount of discontent among rural voters. Griffiths took only 45 per cent of the vote, reflecting voters' frustration with the Klein government, particularly the handling of the teachers' strike and the elimination of Community Lottery Boards. Interestingly, though, the two major Opposition parties in the province – the Liberals and the New Democrats – were not the primary beneficiaries of the swing away from the Conservatives. The Liberals finished third and the New Democrats finished fifth. The fledgling Alberta First Party finished second with 26 per cent of the vote. The failure of either the Liberals or the NDP to establish themselves as a clear alternative to the Progressive Conservatives indicates that whatever frustration there was with the Klein government, neither party had done a good job of positioning itself to take advantage of the situation. The election results were particularly sobering for the Liberals. Although Wainwright was not a strong place for the party – it had finished third in 2001 – the Liberals showed no sign of rebounding, despite the apparent discontent with the government and the leadership of Nicol, widely perceived as being far more palatable to rural Alberta than were his predecessors. If the Liberals were on the road to recovery, the 8 April by-election revealed that the road ahead would be windy, difficult, and treacherous.

The fall saw a new entrant into the already crowded right wing of Alberta party politics. In September former Social Credit leader Randy Thorsteinson announced the formation of the Alberta Alliance. The new party – which, despite its name, had no formal relationship with the national Canadian Alliance – was emphasizing fiscal conservatism and a vigorous defence of provincial rights. The party had planned on holding a founding convention in October, but that was delayed until February to coincide with a leadership convention. In the meantime, Thorsteinson was serving as interim leader. Little else was known about the new party, including its relationship with the existing Alberta First and Social Credit parties.

The economy

Alberta's economy grew by about 2.5 per cent in 2002, which was a respectable if not stellar showing. For the first time in a few years Alberta trailed the rest of Canada in economic growth. The slow economic recovery in the United States, the drought, and depressed prices for natural gas all combined to clip the wings of Alberta's economy. The economic difficulties should not be overstated, however. Alberta's employment situation and consumer spending remained strong. The speculation about an impending war in Iraq drove up natural gas and oil prices in late 2002, suggesting that 2003 would be a better year.

Without question, the Alberta business story of the year was the merger of PanCanadian Energy and Alberta Energy. In late January the two companies announced their plan to join together to form EnCana, a $27 billion company that would be the largest independent petroleum producer in the world. Besides its impressive North American assets, EnCana had significant international oil and gas holdings as well. The new company would be based in Calgary and Alberta Energy's Gwyn Morgan assumed the job of chief executive officer of the new entity.

The stock prices of both PanCanadian and Alberta Energy soared after the announcement of the proposed merger, which was finalized after the approval of shareholders of both corporations, in April. EnCana became the third largest publicly traded industrial corporation in Canada, trailing only Nortel and BCE.

Another important oilpatch story was the announcement that Calgary's Talisman Energy was selling its stake in Sudan. Talisman's Sudan holdings had been a public relations nightmare for the company, as human rights and church groups had charged that the revenues generated by Talisman's operations were helping to fund a civil war in that country. The buyer, India's ONGC Videsh, paid $1.2 billion for Talisman's Sudan operation.

Miscellaneous

The death of four Canadian soldiers in a 'friendly fire' incident in Afghanistan in April shocked all of Canada, but it had special resonance in Edmonton. The four soldiers were part of the Princess Patricia's Canadian Light Infantry, based out of Canadian Forces Base Edmonton. A memorial service for Sergeant Marc Leger, Corporal Ainsworth Dyer, and Privates Nathan Smith and Richard Green, at the Skyreach Centre in Edmonton, was attended by over 16,000 people, including Prime Minister Jean Chrétien and Governor General Adrienne Clarkson.

JOSEPH GARCEA

Saskatchewan

Saskatchewan is constantly being challenged by climatic and economic factors over which it has no control: 2002 produced a set of challenges that were all too familiar to the government and people of this province. It is not surprising therefore, that in 2002 the provincial government produced a budget entitled 'Meeting the Challenge for the Saskatchewan People' and a massive national media promotional campaign for the province named 'Wide Open Future.' These two titles reflected what historically have been and continue to be the two key components of the social and political psyche of the people of Saskatchewan – determination and optimism.

Elections

The province was relatively quiet on the electoral front in 2002. The only major events were a provincial by-election and deliberations related to the recommendations of the federal Electoral Boundaries Commission. The provincial by-election, held in October for the Kindersley constituency, was precipitated by the resignation of the prominent and powerful Saskatchewan Party MLA Bill Boyd. The Saskatchewan Party managed to retain the constituency, and so there was no effect on the distribution of the fifty-eight seats in the Legislative Assembly. After the by-election the NDP still held twenty-nine seats, the Saskatchewan Party once again had twenty-six seats, the Liberal Party, one (North Battleford MLA Jack Hillson). The remaining two seats were held by independents: former Liberal leader Jim Melenchuk and Ron Osika, both of whom remained in the cabinet of the NDP–Liberal coalition government.

The notable event related to federal elections was the appointment of the independent commission mandated to redistribute the fourteen federal constituencies in Saskatchewan. The commission proposed the elimination of some of the rural-urban constituencies, adjustments to the boundaries of others, and the creation of entirely urban seats for Regina and Saskatoon. The more radical components of the proposal were eventually abandoned as a result of the protestations by members of Parliament from the Opposition parties, particularly Dick Proctor of the NDP, and Lynne Yelich and Carol Skelton of the Alliance Party, who complained that the proposed changes would result in extraordinarily large rural ridings that would accentuate the existing political divide between urban and rural voters in the province.

The political parties

During 2002 the major political parties were preparing for the provincial election that was expected in 2003. Towards that end they concentrated on getting their internal affairs in order and on criticizing each other. For his part NDP leader Lorne Calvert accused the Saskatchewan Party of having an 'extremist agenda,' which focused on cuts to health care, the civil service, and the selling off of Crown corporations. Saskatchewan Party leader Elwin Hermanson, in retort, charged that the government's incompetence was evident in, among other things, the long waiting lists for surgery, a worsening budget situation, and a poor job creation record. He usually ended his criticism with an appeal to Liberal Party supporters to vote for his party in the next election so as to prevent the vote splitting that he claimed handed the NDP the 1999 election victory.

The Saskatchewan Party devoted considerable effort to portraying itself as being ready to govern. As part of this campaign, party leader Elwin Hermanson announced that when his party formed the government it would do the following: launch an efficiency review of all government operations to reduce waste and improve the quality of service; introduce substantial tax reductions and other economic development initiatives designed to stem the flow of people leaving Saskatchewan; and put a plan in place to increase the province's population by 100,000 people, and attract business with strategic tax reductions.

The provincial Liberal Party continued to be hobbled by internal divisions as its new leader was preparing to lead it into the next election. The former leader, Jim Melenchuk launched a court action against the Liberal Party to recoup what he described as approximately $209,000 in unpaid salary and expenses and some additional money that he had used to cover some party expenses.

The New Green Alliance was also preparing for the pending election. It selected a new leader, Ben Webster, a student at the University of

Regina. Webster criticized the provincial government's stance on the Kyoto Protocol and suggested that this was an issue that his party could use to attract voters.

The federal parties' machinations also generated some interest in Saskatchewan. Two MPs from the province, Ralph Goodale of the Liberal Party and Lorne Nystrom of the NDP, were prominent in the political news. Goodale, Saskatchewan's only federal cabinet minister, was moved from the Ministry of Natural Resources to the position of Government House Leader. Lorne Nystrom, a veteran New Democrat, was the fifth candidate to enter the race for the leadership of the federal party, which was scheduled to culminate with a vote in January 2003. This was the third time that Nystrom had run for the leadership. As the year came to an end it became increasingly clear that it was unlikely that he would be any more successful this time than he had been during his previous attempts.

The legislature and government

The Speech from the Throne portrayed Saskatchewan as a province of opportunity. The government indicated that, although revenues had declined as a result of the previous year's drought, it would continue to invest in developing the province's economy by focusing on four areas: private and public sector investment in the economy and the environment, infrastructure, education, and support for families. The government indicated that the key objectives of its plan were to create new education and employment opportunities. Some of the most notable initiatives outlined in the speech were: the development of the ethanol industry; the implementation of a rural revitalization plan based on the final report of the Action Committee on the Rural Economy; the reconstruction and paving of more than 700 kilometres of highway; the extension of high speed Internet to more than 191 communities; the expansion of online distance education programs for high school and post-secondary education; the implementation of reforms outlined in the action plan on health care; and a significant funding boost to health-related research in the province.

More than seventy pieces of legislation were adopted during the spring session. This included legislation to: protect children from sexual abuse; change the regulation of parole and sentencing; make it easier for oil producers to do business in Saskatchewan; increase the production and lower the taxation of ethanol fuel; empower cities by introducing a separate statute for them designed to increase their authority and autonomy in governing their municipalities and in the management and administration of their assets.

The spring session was characterized by the usual level of criticism of the government by the Opposition parties concerning various controversial issues. Some of the more contentious matters included the government's plan to hike fees for seniors and disabled persons in public nursing homes, as well as the planned development of the ethanol industry – although it was to be largely financed by the private sector, it entailed a potential liability of as much as $100 million for the provincial treasury. These issues along with some others made for an uncomfortable session for the government, which one columnist at the *Star Phoenix* described, on 28 June, as being in a constant state of crisis.

In 2002 there was a fall sitting of the Legislative Assembly. The eight-day sitting held in early December focused on two major issues. The first was the report by the independent provincial Constituency Boundaries Commission, which recommended that Saskatchewan's fifty-eight provincial constituencies be redrawn to give Saskatoon one additional seat and rural Saskatchewan one less seat, to reflect shifts in the province's population. The legislature concurred with the recommendations of the commission and enacted the Representation Act.

The second major issue debated during the fall sitting was the province's position on the Kyoto Protocol related to the reduction of greenhouse gas emissions. The debate was sparked by the ratification of the Kyoto Protocol by the House of Commons. The Saskatchewan Party maintained that ratifying the Protocol would cost the province thousands of jobs and implored the provincial government to oppose it. The provincial government's position was that, although it supported the principle of reducing greenhouse gas emissions, it was not satisfied either with the federal government's consultation process or its plans for meeting the targets.

Two other issues of note that were the subject of question period during the fall session were the ongoing 'Spudco' saga regarding the $28 million provincial government investment in a failed potato marketing operation, and the serious financial troubles faced by the Saskatchewan Wheat Pool in the aftermath of the previous year's drought.

Premier Lorne Calvert shuffled his cabinet, consolidated some departments, and eliminated two cabinet positions. The two positions were abolished largely to show that the provincial government was cost conscious in its operations. Accordingly, the premier noted that the reduction gave Saskatchewan its smallest cabinet since 1974 and the smallest cabinet west of Atlantic Canada. Judy Junor, who had served as minister responsible for seniors and the status of women, and Kim Trew, who had served as minister responsible for Gaming and the Saskatchewan Property Management Corporation, were purged from cabinet. As part of the government's cost-saving measures the premier also announced that a government reorganization would be undertaken that would result in the elimination of 350 public service jobs for a savings of $16.6-million in the coming year. The other cabinet change occurred when the premier decided to take the environment portfolio from Pat Lorje, who had a highly publicized dispute with a staff member, and to give it to Northern Affairs Minister Buckley Belanger.

The budget

The budget presented by Finance Minister Eric Cline consisted of a combination of good news and bad news. Although it was the ninth consecutive balanced budget for Saskatchewan, the projected surplus was only $45,000. What led the government to project a $45,000 surplus is unclear, but undoubtedly it had more to do with political than economic considerations. Premier Calvert attributed the slight surplus to unpredictable events such as severe drought, the economic slowdown created by the 2001 terrorist attacks in the United States, and the softwood lumber trade dispute.

The budget consisted of a combination of cuts in some taxes and increases in others. The government continued with its four-year plan to cut income taxes, but increased the so-called sin taxes on alcohol and cigarettes. In an effort to reduce its costs, the government also raised the fees charged to seniors and disabled persons in long-term care homes. The fees were increased from a maximum of $1,561 per month to $3,875 per month, and the province also eliminated the prescription drug deductible for families with annual incomes over $50,000.

The government cut expenditures, reducing the global budget for its departments, and asking them to reduce their staffing levels. It did, however, increase both health care funding by 5.8 per cent, and municipal revenue-sharing grants by $10 million. In response to calls for more money to fight crime the government provided some funding for hiring more police officers.

The opposition Saskatchewan Party levelled its usual criticism against the government for not having the right budgetary priorities and even charged that the NDP coalition was cooking the books by claiming it had a small surplus when it was actually relying very heavily on internal financial transfers from the Fiscal Stabilization Fund and Crown corporations. The Opposition noted that of the $6.09 billion in revenues, $300 million was taken from the profits of Crown corporations and $225 million was taken from a transfer from the FSF. Only these monies, the Opposition asserted, allowed the government to post a surplus.

The official Opposition was not alone in questioning the government's budgetary framework. The government was also criticized by Saskatchewan's Provincial Auditor Fred Wendel, who chastised the government for suggesting that it was producing a surplus budget when it was actually running a $483 million deficit for 2002. He boldly accused the government of living beyond its means and thereby stifling the economic growth of the province, and urged it to produce budget statements that provided the public with a clear and accurate picture of its revenues, expenditures, surpluses, deficits, and debt. Unlike the official Opposition and the provincial auditor, the bond markets were clearly not concerned with the accounting practices of the provincial government, as they gave the province its tenth straight positive credit rating.

The economy

For Saskatchewan's economy 2002 was not a very positive year. The economic slowdown attributable to the terrorist attacks of 9/11 and the drought experienced by Saskatchewan the previous year had negative effects on the provincial economy. The drought was particularly costly. Agricultural production was down 46 per cent from the average over the previous ten years, and government compensation payments for the year totalled $1.09 billion. The government also had to pay $25 million as part of the assistance program for livestock producers. The drought also resulted in an unusually high number of forest fires, which, in turn, produced abnormally high firefighting costs, as the bill for 2002 was $118 million compared with an average of $55 million in previous years.

The prospects of a quick turnaround in the farm economy were dimmed by the agreement among U.S. politicians on farm subsidies under their Farm Bill. The agreement was that base level subsidies for U.S. farmers would be increased by 78 per cent for the next six years. Premier Calvert estimated that this initiative would have an adverse effect on up to 94 per cent of the province's total crop production. In an effort to take measures against the bill, Premier Lorne Calvert met with Manitoba Premier Gary Doer. Both concurred that this action by the

United States violated its subsidy reduction commitments under the World Trade Organization Agreement on Agriculture.

Despite the overall economic slowdown, some areas of Saskatchewan's economy did experience growth. The notable improvements were in the oil and gas sector, where investment and revenues continued to grow: 3,511 wells were drilled in 2002 compared with 3,333 in 2001. Had it not been for the positive activity in the energy sector, the year would have been truly dismal for the provincial economy. Not only would the revenue and expenditure streams of the provincial government have been adversely affected, but so too would have been the already relatively high unemployment rate and the continuing decline in the province's population in recent years.

In an effort to promote economic development in the face of the various economic challenges, the provincial government launched a promotional campaign entitled 'Wide Open Future' that included television, radio, and print ads. It also featured a tour by Premier Lorne Calvert to various Canadian cities to meet with investors, entrepreneurs, graduates of Saskatchewan universities, and other former residents of the province, to encourage them to consider what opportunities existed for them in Saskatchewan. The core message was that they could be instrumental in rebuilding the province and that it was a place where they could build their businesses and careers, raise their families, and enjoy a good quality of life.

The judiciary

Judicial salaries were again on the policy agenda after judges started calling for substantial pay increases because only their Newfoundland counterparts were being paid less. One of the most interesting legal cases of the year focused on the scope of municipal liability for accidents caused by road hazards. The Supreme Court of Canada ordered the Rural Municipality of Shellbrook to pay Paul Housen $2.5 million. He was left paralyzed when the truck in which he was a passenger slid off a muddy curve. Housen sued Shellbrook for failure to erect a sign to warn drivers of the curve in the road. The case ended up in the Supreme Court of Canada after the Saskatchewan Court of Appeal overturned the decision by the Court of Queen's Bench to award Housen damages. The court decision had the dual effect upon municipalities of increasing their vigilance related to signage and their obtaining appropriate insurance policies.

Intergovernmental relations

Intergovernmental relations produced the usual mix of excitement and intrigue. Continuity was much more prevalent than discontinuity with regard to the key items and dynamics both in federal–provincial and in provincial–municipal relations.

The drought set much of the agenda for federal–provincial relations during 2002. Saskatchewan's minister responsible for agriculture, Clay Serby, accused Ottawa of cheating the province out of crop insurance money. In response to that accusation, his federal counterpart, Lyle Vanclief, said that the reason for the paucity of funds for crop insurance was that the scope of the 2001 drought and the resulting crop insurance payouts had already consumed much of the money that had been set aside for 2002. This marked the beginning of a strained relationship between the federal and Saskatchewan governments for the year. The relationship was strained even further when later that year the federal government announced a new agriculture safety net program that would cost the federal government $5.2 million over five years. The Saskatchewan government argued that the proposed program would meet neither the needs nor the expectations of farmers in the province. For several months the Saskatchewan government refused to sign an agreement related to the program because it felt that the federal government should increase its financial contribution to it. By the end of the year, however, the provincial government indicated that despite still being dissatisfied with the terms of the proposed agreement, it would likely sign it sometime within the next year.

Provincial–municipal relations were better than they had been during the previous two years, but some tensions persisted. As in the past, financial considerations continued to be irritants. Both the Saskatchewan Urban Municipalities Association, and the Saskatchewan Association of Rural Municipalities criticized Premier Calvert and his cabinet for the cuts that the province had made to the annual revenue-sharing grants to Saskatchewan over the past decade and asked the government to make a commitment to increasing the size of the revenue-sharing pool and also to sharing the gas revenues. SARM also demanded that the provincial government increase its financial commitment to at least three other programs. This included an extra $10 million to municipalities for repairing their roads, a larger and more predictable rebate for the education proportion of the property tax on farm properties, and a reduction of the proportion of education costs to be covered from the property tax base. One proposed change regarding the calculation of property taxes that SARM did support was basing the valuation of farmland on its generation of income rather than on its market value.

The year witnessed a change in SARM's leadership. Sinclair Harrison, who had served as president for eight years, resigned. He was replaced by Neal Hardy who was acclaimed. Hardy had served as SARM's vice-president for several years and prior to that he had served as a cabinet minister in Premier Grant Devine's Progressive Conservative government during the 1980s. This change in leadership may have resulted in a change of leadership style, but it did not change SARM's basic agenda at the provincial–municipal negotiating table.

Aboriginal affairs

The highlights in Aboriginal affairs this year were more land settlements for First Nations, and the elections of the Federation of Saskatchewan Indian Nations. The Kahkewistahaw First Nation, based in southeastern Saskatchewan, and consisting of approximately 1,385 members, received a $94.65 million land claim settlement. The money was for the approximately 13,300 hectares of land that the band surrendered in 1907. The settlement came about based on the findings by the Indian Claims Commission that the government had never provided the Kahkewistahaw Nation with the land that it had been promised in 1907.

The FSIN held elections for second and fourth vice-chiefs in 2002 and these proved interesting; however, ultimately the incumbents retained their posts. The two contestants for the position of second vice-chief were incumbent Guy Lonechild and Todd Seeseequasis. The position of fourth vice-chief was contested between incumbent Lawrence Joseph and Henry Daniels, a former FSIN vice-chief in the 1980s. Both Lonechild and Joseph easily retained their positions. Lonechild promised to address provincial taxation infringement on areas of First Nation jurisdiction. Joseph saw his re-election as an affirmation of his strong position on negotiations with the various orders of goverment.

Two other notable events occurred at the start and at the end of the year. In January, after several years of lobbying the provincial government, Saskatchewan's Metis and their governments received official statutory recognition with the enactment of the Metis Act. The act diminished the extent to which the Non-Profit Act applied to the Metis Nation Saskatchewan. In speaking about the act at a proclamation ceremony, Aboriginal Affairs Minister Chris Axworthy said that it was valuable both at the symbolic and substantive levels in that it committed the provincial government to work with the MNS both in relation to governance and in providing services to Metis communities.

In December the provincial auditor criticized the Saskatchewan Indian Gaming Authority for its failure to improve its financial accountability frameworks as he had recommended in a report that his office had produced two years earlier. In that report, both the Saskatchewan Liquor and Gaming Authority and SIGA were accused of allowing lavish spending with few rules regarding conflicts of interest.

Other major issues and events

One of the major events in 2002 was the release of the report produced by the provincially appointed independent commission into the serious and potentially tragic problems that had emerged in North Battleford's water supply the previous year. At the time, approximately 7,000 individuals had been affected by the outbreak of an intestinal illness caused by cryptosporidiosis. The commission had been mandated to investigate what factors led to the outbreak, the roles and responsibilities of various agencies and officials both in relation to that outbreak and in the handling of it, and to make recommendations to minimize the risk of such an occurrence in the future. The commission delivered a scathing criticism of Saskatchewan's water inspection system along with twenty-eight recommendations for improving the safety of the water supply.

GEOFFREY LAMBERT

Manitoba

The New Democratic Party continued to govern quietly, making few errors, and apparently alienating very few voters. Perhaps there was a sense in 2002, here and there, that Premier Gary Doer's government had little of the radical edge one normally associates with social democrats. Or perhaps there was a suspicion in some quarters that the real Doer was different in private from the highly extroverted and warm persona that he projected in public. Still, every piece of available evidence suggested that the New Democrats were going to be in power for quite some time yet.

The legislative sessions

The Legislative Assembly reconvened in April and sat until early August. The volume of legislation was not excessive, nor the significance of it overwhelming. The comparative length of the session reflected rather close Opposition scrutiny, and ill-concealed bad blood between the two caucuses.

The budget was brought down by Finance Minister Greg Selinger on 22 April. He expressed satisfaction with the performance of the provincial economy compared with those of other provinces, and reminded the assembly that some economic and financial specialists had forecast that the rate of economic growth in Manitoba would be the third highest among the provinces in 2002. It was also widely anticipated that the provincial unemployment level would continue to be the lowest, or close to it, in the country. Selinger did warn, however, that the affect of slumping U.S. and world markets, and the aftershock of the terrorist outrages in New York City the previous September, were already imposing some restraints on the economy's potential. Also, there remained the unsettled question of whether the province would have to repay the $408 million that it had received from the federal government some years previously, but to which it had not been entitled. There had been a miscalculation somewhere. Happily, the province was eventually allowed to keep the money.

Selinger told the assembly that the government had to be somewhat cautious in its spending this year. The government would continue to emphasize as its top priorities health and education. Health remained the largest item of expenditure for the government, and the finance minister was clearly proud that fully 39.6 per cent of the budget now went to health care. He excoriated the federal government for its reduced transfers, claiming that, by the province's reckoning, although not by the federal government's, Ottawa's share of the cost of medicare now amounted to only 14 per cent.

Government revenues for 2002–3 were estimated at $6.803 billion, slightly less than the amount for the previous year. Revenue from both personal and corporate income taxes was expected to decline, or at best break even. This possible shortfall would be offset by some increases in sales tax revenue, and a rather substantial hike in the excise taxes paid by tobacco users. Expenditures were set at $6.625 billion, about 3 per cent higher than the previous year.

What this meant was that the government, to maintain its commitments to health and education, and also reduce the accumulated debt ($96 million was set aside for debt repayment), would be forced to reduce allocations to most other departments. A significant component of the government's contribution to education was the maintenance of the freeze on university tuition fees, which had originally been imposed shortly after the NDP had come back to power in 1999. The government claimed (and the universities accepted) that holding the line on fees opened doors for students who would otherwise be excluded. Where the universities and the government disagreed was on whether the government grant to the universities was sufficient to make up the difference. Certainly, given the creation of the Canadian Mennonite University (by the former Progressive Conservative government) and the announcement of a proposed University of the North (by the Doer government), there were fears that perhaps the government was spreading the postsecondary dollar too thin.

There were no major tax changes in 2002, except for the significant increase in the tax on tobacco products. The government was also able to reduce taxation levels in a number of areas.

The budget speech (like the budget itself) demonstrated the NDP's concern for inclusiveness, with Selinger using the speech to recapitulate a number of the government's promises to a broad range of groups. It was received with perhaps predictable commentary. The Opposition

Tories decried the lack of major tax cuts. The business community echoed this. Institutions dependent on the public purse decried the 'inadequacy' of government support, as something clearly (at least to the supplicant groups) undermining the government's claim to be on the side of the little folk.

The session did not end until early August, which became somewhat of a problem given the limited air-conditioning in the august old building, as well as the ill-will between the two sides of the legislature. It seemed that the government was attempting to get as much legislation out of the way as it could to clear the decks for a new Speech from the Throne and a new budget, as preludes to a general election that was expected towards the latter part of 2003.

The legislature returned on 27 November to hear the Speech from the Throne. Comparatively short, the speech touched on a number of familiar themes, indicating that the government was seeking to reinforce its traditional support base. Much of the content of the speech had been announced ahead of time, and very little of the new material took the government in a new direction.

On 25 September the premier announced some changes in the cabinet. Nobody new was appointed, and the shuffle was indeed just that, a shuffle. It did, however, provide observers with a chance to speculate about who was rising and who was falling in power and status after nearly two years of NDP incumbency.

One of the rising stars was obviously the Reverend Tim Sale from Fort Rouge. Long thought of (at least by Tories) as a radical menace, he had done well in family services. He became one of fortune's blessed when the premier appointed him to head a new and very important department, that of energy, science and technology. Another bête noire (or bête rouge) of the Tories, Steven Ashton, the fire-tongued MLA from Thompson, became conservation minister, important in the new context of the Kyoto Protocol and its consequences. Ron Lemieux took on the education portfolio; Eric Robinson became minister of culture, heritage and recreation; and Scott Smith was moved to the transport portfolio. Two ministers who appeared to be losing favour with the premier were Oscar Lathlin (now Aboriginal and northern affairs minister) and Drew Caldwell (now family services). The former had occasionally seemed lackadaisical in his approach to his duties, while the latter was sometimes referred to as 'motor-mouth.' From this designation, one may readily infer that Caldwell was considered to be too outspoken on too many issues. Why the premier did not bring new blood into the cabinet was not immediately apparent.

Civic politics

Civic politics enjoy the same attention and level of interest in Manitoba as elsewhere, namely, not much. But in 2002 there did seem to be a little more going on at the local level than had been usually the case. Much of this unusual level of activity resulted from the rather dynamic performance of the mayor of Winnipeg, Glen Murray. In his four years in office, Murray had substantially reorganized the workings of city hall, making the mayor and the city council more powerful. He had large ideas for the city, promoting developments that he believed would bolster Winnipeg's profile and reputation. A former New Democrat, he had become friendly with the Liberals, perhaps facilitating a better relationship with the federal powers that be. Indeed, it was rumoured that Murray was under some pressure to run for the party federally.

Murray enjoyed a wide measure of popularity, and it appeared at the outset of 2002 that there would be little or no significant opposition to his attempt to secure a second term in the elections set for 23 October. But, in a year otherwise notable for the city council's perpetuation of the status quo on the council, he had to run in the end against unexpectedly formidable opposition. Murray's major opposition came from former Councillor Al Golden, who had left the council because of some financial irregularities, and had failed to gain re-election. Golden, an outgoing and feisty populist, accused Murray of elitism, back-room decision-making, and other assorted crimes against the little guy. He enjoyed some success with this line of attack, since Murray refused to participate in the town hall meetings held during the campaign. Murray's explanation was that such events are seldom accompanied by the calm, thoughtful atmosphere that should attend the discussion of public issues. Instead, he saw them as little more than forums allowing his opponents to 'gang up on Glen.' Other candidates for the mayoralty were David Lettner, an active ecologist and strong opponent of the destruction of Eaton's downtown store to make way for a modern arena; Metis activist Chris Henderson; and veteran agitator Nick Ternette.

Murray did win (with about 51 per cent of the vote to about 38 per cent for the surprising Golden) but without the sweeping endorsement that he had probably hoped for some months previously. Turnout was 49 per cent, higher than usual. Apart from that, the voters returned incumbents in most parts of the province, prompting the *Winnipeg Free Press*, in sheer frustration to once again raise the question of imposing term limits on elected municipal officials. The paper's complaint essentially was not only that the existing Winnipeg City Council was prone to a lack of imagination, but also that it was difficult for challengers to break through a systemic bias in favour of even lacklustre councillors, who now had publicity budgets with which to promote themselves.

The smoking ban

On 1 January new ordinances to control smoking in public places came into effect in both Winnipeg and Brandon. The Brandon by-law prohibited smoking in all public places, without exception. In Winnipeg, however, only facilities likely to be frequented by children (i.e., persons under eighteen years of age) were forced to ban smoking on the premises. (This provision, incidentally, also encompassed taxis.) Those establishments that catered exclusively to adults were still free to designate smoking areas in their places of business. In the eyes of a lot of people, this was not a satisfactory way of doing things.

Some businesses, fearing the loss of patrons, bit the bullet and banned the admission of minors, thereby enabling them to permit smoking on their premises. Others were forced to lay off workers who were under eighteen years of age . Many said the restaurant business would suffer and sought an abandonment of the new law. Others felt that a total ban on smoking in public places ought to be in effect. During the municipal elections held later in the year, the smoking issue remained highly controversial, with the strong possibility emerging of a total smoking ban being enacted in Winnipeg.

The royal visit

This was, of course, the year of Queen Elizabeth II's golden anniversary, and Winnipeg was included in her Canadian tour. The Queen spent only one day in the city, but this attracted considerable attention, not necessarily of the most favourable kind.

The Queen, while in Winnipeg, lit up the restored Golden Boy, newly returned to his perch at the top of the Legislative Building after being thoroughly cleaned and refinished after eighty years of exposure to Manitoba winters. There was a state dinner with a guest list somewhat more democratic than sometimes is the case with such events. There was a spectacular fireworks display. Manitoban artistic talent, ranging from Loreena McKennitt to the Hula-Hoop Dancers of Flin Flon, was showcased. And Prince Philip went off to present some of his awards, and visit a barracks.

But it was not these wholesome if mundane activities that gained publicity. The weather was cold (although not such that Winnipegers were much concerned), yet many events were held outdoors. Some of the British press corps following the visit waxed indignant about this lack of sensitivity to what they called the 'elderly English couple' in their midst. Worse still, the engine on the boat carrying the royal couple across the river the very short distance to Saint Boniface stalled, and a rescue mission had to be mounted. In all, rather blush-making, and exaggerated by members of the British press corps, who tend to be rather superior in their attitudes to such colonial fiascos.

Perhaps the best perspective on this mini-crisis came from Steve Ashton, a member of the Doer cabinet and himself a Londoner by birth. He observed, in a letter to the *Times* (London) that nothing on earth was as cold as those damp, clinging Winters one can spend in the 'island kingdom.' And someone else pointed out that there should have been no worry about the boat, since one of the party aboard was an admiral of the fleet.

Politics and political parties

The other Murray, PC leader Stuart Murray, must have envied his clansman's success. The early days of the new political financing legislation (passed the year before) saw his party's income drop catastrophically. Office staff had to be laid off, and other savings made. He and his caucus put up effective opposition, but it failed to generate much attention. Late in the year it was revealed that he had hired Taras Sokolyk to provide strategic advice at a price of 25,000 hard-to-find dollars. Sokolyk had been chief-of-staff to former Premier Gary Fillmon, and one of the principals in the 'vote-splitting' scandal investigated by the Monnin Inquiry in 1998–9. The fallout from that investigation was regarded as one of the major factors in the defeat of the PC government in the last election. Murray and Sokolyk had worked together in the past. Both are able men, sharing a mutual respect. In short, whatever strategic advice was given was probably good. But the decision to hire Sokolyk seemed to demonstrate a strange political judgment on Murray's part. It also transpired that Murray had reached his agreement with Sokolyk while bypassing regular channels. He should have put a matter carrying so high a price tag to the party executive. In response, the party treasurer, Trevor Sprague, resigned, and there were some mutterings about a leadership review.

Liberal leader John Gerrard continued to be dogged by a low profile and rather low public expectations. However, he must have been cheered by the appearance of published opinion polls, commissioned by the *Winnipeg Free Press* and carried out by Probe Research of Winnipeg, showing his party making gains from the Tories. The polls confirmed that the NDP had largely held its support base from 1999. Nonetheless, there was one cautionary note for those ready to write off Murray and the Manitoba PCs: at a by-election in Lac du Bonnet riding following the resignation of Darren Praznick, the Tories held on to the seat by about the same margin of victory as in the preceding general election.

The economy and economic developments

The provincial economy's major asset, its diversity, stood the province in good stead again in 2002. Manitoba's economy grew by 3.1 per cent, and its nominal gross domestic product reached almost $36 billion. Unemployment levels were the lowest in the Canada, averaging 5.2 per cent over the year. The rate of employment among 15 to 24-year-olds was also the best in the country. The new jobs this represented, however, were overwhelmingly part-time in nature. Earnings grew, albeit slowly; inflation was under control, and most Manitobans no doubt felt content with their situation.

The province's population continued to grow, if very slowly. (This point is taken up later in a discussion of the census reports.) Natural increases and international migration were just enough to give the population some sort of increase, since Manitoba continued to suffer from a net migration of its younger citizens to other parts of Canada. Hence, there were shortages of labour in some areas such as meat-processing, garment manufacturing, and nursing. Further to this, there were discussions in the media regarding Winnipeg's deficiencies as a centre of high-technology jobs, and about the absence of a large community of creative individuals. In short, not even the Asper family's moving of a few senior positions in the CanWest empire to Winnipeg could, in the short run, break its reputation as a 'blue collar city.'

The manufacturing sector, the provincial economy's largest single component, registered some gains, and some losses. Food products (Manitoba's largest manufacturing sector) did well, but the most dynamic was transport equipment. Indeed, Manitoba is now this continent's largest supplier of buses. In light, however, of the uncertainties for the commercial airline industry following what is usually succinctly referred to as '9/11,' the aeronautical industry did not have a good year. Other areas, such as wood products, did less well this year than in 2001.

In some areas most of Manitoba's external trade is with the United States. In common with other parts of Canada, about 80 per cent of provincial foreign exports go to our southern neighbours. In light of the U.S. economic slowdown, there was some diminution of trade in that direction.

In 2002, the mining sector of the economy had, as always, its ups and downs, along with the boom-or-bust mentality of mining towns. Still, the year was largely one of declines and uncertainty, reflecting international demand. Farming did better this year, particularly in its grains component. In the livestock area there were some winners and some losers. Hog production has been gaining an increasing hold on economic life in Manitoba, and its attendant and generally unpleasant problems have begun to cause some concern.

Housing construction and the retail trade both did very well in 2002. Winnipeg's housing market has remained dynamic for a number of years. Both new housing construction and the resale market continued at a high level. The retail trade figures suggested that Manitobans, notoriously frugal though they may be, were still optimistic enough to spend money on automobiles, appliances, and so forth, taking advantage of low interest rates.

Capital investment increased, although private investment was sluggish. Public projects were there in a goodly number. Hydro production increased, but external sales decreased; however, there were some significant omens in this area. First, Manitoba Hydro purchased Winnipeg Hydro and promised to construct a handsome new building in downtown Winnipeg, an important proposal, given the city's (if not the province's) obsession with rejuvenating the capital city's inner core. Major deals appeared to be on the horizon, such as one with Xcel Energy of Minnesota, a major market for Manitoba energy.

The Kyoto Protocol and the various discussions surrounding it placed the spotlight on the province's major economic asset. Clearly, in the most stringent interpretations of the Protocol, hydro-electrical power would play an important role in replacing other, polluting, sources of energy. One issue that faced Manitoba planners, however, was how much new, extremely costly, construction should be undertaken on the basis of demand estimates that were inherently uncertain.

The province's tourism industry did well, somewhat better than its counterparts in the rest of the country. Both the number of tourists and the number of dollars that they spent increased. A lot of attention was paid to the province's modest film industry, the tax credit available to film-makers inducing a number of U.S. producers to make movies, or parts of movies, in Manitoba. Apparently, a singular attraction (quite apart from the tax credit) was that Winnipeg has, in its downtown area, a large stock of late Victorian and/or Edwardian buildings, which enables it to resemble Chicago or other large cities that had themselves torn down all their nineteenth-century edifices. But the moviemakers did not confine their attention to the provincial capital. No less a figure than Harrison Ford graced Gimli with his presence when shooting a film about a distressed Soviet submarine.

It is a constant in Manitoba politics that politicians and others yearn for a more exciting economic landscape. Low unemployment and a relatively modest cost of living, allied to the diversity of the economic base, provide stability. Some long, though, for booms the likes of which are generally only present in Alberta, or for local high-tech versions of Silicon Valley North. People do not enjoy seeing their children take off for Calgary, Vancouver, or Toronto. Often, it is claimed, there is not the quality of life or sufficient variety of leisure activity to suit the more aggressive of the province's youth. Yet, Manitoba cannot produce mountains to ski down or bring back the Jets. And clearly, some cultural institutions, such as the Winnipeg Symphony, cannot fill the void, judging from the scant attendance and large losses. Somewhere there is, no doubt, a solution. But for now the lament will continue.

Some census fragments

The release of some of the 2001 Census data pointed to a number of issues that Manitoba's decision-makers will have to grapple with if they wish to ensure the province's prosperity.

First, the rate of growth of population was the slowest of any province, although the Northwest Territories' population actually declined. Manitoba's population of 1.15 million was only 0.5 per cent higher than it had been five years before. The population and the tax base were threatened. True, the Aboriginal population was growing fast enough to enable the overall totals to go up. But Manitoba will have to pursue a larger share of foreign immigration if the population is to rise.

The figures also pointed to substantial variations between different parts of the province. Major growth was registered in the prosperous small towns and surburbs that provide homes for those many Winnipeg commuters fleeing the high property taxes of the capital city. Winnipeg itself (with about 677,000) grew as slowly as the province overall. It was a matter of concern, though, that large areas of Manitoba were being slowly depopulated, and the rural way of life threatened.

The population was short of young people and potential taxpayers. The median age of Manitobans was 37.4 years. This fact had major ramifications for such issues as the demand for and availability of health care services.

Manitoba's cultural diversity was becoming even more marked. It has long been, apart from Quebec, the least British of the provinces. Only 38 per cent now claimed British descent. What was found as well in the 2001 Census was that, although English remained the dominant language, some other European languages were losing their place. French, in spite of its constitutional protection, was losing ground. German remained a respectable second, because of the many Mennonites in the province. But Ukrainian seemed, if not moribund, at least in need of revival. Reflecting a major recent trend in the settlement of the province, the fastest growing language was Tagalog, the mother tongue of Manitoba's vibrant and growing Filipino community. Chinese, in its infinite number of dialects, seemed also to be on the rise.

KEN COATES AND GREG POELZER

The Territories

The three northern territories – the Yukon, the Northwest Territories, and Nunavut – faced a continuation of their long-term struggles in 2002. They are still waiting for a resolution of the debate over the route and construction of a natural gas pipeline from the North, coping with the demands of accelerated political reform, adapting to the political and administrative realities of the post-land claims settlement era, and seeking an end to the boom and mostly bust cycles that continued to plague the northern economy. Nunavut bathed in the continued glow from its status as Canada's newest territory – the only one with an Aboriginal majority. The Northwest Territories enjoyed the growing prosperity associated with the exploitation of sizeable diamond mines, and the Yukon looked forward with anticipation to the redrafting of its founding legislation, the Yukon Act, and the devolution of substantial powers from the federal government.

To a degree that few Canadian recognized, the northern territories continued a process of unprecedented political and administrative transformation. Only two decades earlier, the Yukon and the Northwest Territories were effectively colonies of the federal government, lacking assured political authority and fully dependent upon federal grants and direction. Over a short period of time both jurisdictions secured and exercised self-government and established autonomous political systems. Nunavut, controlled by the Inuit population, was carved out of the Northwest Territories and became a flagship for Indigenous self-government in Canada and internationally. The settlement of a series of Aboriginal land claims, including major agreements covering the Inuit and the Council for Yukon First Nations, ensured Indigenous peoples of a permanent plan in northern politics and administration. Add to this the continued and at times rapid devolution of political authority from the Government of Canada to the territories, with the Yukon leading the way, and the scale and scope of the transformation of the North becomes evident.

The North in national affairs

The changes in northern governance, perhaps surprisingly, came at a time when northern issues were not high on the national agenda. With the exception of the development of the diamond mines in the Northwest Territories, which briefly caught the public's imagination, northern developments attracted only passing attention across the country. Even the lingering debate over the possible route for the Mackenzie Valley Pipeline had shifted to the business pages, a matter of funding, politics, and commercial considerations, and of steadily declining public interest. Federal Minister for Indian and Northern Affairs Canada Robert Nault focused his efforts primarily on Aboriginal issues, many of which had a northern element. He held onto his post during a midyear cabinet shuffle by Prime Minister Jean Chrétien, a sign that his tough-speaking and hard-nosed approach to Aboriginal governance and regional development remained in favour in Ottawa. He was best known for his demands for greater accountability by Indigenous governments. Nault's request for audits of spending by such organizations revealed that the Northwest Territories (only twelve out of thirty-three conducting audits) and Nunavut (zero out of ten) were a matter of particular concern to the minister. (In the Yukon sixteen out of twenty-one Aboriginal organizations produced audits; across the country, approximately one-quarter of all groups was not audited.)

Nault and INAC officials remained deeply involved in land claims negotiations involving Indigenous groups in the Mackenzie River Valley and the Yukon. Anxious to press matters to an appropriate resolution, the federal government announced that it would hold firm to a 1 April deadline for the signing of final agreements in the Yukon. Ta'a Kwach'an signed their agreement in January, one hundred years after a former chief, Jim Boss, first approached the king of England on the matter. The group agreed to a payment of $26.9 million over fifteen years (less the $10 million borrowed for the negotiations), plus $3.4 million in re-indexation money, ownership of 785 square kilometres (with subsurface ownership of half of the land). There were other one-time payments, including $4.2 million for economic development. Ta'a Kwach'an opponents challenged the agreement in court, but their arguments were dismissed. Elder Frances Wollsey commented, 'From the days when the gold rush brought massive and irreversible change to the land, the people of Ta'an have struggled to find a balance between the old ways and the new, to welcome newcomers and new ideas, while holding on to our cherished traditions, our languages, land and our beliefs. Today we can be proud of what we achieved as a people' (*Whitehorse Star*, 14 January).

This agreement still left a number of claims unresolved, with the government holding firm on the deadline. On the last day of March, Kluane agreed to a settlement. Kluane Chief Daniel Tlen, said, 'To me, this is a bitter-sweet moment because we are letting go of our old ways and our old rights and moving ahead with new conditions and new terms. So it is an exciting moment; a momentous time in Kluane's history' (*Whitehorse Star*, 1 April). Nault signed a final agreement with the Salt River First Nation in the Northwest Territories in June, and allowed negotiations with the Kaska in the Yukon to continue because of family crises affecting the Kaska negotiating team.

The North entered the national agenda on a variety of issues, ranging from public presentations to the Commission on the Future of Health Care in Canada, chaired by Roy Romanow, to continued regional protests about the national gun registry (which included a Nunavut court challenge that secured a temporary stay in the implementation of the registry in the North). Northern leaders lobbied, without specific success, for northern economic development to match other regional initiatives, like the Western Economic Development Fund and the Atlantic Canada Opportunities Agency. The Yukon and the Northwest Territories, in particular, jostled with Ottawa over the preferred route for a natural gas pipeline, with the Yukon angered by the federal government's evident support for the all-Canadian route down the Mackenzie River valley. Northern premiers cooperated more fully on a campaign to secure greater federal funding for Aboriginal health care – the Yukon claimed unpaid bills amounting to $25 million – but a resolution remained elusive. The federal government announced in the fall of 2002 that a new national park would be created, Wager Bay, covering 20,000 square kilometres; the area is highly regarded for its abundant wildlife, including polar bears, beluga whales, and seals.

Issues of Canadian sovereignty remained, as in the past, a matter of contention, particularly as the retreat of the polar icecap had the potential of opening up the Northwest Passage to ocean navigation. In April the 1st Canadian Ranger Patrol Group, with representation from all three territories and a substantially Aboriginal staff, undertook a 1,700 kilometre patrol from Resolute Bay to Cape Isachsen, the approximate site of the magnetic north pole. The expedition's purpose was to assert Canadian sovereignty over the little-used and little-known lands of the Central Arctic, and to thereby hold at bay U.S. expectations that the northern passageways be opened for navigation.

Politics and policy

Yukon

The defining constitutional moment of 2002 for the Yukon came on 22 March, when the Government of Canada passed the revised Yukon Act. The Yukon's founding legislation, initially passed in 1898 and revised minimally in subsequent decades, did not recognize the existence of responsible government in the territory, among its other shortcomings. Although several First Nations expressed concerns that the new Yukon Act would imperil land claims negotiations, principally by passing control over land and resources to the territorial government, there was widespread support for the modernized legislation. The new Yukon Act was slated to come into effect on 1 April 2003, giving the governments of Canada and Yukon an additional year to work on the details of a complex devolution plan. In anticipation of the shift over 250 federal employees were offered new jobs and 245 accepted. The arrangement was not without its critics, including the Public Service Alliance of Canada, which declared that the employees had little actual choice. It is surprising that this very important change did not attract more attention in the territory.

The Liberal Party led by Premier Pat Duncan was elected, somewhat surprisingly, in April 2000 and seemed poised to govern the territory with a sustainable majority. The government started the year by announcing tax reductions and an extensive administrative reorganization in anticipation of the forthcoming devolution of federal authority. The reorganization sparked conflict with the Yukon Employees Union, which questioned the cost of the restructuring and suggested that layoffs and reclassifications would cause considerable hardship. The activist government fired three deputy ministers in January, pulled funding from the Yukon Schools Council, continued to work on a Yukon Permanent Fund, and changed the operations of the Yukon Lottery Corporation. Premier Duncan soon faced considerable difficulty with her caucus. Sue Edlerman was forced to resign as minister responsible for the status of women (holding onto her post as health minister) after referring to the Yukon women's movement as 'femi-Nazis' in an email. Duncan dismissed two cabinet ministers, Don Roberts (health and social services) and Wayne Jim (government services). The restructured cabinet was the first in Canadian history with more women than men.

Duncan's government, under increasing public criticism, fell into crisis in April. The two demoted cabinet ministers, Jim and Roberts, left the Liberal caucus, as did backbencher Mike McLarnon. As Jim said of the premier, 'It was her way or no way. That was it; bottom line' (*Whitehorse Star*, 2 April). Duncan said that she had rejected the 'bullying demands' of the three backbenchers; the dissidents declared that they had been expelled. The Liberal government survived the budget debate when the sole Yukon Party member, Peter Jenkins, opted to support the government. Legislative debate was tough-minded and spirited, focusing on such issues as an electoral boundaries act and plans to build a school on the outskirts of Whitehorse. As the session proceeded, stories emerged about the government's attempts to prop up their minority administration by offering the speaker's chair, variously, to one of the Liberal dissidents and two different NDP members.

The situation on the Opposition benches was not much better. Yukon Party leader MLA Peter Jenkins called on other party members to come forward if they wanted to contest his leadership. Watson Lake MLA, NDP house leader, and former NDP cabinet minister Dennis Fentie surprised the territory by resigning from his caucus and announcing his decision to run for the leadership of the Yukon Party. The announcement, in turn, revealed the news that Fentie had earlier been in discussions with the Liberals about crossing the floor. A third candidate, Darcy Tkachuk, former Yukon Party president, entered the race, declaring, 'It's become a tragedy when our Yukon has become the Newfoundland of the North; when our primary export is our young people' (*Whitehorse Start*, 16 May). Fentie won the mid-June contest on the first ballot, securing exactly the number of votes necessary to win.

The New Democratic Party found itself in comparable shape to the other parties. Although party leader Eric Fairclough declared that Fentie's departure was not an indictment of his leadership, the party was uncertain about its direction. Fairclough called for a leadership review, placing in doubt his position as the first Aboriginal to lead a mainstream Canadian political party. Two others entered the contest: Todd Hardy, former MLA and unsuccessful Whitehorse mayoralty candidate, and Mike Travill, a workers' advocate. Fairclough subsequently withdrew from the race, and Hardy won the late-September vote, becoming the sixth NDP leader in twenty-four years but the fourth in thirty months.

With a weak and divided Liberal Party in office, and with both Opposition parties with new leaders, Yukon politics remained at a fever pitch through the fall. Much of the discussion focused on the Grey Mountain Primary School, which Opposition members derided as flagrant vote-buying. The Liberals recruited high-profile First Nations candidates for the anticipated winter election, attracting First Nations Chiefs Paul

Birckel, and Pat Van Bibber, as well as former Commissioner Judy Gingell. Anticipating defeat on the Liberal budget, Premier Duncan called an election for 4 November, only two-and-a-half years into her government's mandate.

The election campaign was heated and intense. It featured several independents and much discussion of the revelation that Fentie of the Yukon Party had served seventeen months in jail on a drug sentence before receiving a full pardon. Anti-Liberal sentiment mounted, however, and the Liberals were routinely criticized for high-handedness and for failing to address the territory's economic woes. The Yukon Party won handily, taking twelve of eighteen seats and 40 per cent of the vote. The Liberals were decimated, with only Pat Duncan holding onto her seat. The NDP became the official Opposition, with Todd Hardy leading the five-member delegation into the territorial legislature. Fentie moved quickly to quell suggestions that the Yukon Party had a right-wing agenda, pointing to his record on social issues, pledging support for land claims, a Yukon hire policy, and environmental and sustainability measures. The Yukon Party had clearly shifted from the right to the centre.

Aboriginal issues continued to feature prominently in territorial political affairs. The public at large followed First Nations elections with greater interest, as the chiefs and councillors played increasingly prominent roles in territorial public affairs. The Kaska First Nation, in the southeast corner of the territory, presented the most formidable challenges, as it continued to negotiate complex transboundary issues, demanded attention to its outstanding land claim, and sought agreement on a forestry management plan. A Forestry Stewardship Memorandum was signed with the Kaska in July, creating the Kaska Forestry Stewardship Council, with a seven-member board assured of three Kaska members. The Kaska did, however, continue to express concerns about the state of territorial devolution, threatening to challenge the process in court if its concerns were not addressed before the 2003 implementation of the Yukon Act.

Northwest Territories

In a year of rapid economic expansion and continued transition following the separation from Nunavut, the Government of the Northwest Territories decided early in 2002 that it would close off a long-standing debate over the renaming of the territory. Two efforts to identify a new name had resulted in the same two leading suggestions – Northwest Territories and Bob. The government opted to kill the effort. On a more serious front, political life in the territory was dominated, even more so than in the Yukon, by debate about the location of the natural gas pipeline. The economic development plans of the territorial government and several First Nations rested on the selection of the Mackenzie Valley pipeline route, a strategy strongly opposed by several groups in the southern Northwest Territories. This hotly contested issue caused friction with the Government of Yukon but attracted cautious support from federal authorities.

The most sustained battle with the federal government focused on Premier Steven Kakfwi's demand for more than $200 million in investment in infrastructure and economic development funding. The booming mining sector, based particularly on diamonds, had accelerated demands on the territorial government and strained the regional infrastructure. Facing the prospect of the early start on a $3 billion natural gas pipeline, Kakfwi indicated that the Northwest territories needed additional resources to cope with the pressures, or else they would lose interest in encouraging large scale developments. To this end, the territorial government started talks with the federal government about royalty revenue-sharing, designed to ensure the territory a significant return from economic activity in the region.

The bitterest political conflict in the territory involved the termination of – and paying of severance to – two government employees. Critics alleged that Premier Kakfwi had overpaid his former chief of staff and former principal secretary by more than a quarter of a million dollars. The heated debate resulted in a motion to demand the premier's resignation, which failed to pass following a vote of 5 to 10.

The Northwest Territories, while attending to the reality of a widely dispersed population, did not pursue an aggressive decentralization plan, as in Nunavut. In a slight step towards greater administrative efficiency, the government created a Joint Health Leadership Council (including the minister of health, deputy minister, and chairs of the health authorities) and a Joint Senior Management Committee (department managers and chief exectuive officers of the health authorities) to promote greater collaboration and improved efficiencies. There was considerable debate about the need to refine the social welfare arrangements in the territory, sparked by the release of a major report entitled on the subject *Social Agenda: A Draft for People of the NWT.* The report's ten recommendations called for (among a variety of administrative measures): made-in-the-North policies, greater internal flexibility, more emphasis on the prevention of poverty, and greater public debate about social welfare arrangements.

Health care and education remained crucial issues, with considerable effort in both fields to attend to the unique needs and expectations of the territory's large Aboriginal population. Staffing issues remained paramount. In August 2002 the intensive care unit at the Stanton Territorial Hospital in Yellowknife was closed because of staff shortages, sparking concern that the obstetrics unit might also have to close. (This was a particular concern as many expectant, near-term mothers from the smaller communities relocated to Yellowknife to have their babies.) The government paid for the cost of flying critically ill patients to southern hospitals and declared its intention to recruit enough nurses to keep the Stanton UB unit fully operational. The shortage of nursing staff was attributed, at least in part, to the removal of recruitment and retention bonuses in March. The problems with the Stanton facility had repercussions throughout the system, as hospitals from the outlying communities had to arrange for the patients to be flown south, typically to Edmonton. The shortage of medical specialists in Yellowknife meant that those who remained in the territory made fewer visits to the communities. Health Minister Michael Miltenberger's announcement in October of an external review of the Stanton Hospital drew angry criticism from medical personnel and community members who demanded prompt action.

In one of the most important infrastructure developments in the history of the territory, the Government of the Northwest Territories also took major steps towards the construction of a bridge across the Mackenzie River. The planned $55 million bridge, to be funded in part by tolls on commercial traffic, promised significant improvements for life in the territory, including uninterrupted road travel to the south and significant savings on food and supplies. (A ferry moved cars and trucks across the river, with an ice bridge operating after freeze-up in the winter; this left Yellowknife without secure road access to the south for several months each year.) In mid-November the territorial government and the Fort Providence Combined Council Alliance signed an agreement to move the Deh Cho Bridge to the next stage of planning, the most significant step yet in the effort to construct the long-desired bridge.

Despite the resource boom under way in the territory, the Government of the Northwest Territories was far from flush financially. The federal–territorial financial arrangements left Ottawa in control of resource revenues, meaning that there was no assured connection between territorial resources and the vitality of the economy. The NWT government's budget for 2002–3 called for a $12.1 million deficit, with only modest improvements in social programs (including a $1 million boost in day care subsidies). The government had revenues of over $850 million, with almost $390 million coming from federal grants and another $55 million in transfer payments. Corporate ($264 million) and personal ($47 million) income taxes fell short of the federal revenues as a percentage of the total.

The Northwest Territories continued to provide strong evidence of the unique 'politics of smallness' in the Canadian North, particularly at the band council level. Northern politicians repeatedly discovered that the intense focus of local politics, with the added elements of land claims and self-government negotiations, proved extremely difficult for political leaders. In 2002 three Northwest Territories Aboriginal leaders clashed with their communities. At Colville Lake, the band council had voted (in 2001) to remove Dora Duncan and her daughter, Jennifer, from the council. The Duncans went to court to fight their ouster; in May 2002 the Federal Court stopped a planned by-election to give the Duncan appeal time to proceed. At Wrigley, Chief Percy Hardisty was ousted from office by his council, and a new election was called. Tim Lennie was elected; Hardisty opted not to run in order the protect his legal case. Salt River Chief Victor Marie was elected in August and voted out of office in October, his council turning on him after he elected his sister, former MLA Jeannie Marie Jewell, as interim band manager. He was returned to office the next month following a community vote.

The turmoil highlighted a continuing problem in the Northwest Territories. In southern jurisdictions, band council elections operate under the Indian Act. Since there are no reserves in the Northwest Territories, First Nations in the territory rely on customary elections. Some use secret ballots; others rely on a public 'show of hands' (as in the Salt River reaffirmation of Marie). In November 2002, Indian and Northern Affairs Canada proposed the implementation of formal election codes for each community (offering funding to support the process as well), in the hope of heading off continuing conflict and controversy. The federal approach was greeted warily: 'I think it should be left up to the communities,' commented Colville Lake Band Councillor Alvin Orlias. 'The communities know what they want' (*News of the North*, 9 December).

Nunavut

In October Queen Elizabeth and Prince Philip visited the newest political jurisdiction in the realm. The event, which drew large crowds to the streets of Iqaluit, proved to be the highlight of a contentious and difficult year for Nunavut. The government of Premier Paul Okalik continued with the difficult transition to territorial status and the attendant challenges of regional self-government. The Inuit-dominated government had set an ambitious agenda, focusing on increasing Inuit participation in administration, improving educational opportunities, and building a strong economy. Nunavut proved to be a costly project for the Government of Canada, and 2002 saw renewed evidence of federal concerns about the escalating expense of the territory and the difficulty of addressing Nunavut's complex social, cultural, and economic needs in a timely fashion. Efforts by Nunavut mayors to secure additional funding for their communities, for example, were met with warnings by Minister Robert Nault that the federal government could not possibly meet all of the territory's needs in a short period of time. The minister also made it clear that the full transfer of land and resources to the Government of Nunavut – a process nearing completion for the Yukon – was not likely to happen in the near future. One writer observed that "since they came to power in 1993, the Chrétien Liberals have demonstrated an unwavering commitment to two principles: one, deprive the government of Nunavut of the means required to meet its people's basic needs, and two, lie about it to the rest of the world.' (*Nunatsiaq News*, 4 October).

The leaders and people of Nunavut worried Canada's long-term aspirations for the Arctic, particularly in light of major debates about the impact of climate change on the North and increasing U.S. challenges to national sovereignty in the region. As the *Nunatsiaq News* editorialized in February,'Canada is now well on its way to becoming an economic and military colony of the United States, utterly dependent on the U.S. to protect its borders, and a sovereign nation in name only. If current trends continue, it won't be long before the Canadian government's relationship with the U.S. resembles the Greenland government's relationship with Denmark' (*Nunatsiaq News*, 1 February).

The Nunavut government faced considerable internal tension throughout 2002, in large measure because of the rapid pace of change and the consequently heavy demands on politicians and administrative staff. There were battles over the territory's aggressive Nunavut-first policy. Abraham Tagalik, president of the Qikiqtaaluk Corporation, quit his position after he rejected pressure from its board of directors to award a major hospital construction contract to the Nunavut Construction Corporation, saying that a competitive non-Inuit bid was far superior. Two other employees resigned at the same time. Less controversial, but equally challenging, was the government's commitment to Qaujimajatuqangit, to increase respect for and awareness of Inuit culture in the administration of public affairs. Nunavut's Language Commissioner Eva Aariak introduced proposals for a broad expansion of Inuktitut language rights in the territory and suggested that the government's goal of becoming Inuktitut by 2020 was unlikely to be accomplished. (The language commissioner also pointed out that Nunavut was not honouring its obligation to provide government services in French.) The Special Committee Reviewing the Official Languages Act endorsed the commissioner's proposals and called on the government to act promptly in this highly symbolic area. A revised Education Act was passed in May 2002, redefining the role of the District Education Authorities and expanding the age of compulsory education to 5–18 years, but earning criticism from the DEAs for leaving too much authority in the hands of the minister of education. The government released a major report, entitled *Aajiiqatigiingniq*, on the expansion of Inuktitut instruction in territorial schools, after holding the document for more than two years. The controversial plan called for the development of a fully Inuktitut school system within ten years.

The Nunavut government announced that planning was under way for the formation of a new Crown corporation, Qulliq Energy Corporation, to manage the territory's diverse energy requirements. Subsidies in this sector consumed more than 20 per cent of Nunavut's annual budget. Establishing QEC also meant the transfer of jobs from Ranklin Inlet to Baker Lake, a hotly contested issue in the former community and a reflection of the continuing tensions in Nunavut over decentralization strategies. In a significant step designed to bring Nunavut into line with the rest of Canada, Premier Okalik introduced the first draft of Nunavut's human rights legislation in November. The government also revised the Nunavut Elections Act, which, along with other changes, shortens the campaign period and allows electors in remote regions to phone in their votes.

The non-partisan Legislative Assembly, which operates on a consensus model and without political parties, invited public criticism when, early in March it passed a revised pension plan for MLAs, at a cost of $2.7 million over four years. Three MLAs from Iqaluit voted against the bill, which passed in the face of considerable public opposition. The MLAs later agreed to grant a severance allowance to departing territorial politicians. Equally controversial was a lengthy public outcry about the sale of contaminated gasoline by the Government of Nunavut. The gasoline damaged numerous snowmobiles and other equipment and led to the government's decision to provide compensation for damage caused by the bad gas. For all of this activity, the government and legislature received mixed reviews, as a *Nunatsiaq News* editorial reveals: 'Without a doubt, the sitting of the Nunavut Legislative Assembly that MLAs inflicted upon us between Feb. 20 and March 6 was an unmitigated embarrassment. The session began with a series of attacks on battered women and the under-funded shelters set up to protect them, and ended with MLAs voting, not only for a $70,000 transition allowance for those who leave office, but for an obscenely enriched supplementary pension plan that will provide most of them with incomes for the rest of their lives. For those who believe in the potential of the Nunavut Legislative Assembly, it was a disappointing time.' As the editorial continued, however, the second sitting of the assembly, which ended in May, produced much more refined debate and clear evidence of maturation in the political life of the territory (*Nunatsiaq News*, 17 May).

Decentralization, a major pillar in the Nunavut government's strategy for community development, remained a disappointing work in progress. The issue had been with Nunavut from the beginning, and reflected lingering resentment over the dominance of Yellowknife in the affairs of the old Northwest Territories. A report produced by retired government official Ken Lovely and three Nunavut officials noted the following Problems: many of the jobs slated for relocation to the smaller communities remained unfilled; morale was very low among government workers; difficulties remained with communication and lines of authority; and the costs of the decentralization were impossible to calculate with precision. Many Government of Nunavut workers did not wish to relocate outside of Iqaluit. As a result most of the positions were filled by Inuit workers, at lower and less-skilled levels. The politicians remained committed to the concept, given that government jobs were viewed as the cornerstone of community economies. The government announced plans to move more than seventy additional jobs to seven communities, bringing the total positions relocated to almost 430. The movement of jobs and the emphasis on recruiting Inuit resulted in a very rapid turnover in the civil service, with almost one-third of employees leaving between 2001 and 2002. In the Department of the Executive, fourteen of fifteen workers left their positions, and even Nunavut Arctic College had more than half (59 of 112) of their employees leave their posts.

On the surface, Nunavut's finances appeared to be in order, with the government forecasting a modest surplus in their May budget, even in the face of skyrocketing health care costs (up by more than 25 per cent), and establishing the lowest personal and corporate income tax rates in

Canada. By November revised budget estimates forecast a significant shortfall, largely as a result of a doubling of the territory's capital budget. Even more critically, federal Auditor General Sheila Fraser issued a stern evaluation of Nunavut's finances in February, indicating that the shortage of skilled managers placed the ambitious decentralization plan at risk and calling on the territory's government to recruit more highly qualified personnel. She also questioned the government's expenditures, particularly on leased facilities.

Many of the issues faced by the Government of Nunavut were very basic. Education remained a top political issue, with clear evidence of staff shortages, inadequate facilities, and serious problems with student performance. Most children in Nunavut learned in Inuktitut for the first three years and then faced an abrupt language transition to English. The system did not appear to be working, sparking plans to redraft the Education Act. National tests of educational attainment continued to draw attention to the weak performance of Nunavut students, a problem officials ascribed to cultural problems with the surveys and examinations, the fact that most Nunavut students were Inuktitut speakers, and the challenges of staffing and supporting the territorial education system. Estimates of food costs in Nunavut ran close to twice the national average, leading Health Canada, Canada Post, and Indian and Northern Affairs Canada to implement a pilot project designed to reduce the cost of bringing nutritious food to the territory.

As with the Yukon and the Northwest Territories, Nunavut wrestled with the realities of INAC funding for health care, which targets on-reserve Aboriginal people and leaves the northern territories (where there are few reserves) with less support than received by comparable provincial districts. The Romanow Commission on the future of Health Care in Canada heard stinging indictments of health services in the North and demands for rapid and determined action. As Jose Kusugak, president of Inuit Tapiriit Kanatami, said, 'The health-care system you are reviewing barely exists in the Arctic. It is so far removed from our needs and our reality that as I read the commission's interim report I often felt as though I was reading about a different country' (*Nunatsiaq News*, 5 April). Nunavut political leaders embraced the final Romanow Report, which called for a substantial increase in support for northern health care, with the Nunavut leaders arguing that the per capita approach used to finance health care left the North at a serious disadvantage. Representatives of Inuit Tapiriit Kanatami, the national Inuit organization, and Pauktuutit, the Inuit women's association, led a spirited critique of federal programs for Aboriginal people in the North, arguing that the southern Canadian approach did not suit Nunavut circumstances.

Similar challenges existed in the mental health field. A major report presented to the Legislative Assembly in May outlined the extent of Nunavut's challenge in this area. Entitled *Nunavut Addictions and Mental Health Strategy,* the report called for culturally based healing programs, drawing on traditional knowledge, and the construction of new facilities. The report documented the territory's soaring suicide rate, incidence of child abuse, and crime rates; the shortage of qualified mental health professionals; emergency shelter admissions (that were eight times the national average); and serious problems with maternal drinking during pregnancy and fetal alcohol syndrome (which affected almost two-thirds of all prison inmates).

Nunavut politicians faced considerable pressure to attend to regional, national, and international issues. Inuit politicians remained heavily involved with the Inuit Circumpolar Conference, which held its August meeting (including an international elders' conference) in Kuujjuaq. Cathy Towtongie, newly elected president of Nunavut Tunngavik Incorporated, challenged political leaders to address issues of greatest importance to the people of the North: 'Social issues are making our people unsure of the future; they are zapping our strength. They are overwhelming those we serve – we cannot avoid them or downplay them. We must turn our attention to suicide, addiction, abuse, crime, illiteracy, family dysfunction and violence. All of these barriers to our mental and emotional health have multiplied during many of the leadership's great silence about them' (*Nunatsiaq News*, 5 April). Premier Okalik found himself in a bitter and public disagreement with the federal government over offshore fishing rights granted to the Makivik Corporation, rights that the premier argued interfered with Nunavut's aspirations to secure additional resource opportunities in the Davis Strait region.

Nunavut Tunngavik Incorporated, charged with implementing the land claims agreement in the North, continued its transition. Arrangements were introduced for the management of hunting and harvesting activities, although suggestions for mandatory hunter training were roundly criticized in community meetings. Nunavut gained increasing experience in the self-administration of resource use and management, including imposing a ban on boats on the Sylvia Grinnell River, designed to rebuild the Arctic char population. The Nunavut Wildlife Management Board recognized the Igloolik and Hall Beach bowhead hunt in June, sparking strong community interest in the activity. There was vigorous debate about the assignment of hunting rights to another

Inuk of 'spouse of a person cohabiting as the spouse of an Inuk,' with the discussion focusing on eligibility for harvesting rights. Nunavut Tunngavik abolished the Nunavut Social Development Council in March, claiming that the organization charged with making recommendations on social, health, housing, and cultural issues was not performing its work. The NSDC fought back, claiming that it had not been given appropriate direction and pleading for additional time to produce more effective results. NSDC was reconstituted as a department of NTI.

Many of the land claims issues and concerns were resolved at the regional level. Qikiqtani Inuit Association, for example, managed the land claims implementation for Baffin Island. This organization went through an extensive reorganization in 2002, building around a vision statement entitled *Protecting and Promoting Inuit Rights and Values.* December elections involving beneficiaries produced a new executive and renewed determination to address the challenges of adapting to and implementing the land claim. The association had had a troubled two years, removing presidents in both 2000 and 200,1 and appointing Archie Alikatuktuk as interim president. A highly regarded artist from Pangnirtung who had resurrected QIA from its disarray, Alikatuktuk was confirmed as president in the December vote, which attracted only one-third of eligible voters (in part because of a blizzard that hit several communities).

Economy

Yukon

In the Yukon the economy continued to limp along, with growth lagging behind the rest of the country. Housing prices in Whitehorse fell. Federal employment figures revealed that several hundred additional Yukoners had found work, although commentators declared that many had had to leave the territory to do so, finding mining employment in the Northwest Territories or in the Alberta oil sector. Yukon government statistics verified this assertion, and indicated that 500 fewer people were working in the territory. Tourism suffered from the post–11 September 2001 downturn and rising gasoline prices. Mineral exploration fell from $54 million in 2001 to $40 million in 2002. The government made a concerted effort to restart the Else Mine, and the purchase of United Keno Hill Mines' assets by AMT Canada seemed to suggest that production would begin. A prolonged battle over environmental licences and the costs of reclamation at the mine site stalled the development several times and had AMT Canada on the verge of pulling out. The closure of the Faro Mine, the long-time mainstay of the Yukon economy, appeared likely to wind up that chapter in the territory's history. The Yukon's unemployment rate for the year was 8.9 per cent. The territory also claimed one of the highest median annual incomes: at $26,000, the Yukon rate was significantly higher than the $21,600 national average, although still behind the Northwest Territories, where it is $27,800.

Northwest Territories

The economy of the Northwest Territories remained robust throughout 2002, fuelled by continuing interest in northern resources, the expanding diamond sector, and anticipated developments in oil and gas. The matter of the Mackenzie Valley pipeline remained unresolved, with U.S. politicians supporting the Alaska Highway route (including a much disliked subsidy plan that angered NWT leaders) and with favourable but far from overwhelming backing from the Canadian federal government for the Mackenzie River route. Prime Minister Jean Chrétien did intervene to protest the U.S. plan to subsidize the Alaska Highway proposal, arguing that the market should decide. Natural Resources Minister Herb Dhaliwal made it clear that the federal government favoured the Northwest Territories option, but quashed a request for federal loan guarantees to Aboriginal groups who wish to participate in the project. The alliance of energy firms, Aboriginal groups, and the Northwest territories government held firm throughout 2002, although Dene communities from the southern part of the territory continued to raise doubts about the project. The emergence of competing proposals, continued competition from Alaska and the Yukon, and the prospect of opposition from the Dene, as well as a complicated National Energy Board review hearing, meant that uncertainty remained the order of the day in the pipeline sector.

On the supply side, continued activity in the Beaufort Sea and Mackenzie River delta augured well for the future of the oil and gas industry. A well drilled by Devon and Petro-Canada south of Tuktoyaktuk produced extremely well – thirty times the Canadian average for a gas well – and increased the prospects of the Tuktoyaktuk region. The Inuvik area enjoyed substantial economic growth, much of it based on the engagement of locally owned firms in the oil and gas industry, in sharp contrast to the early oil-and-gas–led booms in the region. Many local companies, a significant number Aboriginally owned, were engaged in transportation and supply operations for the oil rigs, fuelling an expansion in the Inuvik economy. In 2002 the Mackenzie Delta was host to seven companies operating out of twenty different camps. A total of over 2,000 workers were engaged in the sector, almost all of them drawing heavily on Inuvik for supplies and support. Further evidence of the vitality of northern exploration came from the announcement that Beaufort Sea licences had been issued to two groups: Chevron Canada / BP Canada Energy and Devon ARL / Petro-Canada. Further south, Parmount Resources continued its work on the Cameron Hills oil and gas field.

Mining attracted a great deal of interest in 2002. The success of the Northwest Territory's diamond mine, BHP Diamonds Inc.'s Ekati property, producing about 4 per cent of the world's diamonds in 2002, drew prospectors and investors to the North like bees to honey. Exploration ramped up and 'diamond fever' ran rampant throughout the region. A second diamond mine, Rio Tinto PLC of Great Britain and Aber Diamond's Diavik property, opened in the autumn, having cost some $1.3 billion to bring into operation. Promising returns from the Kennedy Lake exploration, undertaken by Mountain Province Diamonds Inc., suggested that another mining operation might well proceed. In addition to the diamond activity, the Cantung tungsten property (just inside the Northwest Territories' western border and accessible by road only through the Yukon) reopened. Miramar Mining Corporation kept its Yellowknife mine in operation, even though gold prices remained low.

The impact of the resource boom could be seen throughout the Northwest Territories, but particularly in Yellowknife. The territory's unemployment rate stood at 8.6 per cent early in the year, the higher than average rate largely attributable to continued economic difficulties in many First Nations communities. Developers struggled, without success, to keep pace with demand for housing in Yellowknife, with a resulting surge in construction activity, low vacancy rates, and soaring house prices.

Perhaps of greater long-term significance than the specific mining and oil and gas programs was the radically different nature of Aboriginal participation in resource development in the Northwest Territories. Joint ventures had, by 2002, become commonplace, and new projects invariably had a high level of local involvement. The early development of the Snap Lake property by DeBeers, for example, included an agreement with the North Slave Metis Alliance to provide jobs and opportunities for Metis businesses.

The greatest economic challenge in the Northwest Territories in 2002 remained diversification. Although many of the workers in the mining and oil and gas sectors were northerners – 40 per cent of Diavik's workforce came from the region – employment in the resource field remained largely transient. Efforts at the subsidization of value-added production, principally through the territorial government's NWT Development Corporation, produced few success stories, although 2002 saw a major improvement in the commercial prospects of Fort McPherson Tent and Canvas, including a doubling of the local workforce and the profit forecast for 2003. The northern fur trade continued to rebound, with fur auctions in the spring producing record prices – up to $90 for a seal pelt – and growing interest in northern-produced clothing. NTDC's subsidiary, Arctic Canada Trading Company, represented a variety of Dene-designed and-manufactured items, as did Dene Fur Clouds of Fort Providence, and Just Furs in Yellowknife. The diamond sector provided other opportunities. Tiffany and Company, the famed New York jeweller, spent more than $3 million on a substantial diamond manufacturing facility in Yellowknife, designed to capitalize on the flow of diamonds from Diavik, in which Tiffany is a shareholder.

The most impressive economic success stories in the Aboriginal communities came out of the Inuvialuit Development Corporation, established in 1977 and celebrating its twenty-fifth anniversary in 2002. ICD, operating initially with a $10 million endowment fund, remained a major player in the economy of the Northwest Territories, with over $130 million in assets and revenues exceeding $170 million. IDC owns or has interests in major transportation companies (Aklak Air, Canadian North, Northern Transportation Company, NorTerra, and a joint venture with Canadian Helicopters). IDC operates retail outlets, equipment manufacturing, a catering company, environmental firms, drilling rigs, and the largest computer network operation in the Northwest Territories.

Social and cultural affairs in the Northwest Territories continued to emphasize renewed celebration of Aboriginal life (Dene, Inuit, and Metis). School programs, enhanced language instruction, the terrirory's involvement with Aboriginal television and radio (particularly Indigenous language programming,) and outreach activities continued. These cultural activities were firmly rooted in community life, the education system, and public institutions, and provided high-profile support for the work of elders and others attempting to strength Indigenous language use and traditional cultural practices. The Inuit in the Western Arctic continued to participate in Arctic-wide Inuit activities, capitalizing on the extensive programming undertaken in Nunavut and supporting the circumpolar political activities of Inuit/Eskimo groups from Greenland to Alaska.

The Northwest Territories continued to wrestle with a variety of social and cultural challenges, relating particularly to residents of the remote and small villages. As with the Yukon and Nunavut, the Northwest Territories continued to experience rates of alcohol and drug abuse that ran well above the national average, with comparable problems regarding suicide and violent behaviour. Dr Andre Corriveau, the territory's chief medical officer, released statistics on sexual activity among young people in the territory, drawing particular attention to the rate of sexually transmitted diseases. In the NWT the incidence of STDs is more than ten times the national average. Perhaps most worrying for Corriveau, the incidence of STDs among children aged 12 to14 years had increased by 61 per cent in less than a decade, with comparable increases among older people. In 2002, the NWT also faced serious problems with HIV/AIDS, with the disease spreading among the heterosexual community.

Nunavut

The economy continued to present major challenges in Nunavut in 2002, even though the territorial gross domestic product grew by 3.7 per cent over the previous year – substantially above the national average growth rate of 1.2 per cent. The closure of the Nanisivik zinc mine in 2002, and the news that its owner, Breakwater Resources, had incurred losses of more than $110 million, represented significant setbacks for the territory (and raised questions about the financing of the mine's clean-up). Job creation remained limited, and opportunities for Inuk remain very low. Expanding opportunities in government and with Inuit organizations (such as the decision by Nunavut Tunngavik Incorporated to create eithteen community liaison officer positions) were the most significant developments in the territory. Despite harsh criticisms by the auditor general of Canada, the Government of Nunavut continued to fund the Nunavut Development Corporation. Sustainable Development Minister Olayuk Akesuk justified the continued expenditure, $3.5 million in 2002, arguing that the government was more interested in jobs and training than in short-term profits. Across the territory, active Inuit-first employment strategies were contemplated or implemented, including an effort to recruit more Inuit into managerial positions with the Iqaluit municipal government.

Mining presented a divided picture, with Nanisivik finally closing operations, but with very promising results from Ashton Mining of Canada's Kim diamond property, located northwest of BHP's Ekati mine and Cumberland Resources' Meadbank gold property near Baker Lake. Mining executives suggested that development was possible at Miramar of Vancouver's Hope Bay gold property, Inmet Mining Corporation zinc and copper deposit at Izok Lake, and Kinross Gold Corporation's gold properties at Goose Lake and George Lake, Tahera Corporation's Jericho diamond project, and Wolfden's high-grade copper and zinc property at High Lake. Mineral exploration and producing mines, still relatively small in 2002, created both employment and business opportunities in the Kitikmeot region. The government responded by increasing local training courses and by encouraging the mining companies to hire local workers whenever suitable and possible. The North's diamond rush continued, with more than 2,500 claims staked in the Coronation Gulf region, accounting for more than 5.8 million acres. Cumulatively, mining accounted for 25 per cent of Nunavut's economic activity, although forecasts called for a substantial cooling of the diamond rush and other mineral ventures in the area.

Several new and emerging elements brightened the territorial economic picture. The Nunavut Trust Fund, based on holdings derived from land claims settlements, continued to emerge as a major factor in the economic development of the North. The fund continued to build towards its goal of holding more than $1 billion and supported the work of Nunavut Tunngavik Incorporated (recipient of loans of close to $100 million), Atuqtuarvik Corporation, and the elders' pension plan. Small market opportunities developed, including the following; the sale of seal products to Asia; the development of cruise ship tourism in Pond Inlet, Cape Dorset, Kimmirut, and Pangnirtung; continued growth in the arts and crafts sector; gemstone and jewellery production. These positive developments were offset, in part, by considerable turbulence in the airline industry, which saw reductions and changes to service and continued awareness throughout Nunavut of its dependence on commercial aviation.

The Nunavut government continued with plans for the Bathurst Inlet deep water port and road project (to a zinc and copper project at Izok Lake), estimated to cost over $210 million and requiring close to half that amount in federal support. This all-weather 210 kilometre-long road would have reduced the dependence of mining companies on the long (570 kilometres) Lupin ice road, which operates only in the winter and which adds greatly to the cost of operating properties in Nunavut and the Northwest Territories. Other road-building projects under consideration include the Iqaluit to Kimmirut road, and a connector between Manitoba and Nunavut. The government also continued its effort to encourage Inuit-controlled business, albeit with a high-profile change in policy. Under the Nunavummi Nangminiqaqtunik Ikajuuti, the Government of Nunavut extends a significant preference to specific northern companies. Initially, externally controlled firms had two years to adjust to the new regulations, but in April the government extended the grace period for an additional year. Southern firms expressed concern about the policy, which they said would deter investment and which did not recognize the limited ability of Nunavut businesspeople to invest in regional companies. Several northern firms, including NorTerra Incorporated (and its subsidiary, Canadian North), protested the regulations. Nor Terra was 100 per cent Inuit-owned, but with only 50 per cent Nunavut beneficiary ownership (not the 51 per cent required under the regulations), and it had not had an opportunity to appeal its status. NTI responded to the government's decision by launching a court challenge in June, demanding that the original two-year transition period stay be reinstated and that northern-based businesses be given a better opportunity to compete for business, although the matter was resolved without the case going to court and with assurances about future consultation. Paul Kaludjak, NTI's vice-president of finance, asserted, 'What we are dealing with is an Iqaluit phenomenon, and an invitation for the Inuit of Nunavut and everyone from other communities to continue to be dominated from Iqaluit by a handful of these companies.' (*Nunatsiaq News*, 14 June).

On the demographic front, Nunavut stood out from the rest of Canada, with the youngest average population (22.1 years of age against a national average of 37.6 years) and a very high birth rate that was double the national average. In 2002, almost half of Nunavut's population was under the age of 19, a full 21 per cent higher than the nation as a whole. Young women between the ages of 15 and 19 had a birth rate of 135 children per 1,000 women, well in excess of the 18.7 per 1,000 rate for the rest of Canada among women that age. The territory recorded a net population loss of some 330 people between 1996 and 2001, a figure that masked a nation-high birth rate. Housing continued to be a matter of serious concern across the territory, with low vacancy rates, high rental costs, and an absolute shortage of suitable housing plaguing all communities. Efforts were made to add to the stock of affordable housing, which in Iqaluit in particular, made it difficult to recruit qualified personnel to work in the community. The Nunavut Housing Corporation encouraged the development of condominium corporations, only to have several of the initial proposals meet municipal opposition (a fairly common refrain from developers in the community). The government even investigated the costs and barriers associated with relocating thirty homes from the mining town of Nanisivik, which closed in 2002, to Arctic Bay, as part of a broader campaign to secure infrastructure for their community.

In an important and moving indication of the growing recognition of the Inuit, Canadian soldiers in Afghanistan erected an Inuksuk to honour four comrades-in-arms killed by 'friendly fire.' Jose Kusugak of ITK observed, 'We note in news reports that the soldiers view it as a truly Canadian symbol. To us that's a very moving thing to hear. When the Inuit of Canada recently submitted illustrations for a new logo for our national Inuit organization, many of the designs included the maple leaf as a national symbol. So if a national symbol for the soldiers is an Inuksuk, and a national symbol for Inuit is a maple leaf, I think we're on the same wavelength" (*Nunatsiaq News*, 5 July). In a way that eluded other northern peoples and territories, the Inuit of Nunavut continued to capture the Canadian imagination and continued to enjoy widespread interest and support across the country.

Social and cultural developments in the North

Perhaps the most significant developments in the territorial North were the continued renaissance in regional cultures, particularly among Indigenous peoples, and improvements in relations between newcomers and Aboriginal communities. The Yukon's population declined by close to 6.8 per cent, a decline of 2,000 in five years (with Faro accounting for half of the loss). Territorial figures put the Yukon's population at 30,418, with over 19,000 in Whitehorse. The Northwest Territories was the most populated territory, with a still-tiny population of 37,360, approximately 16,500 of whom lived in Yellowknife. Nunavut's population, the youngest in the country, was only 26,700. The territories remained the only jurisdictions in Canada where men outnumbered women, by a scant 101 to 100 in Nunavut and a more dramatic 105 to 100 in the Northwest Territories. The education challenges facing the northern territories remained in evidence. A study of academic achievement in mathematics released in April revealed that Nunavut had the lowest mathematics scores in the country. Only 11 per cent of 16-year-old children in Nunavut were at age-appropriate levels of reading, compared with a national average of 50 per cent (the NWT rate was 36 per cent and the Yukon 45 per cent.[1]

Nunavut's population continued to expand, with much of the growth concentrated in Iqaluit (to over 5,200 people), the second fastest growing area in the country. The smaller communities grew less rapidly and in several communities (Cambridge Bay and Kugluktuk) the population count actually fell slightly. Very worrisome was Nunavut's high suicide rate. Seventy-nine Inuit killed themselves in 2002, a rate that was almost seven times the national average.

The Yukon Territory remained a robust and active place, noted for the variety of cultural and social programs. The territory secured federal guarantees for the funding of the 2007 Canada Winter Games, to be held in Whitehorse, with a budget of more than $60 million. A wide variety of celebrations marked the 2002 calendar, from Dawson City's centenary in January to the annual Yukon Quest dog-sled race and the Sourdough Rendezvous, held each winter in Whitehorse. Yukon artists participated in a variety of regional and national competitions and festivals, drawing increased attention to a nascent film and music industry. The increasingly well-known Yukon International Storytelling Festival remained popular, as did the Frostbite Festival and other cultural activities, many of which brought Indigenous and newcomer cultures together. The television reality show, *Klondike: Quest for Gold*, brought the region to national attention.

Much the same held for Nunavut, where the efforts to strengthen Inuit culture continued to find considerable national and international interest and support. Zacharias Kunuk's film *Atanarjuat (The Fast Runner)*, released in 2002, won awards and accolades, drawing attention to the film-making capacity in Nunavut (and leading a discussion about producing action figures for Inuit children based on the movie). Production began on an IMAX documentary on Inuit culture, produced by Nuna Media, and operating almost entirely with Inuit staff (save for the IMAX camera operators). Also in 2002, however, Nunavut learned that contracts for the production of *Snow Walker* (based on Farley Mowat's books) had been lost to Manitoba, when that province offered a considerably higher subsidy. Inuit television production continued, including the award-winning *Takuginai (Look at This)*. Long-standing Inuit artistic activities continued, including printmaking and soapstone-carving. Twelve Inuit artists, the largest contingent in any single year, were inducted into the Royal Canadian Academy of Arts.

1 'Alberta teens top rest of country in math skills,' *Globe and Mail*, 4 April 2002.

Efforts to sustain Inuit culture continued in other ways. The Amittuq Bowhead Hunt proceeded in the summer, with hunters from Igloolik and Hall Beach combining to harvest a forty-six-foot whale. The whale was butchered, and the meat packed for distribution to Inuit throughout the region. The Nunavut Social Development Council, wishing to support greater understanding of Inuit culture, released a calendar, featuring the Igloolik seasonal cycles and Inuit moon-months.

Sports figured prominently in Nunavut in 2002. Jordin Tootoo became the first Inuk drafted into the National Hockey League, when he was selected in the fourth round by the Nashville Predators, an event that sparked great excitement across the territory. In a unique example of international collaboration among Inuit regions, Iqaluit and Nuuk, Greenland shared the March 2002 Arctic Winter Games, an event featuring Inuit and other games and cultural activities that was sufficiently large that neither community could host it on its own. Nunavut maintained one of the most aggressive Indigenous language and culture support programs in Canada and the world, including an expanding Inuit-language publishing program aimed at schoolchildren, Inuit-language radio and television, and numerous initiatives designed to support elders and cultural leaders. The year 2002 also saw the completion of a new Inuit translation of the Bible, produced by the Canadian Bible Society and the Diocese of the Arctic of the Anglican Church of Canada, and the installation of Bishop Andrew Atagotaaluk as the first Inuk Bishop of the Arctic (geographically the largest Anglican diocese in the world) in September.

Conclusion

Northern Canada experienced some telling developments in 2002, including the continuation of the mining and oil and gas boom, an increasingly bitter battle over the location of the natural gas pipeline from the North, and the continued renaissance in Indigenous politics and public life. Although social problems remained severe – some would say intractable – the Northwest Territories established new standards and practices for Indigenous engagement in economic development. Nunavut continued the evolution of one of the most Indigenous-influenced governments in the Western world, and the Yukon provided strong evidence of the ability of Indigenous and non-Indigenous peoples to collaborate for the betterment of the regional order. National interest in the North continued to wane, save for the infatuation with Arctic diamonds and Indigenous artwork, even as environmental concerns continued to escalate. Territorial political systems remained works in progress, although the consensus operations of Nunavut and the Northwest Territories demonstrated that partisan politics were not necessary for lively, informed debate and productive governance. In the Yukon, the one territory with political parties at the territorial level, the political culture remained highly volatile, plagued by ejections from cabinet and caucus, leadership changes, party swapping, and yet another one-term government. Although the northern territories attracted much less national attention than they had in the past, the attainment of territorial self-government and, in the case of the Yukon, very rapid devolution of federal responsibilities, meant that northerners had more than enough on their plates.

ROBERT DRUMMOND

Ontario

When Michael Harris announced his decision to step down as Premier of Ontario, there began a leadership contest that seemed critically important to the future direction of the province. Would it continue, and even expand upon, the 'common sense revolution,' under the leadership of Jim Flaherty or Tony Clement, or would it return to the more pragmatic style of the Bill Davis years, under the direction of a candidate like Ernie Eves or Elizabeth Witmer? When the contest was over, Eves was the new leader of the Progressive Conservative Party, but Flaherty had finished a respectable second. The press coverage suggested that Eves would bring a less confrontational style to the province's politics, but the right wing of the party remained optimistic about its chances. Were Eves to falter, the right stood ready to call for a return to the principles that arguably had brought the PCs back to power after the "lost decade" of the Peterson and Rae governments. The provincial government began the new year facing a strike of its public servants, and in the course of the ensuing months, it dealt with problems in the move to privatize electric power generation, a civic workers strike in Toronto, the follow-up to the judicial inquiry into the Walkerton water tragedy, planning for the onslaught of the 'double cohort' resulting from the end of Grade 13, and speculation about the date on which the government would go to the people in search of a renewed mandate. One consequence of the leadership change was the requirement that Eves return to the Legislative Assembly, and while there was speculation he might stand for Harris' Nipissing seat, he elected instead to seek a southern Ontario constituency. Perhaps, Nipissing was viewed as a little too risky with Harris gone, for while Eves won his seat (Dufferin-Peel-Wellington-Grey) handily when by-elections were held, the Conservatives retained Nipissing by less than twenty votes.

The leadership contest delayed the opening of the legislature until 9 May and the provincial budget until 17 June. On 27 June the Legislature recessed for the summer but was called back into session on 11 July to pass back-to-work legislation to end the Toronto civic workers strike. It recessed again on 12 July and reconvened on 23 September. It then remained in session until 12 December. Over the course of the legislative year, the MPPs passed thirty-six public bills. Some could be described as housekeeping or minor amendments to existing laws, while others dealt with the contentious issues of schools, energy, and water safety.

Indeed, apart from the leadership race in the spring, and some issues of expense claims in the summer and fall, the political life of the province in 2002 was engaged with many of the issues that had marked Ontario's history over the previous decade, especially in the areas of education, health, energy, and the environment.

Leadership

The race for the leadership of the Progressive Conservative Party (and by extension for the post of provincial premier) began in earnest at the start of the new year. Separate and apart from the choice of a head of government, there was an early announcement on 10 January, of the new vice-regal representative to succeed Hilary Weston. The twenty-seventh Lieutenant Governor of Ontario would be the Honourable James Bartleman. Bartleman was a career diplomat whose distinguished service in external affairs had included appointments as ambassador to the European Union and high commissioner to Australia and to South Africa. Perhaps more important to Ontario provincial affairs, however, was the fact that he was the first lieutenant governor in the province from one of Canada's First Nations. Bartleman was sworn in formally on 7 March.

On 17 January April Lindgren of Southam News reported on the previous evening's debate among the leadership candidates. Elizabeth Witmer and Chris Stockwell established themselves as the candidates for change, she observed, calling for new policies for the governing party. Tony Clement and Jim Flaherty, by contrast, urged a recommitment to the unfinished 'common sense revolution'. The PCs could not win by running as Liberals, they said. Ernie Eves seemed to remain above the fray, perhaps foreshadowing his emergence as the front-runner.

In early February Chris Stockwell was expressing concern that the party was not using the leadership race to sign up as many new members as might have been hoped. He suggested that the party would be lucky to have 40,000 voting members by the time the decision was to be made; at the time he spoke, there were only 23,000. By 1 March, however, the party reported that some 105,000 members would be eligible to vote for the party leader.

When a candidates' debate was scheduled by CTV and the *Globe and Mail*, Ernie Eves declined to take part unless other media outlets were given access. His fellow candidates accused him of ducking the event. The debate went on as planned without him on 11 February, and Flaherty and Stockwell directed their attacks largely at the absent Eves. Elizabeth Witmer presented herself as a 'uniter,' who could smooth relations with groups like the Ontario teachers (and presumably among the warring factions of her own party). The next debate was scheduled for 27 February, and Eves agreed to take part when CTV agreed that other media outlets could participate if they were prepared to share costs.

Some PC members suggested in early February that Tony Clement should be banned from running for the leadership of their party because of his support for the Canadian Alliance in the last federal election. A party committee rejected the suggestion, because of the independence of the federal and provincial Conservative organizations, and Clement continued his leadership bid.

Flaherty got considerable press attention when he proposed that special police be appointed to get homeless people off the streets. Although some heralded the suggestion as an innovative and direct approach to the problem, others criticized Flaherty for implicitly criminalizing poverty and blaming those who they believed were the victims of the policies implemented by the government of which he was part. He was similarly criticized in January when he suggested that people be limited to two years out of five on the welfare rolls. He was prepared to make exceptions for those who were single parents of pre-school children, those with disabilities, or those caring for someone with a disability, but critics did not accept this implicit differentiation between the 'deserving' and 'undeserving' poor. When Flaherty was quoted earlier that month as saying that the federal government could provide money to deliver health care for 'real people in real towns' if it cut special funds for Aboriginals, David Young, the minister responsible for relations with First Nations, felt obliged to distance himself from the remarks and to express regret (Canadian Press, 22 January).

While the leadership race proceeded, the Ontario Public Service Employees Union called for a strike vote over its negotiations with the province. The union demanded that the government table a final offer in response to its call for a 12 per cent wage increase over two years and a commitment to rebuilding the Ontario public service. The government tabled an offer of 6 per cent over three years and included a plan of performance-based pay. The union president, Leah Casselman, called on OPSEU members to reject the offer, and the union moved to put itself in a legal strike position by 13 March. When the strike came, it proved to be a long one, ending only on 2 May (coincidentally the same day as the by-election returning Ernie Eves to the legislature). At one point striking civil servants occupied Ernie Eves' campaign office; at another they banged on the doors of the legislature while cabinet was meeting. As in many public service strikes, there was debate over what constituted 'essential services,' which had to be maintained in spite of the strike. The government obtained some twenty-eight rulings from the Ontario Labour Relations Board to limit picket line delays and to force essential workers back to work. The focus of attention at an early date was on jail guards, and union president Casselman was cited for contempt of court a couple of days into the strike, when a prisoner was not delivered to court and the judge was advised it was because of jail guard job action. The OLRB ordered jail guards back to work, but the union claimed that they had been locked out by management. Moreover, they accused the employer of trying to calm things down in the absence of adequate jail security by bringing inmates pornography and pizza. The final settlement on 2 May gave corrections officers a 5 per cent increase in addition to the 8.45 per cent over three years awarded to other OPSEU members. Employees at the top of their scale (other than jail guards) got an additional 1 per cent.

On 17 February Colin Perkel of the Canadian Press reported a new poll of committed Ontario voters that placed Eves and Flaherty in a virtual tie (at around 28 per cent each) for the lead in the race to become premier, with Witmer, Clement, and Stockwell each at between 10 and 6 per cent. Jim Flaherty appealed to the right wing of his party in February by lauding the policy of tax relief for parents of private school students, especially as it benefited independent religious schools. Ontario Secondary School Teachers' Federation president Earl Manners had called on his members in the winter edition of *Education Forum* to defeat the PCs in the next election on this very issue, which he referred to as 'two-tier education.' Flaherty also promised, if elected premier, to privatize the Liquor Control Board – an institution frequently cited by critics of the Harris government as a worthy example of public enterprise.

When the sixth and final candidates' debate was held on 3 March, a handful of protestors (Canadian Press estimated fewer than a hundred) braved the cold weather to demonstrate outside the hall in Oakville where it was being held. Some four hundred police officers were present to ensure that protestors did not enter the grounds of the debate site. Inside the hall, the candidates rehearsed familiar themes. Jim Flaherty reiterated his plan to ban teacher strikes and accused Ernie Eves of flip-flopping on the issue of tax credits for private school families. Liz Witmer and Chris Stockwell cast doubt on the viability of further tax cuts, and Flaherty accused Witmer of sounding like a Liberal when she suggested reaching out to those alienated by the Harris government. At times, all the candidates made a point of saying favourable things about the others, knowing that whatever the result on 23 March, there would be a need for party unity when entering a subsequent election campaign.

On 7 March the *Globe and Mail* reported a poll that showed the Liberals would handily defeat a Conservative Party led by Ernie Eves. The poll, conducted on behalf of the *Globe and Mail*, television station CFTO, and radio station CFRB, found that 51 per cent of voters would support the Liberals in such a contest if it were held that day, and only 31 per cent would support the Eves-led PCs. The NDP was at 15 per cent.

In mid-March, with the leadership vote only two weeks away, the campaign momentarily took on a lighter tone, when candidates were asked if they had ever used marijuana. Three of the five candidates said that they had tried it (Clement and Witmer said they had not), and Chris Stockwell (recalling Bill Clinton's assertion that he had smoked marijuana but had not inhaled) said that he had not *ex*haled. No one recalled this discussion in July, at the height of summer pressure on electricity demand, when Canadian Press reported the assertions of local utilities that illegal marijuana 'grow-ops' were using some 500 million a year in electric power.

On the eve of the leadership convention, a poll conducted for the *National Post* found Ernie Eves with a commanding lead – 46 per cent compared with 29 per cent for Jim Flaherty, 13 per cent for Elizabeth Witmer, 9 per cent for Tony Clement, and 3 per cent for Chris Stockwell.

Voting for the leadership took place on 23 March. Protestors from OPSEU, the Ontario Federation of Labour, and the Ontario Coalition Against Poverty promised to converge on the Metropolitan Toronto Convention Centre in Toronto, although balloting was actually distributed across the province. All party members were eligible to vote in eighty-four locations in most provincial ridings. Voters from thirteen of Toronto's twenty-two ridings were expected to vote in the Convention Centre, and indeed any members could vote there but their vote would count as if it had been cast in their home riding. Each riding was assigned a hundred points and those points were to be distributed among the candidates in relation to the proportion of the votes they received in that riding. With 103 ridings, there were 10,300 points to be had, so the first candidate to reach 5,151 would be declared the winner. After each ballot, the candidate with the fewest points would be eliminated, as would any candidate who obtained less than 10 per cent of the votes cast. On the first ballot, Ernie Eves was in front, but with less than a majority. Chris Stockwell, with just over 4 per cent of the points was eliminated, and while Clement (at slightly more than 13 per cent) and Witmer (at just under 12 per cent) remained on the ballot, they both indicated that they were withdrawing from the race. In the end, they split about 7 per cent of the vote, while Flaherty moved from 29 to 38 per cent. Ernie Eves was declared the new leader, and hence premier of Ontario, with 55 per cent of the available points.

A week after the convention, it was reported that Eves and his cabinet would officially take office on 15 April, and that a by-election to secure a seat for the new leader would likely be held on 2 May. Eves named Andrew Hodgson as executive director of the Progressive-Conservative Party of Ontario, replacing Jeff Bangs who was named as Eves' principal secretary.

When Premier Eves announced his cabinet on 15 April, Andrea Baillie of Canadian Press described it as "centrist" and as signalling a move away from the common sense revolution. All of the candidates for the leadership received cabinet posts, with Elizabeth Witmer (who had thrown her support to Eves at the convention) identified as deputy premier. A former teacher and school trustee, she was also given the portfolio of education minister – an area where the government faced considerable challenges in restoring relations with significant stakeholder groups. Janet Ecker, identified as a more moderate and pragmatic member, replaced Jim Flaherty in finance. Flaherty was given a new portfolio – the Ministry of Enterprise, Opportunity and Innovation – combining some of the elements of the energy ministry and the Ministry of Economic Development and Trade. While many saw the new appointment as a means to appease the significant number of party members who had supported Flaherty, others were reminded of the 'superministries' that had gone to candidates defeated for the leadership by Bill Davis in 1971, and the subsequent virtual irrelevance of those ministers, who controlled bureaucracies that had no clear clients outside government and offered no deliverable services to ordinary citizens. Tony Clement was given the health ministry and Chris Stockwell, environment and energy. Several other portfolios were shuffled among ministers, with only two being dropped from cabinet – former Corrections Minister Rob Sampson and former Natural Resources Minister John Snobelen. (Snobelen, who had also served as a controversial minister responsible for post-secondary education, soon began to wind down his political career. By mid-October, Canadian Press reported that he was spending most of his time on his ranch in Oklahoma.) Liberal leader Dalton McGuinty described the new cabinet as 'the same old cast of characters clinging to the same old script' (Canadian Press, 15 April).

Eves came into office carrying a little baggage from the circumstances of his earlier departure to join the private sector. He had received a payment in recognition of pension entitlement of some $800,000 when the legislature's pension arrangements were restructured under his authority as finance minister. Soon thereafter he left the Legislative Assembly. He described the buy-out scheme (which overall cost some $10 million more than had been anticipated) as a bargain for taxpayers, but the issue dogged Eves through the leadership campaign, and in February, Integrity Commissioner Coulter Osborne received a complaint from Liberal MPP Mike Colle and began an investigation. Osborne wondered initially if he had jurisdiction to hear the complaint, as Eves was not a member of the legislature when it was filed. In May, however, days after the by-election that returned Eves to the legislature, Osborne dismissed the complaint. It had alleged that Eves had a conflict of interest because he was finance minister when his own pension buy-out was being determined. Osborne noted, however, that Eves had not benefited any more than had other MPPs who were similarly situated, and indeed, that the Liberals had supported the changes to the pension rules that Eves had proposed.

Later in May Premier Eves was questioned about a $78,000 severance package that he had received when he departed from the legislature as finance minister and deputy premier. He replied that he had paid the money back to the legislature on the eve of his being sworn in as premier, and even though the Liberal leader asked why Eves had concealed that fact for five weeks, the issue faded from view.

Eves' predecessor had been somewhat coy in February about his plans for the future. Harris had said he was not interested in entering federal politics and even suggested he might remain in the Ontario cabinet if his successor asked him to do so. On 2 April, however, Mike Harris retired from the legislature, and on 1 October it was announced that he was joining the Fraser Institute as a senior fellow. On 3 October it was reported that he had joined the law firm Goodmans LLP (despite not being trained in law) as a 'senior business adviser.' In one of his last speeches before leaving the premier's office, Harris addressed the subject of education – an area that had been very controversial during his tenure. He spoke of having made tough choices and having saved the education system from mediocrity. His critics however, such as Earl Manners, president of the OSSTF, claimed that Harris' ideological stance had weakened the education system through underfunding. Kathryn Blackett, of the parents' group People for Education, remarked, 'I am almost apoplectic at hearing this. This is not the truth and this government has a habit of thinking that if they say things people will believe them, and the facts are completely contrary to what the Premier has said' (Canadian Press, 12 February). Education remained a contentious issue for the government after Eves took over.

Education

Education hit the government agenda in a number of areas during the year 2002. Foremost were two issues – teacher certification and testing, and school board budgets and funding. In early January the provincial government announced that it would require teachers to be screened for criminal convictions. Although the information would remain part of the teacher's personnel file and not be made public, school boards would have the responsibility of deciding what to do about the information. All current teachers were to be screened by July 2003, and no new teacher was to be hired after 31 March 2002 without the background check.

The province had already announced mandatory professional development courses for teachers and the required completion of a test for teachers before their initial certification. Some teachers' groups had undertaken to boycott in-class training of student teachers as a protest against the government's required professional development courses for re-certification. In March, however, the public elementary school teachers decided *not* to join the boycott, mounted initially by the English Catholic Teachers Association. They were reluctant to abandon their role in training the next generation of teachers. At the same time, however, teachers turned their attention to the organizations being called on to provide the professional development courses. Faculties of education were already being urged not to cooperate in producing such courses, and now the Theatre Festivals in Stratford (Shakespeare) and Niagara-on-the-Lake (Shaw) were asked to stop providing courses for re-certification.

In mid-March the government sought to make clear its position that the teacher tests for initial certification were not being provided as a pilot project. Student teachers would be required to pass the test if they hoped to teach in the fall. Then in April it appeared to reverse its position and said the tests would not count for 2002. The tests, developed at a cost of $2.6 million, would be required for teachers beginning in 2003. The government, nonetheless, maintained its aim to test existing teachers in three-year cycles.

The rules for the latter appraisals had been passed into law in March and would apply starting in September. While experienced teachers would be tested every three years, new teachers would undergo assessment twice in each of their first two years. Students in upper high school grades would be asked to evaluate the effectiveness of their teachers in helping them to learn, while parents would be asked to comment on the teachers' success in communicating with them concerning their children's educational progress. Many teachers worried that the assessment would not address the real quality of teaching or the conditions under which it was done, and might be little more than a popularity contest.

A considerable amount of attention was paid throughout the year to issues of education funding, including the capacity of school boards to bring in balanced budgets. In February seventy-two directors of education from across the province and from public, separate, French, and English school boards, complained to Education Minister Janet Ecker that they were starved for cash. The *Toronto Star* quoted Scott Browning, an aide to the minister, on 19 February as saying education funding had gone up in every year of the government's mandate, and that "education remains a priority for this government." Earlier in the month, however, a group of parents had formed a new organization called Concerned Parents of Toronto to protest cuts to school budgets. Because their membership included doctors, lawyers, and business people from upscale neighbourhoods like Rosedale and Forest Hill, it was thought that they might have a significant impact on government decision-makers.

On 21 February Andrea Baillie of Canadian Press reported that the education ministry was looking into reports that two public high schools were violating provincial rules by charging students extra fees for workbooks and classroom materials. Annie Kidder, of People for Education, quoted a survey conducted the previous year that showed that 75 per cent of secondary schools were charging fees for labs or classroom materials. In early March several parents' groups reported increases in the use of special fees, as well as increases in the shortage of textbooks.

Later in the year a number of school boards expressed to the ministry their belief that they could not carry out their responsibilities if they were compelled (as they were by provincial regulations) to bring in a balanced budget. On 28 May the Toronto District (Public) School Board defied provincial rules and passed a deficit budget. On 26 June the Ottawa-Carleton School Board also passed a deficit budget, and by then the Hamilton-Wentworth and Thames Valley school boards had approved deficits as well. In early July Colin Perkel of the Canadian Press reported a study by the Canadian Centre for Policy Alternatives that found Ontario school boards had about $2.2 billon less to work with than they had had in 1994.

By early August the education minister (by this time Elizabeth Witmer) was poised to receive reports from accountants whom she had appointed to conduct forensic audits of the school boards that had passed deficit budgets. When the reports appeared, they were highly critical. In particular, the report on the Ottawa-Carleton board blamed trustees for delayed and uneconomical decisions. The report suggested, however, that it was too late to recover and that recommended new targets be established for January or September 2003.

In Toronto five school trustees called for an open public inquiry to be conducted by Al Rosen, the forensic auditor appointed to look into the Toronto board's budget. Parents' groups urged Rosen to look 'beyond the bottom line.' When Rosen's report appeared, it was roundly attacked by employees of the Toronto District School Board. On 18 November Canadian Press quoted John Weatherup, president of CUPE Local 4400, which represented some twelve thousand non-teaching school board employees, as saying that the report did not resemble an audit. "It is a politically motivated attack," he reportedly said, 'mixing lies with distortions.' For their part, the Elementary Teachers Federation cancelled an invitation to the minister to speak at their convention. They gave NDP leader Howard Hampton a warm reception instead. By August 13 Hamilton-Wentworth board staff had begun to make budget cuts that the board had rejected.

By September 1 the ministry had taken over the school boards in Toronto, Hamilton, and Ottawa, and parents' groups were expressing concern that budget cuts to be imposed by ministry-appointed supervisors would seriously diminish the quality of education. A survey of elementary schools reported by People for Education (and cited by Marlene Habib of Canadian Press) found that schools were increasingly relying on fundraising to provide basic materials for students, and members of the group were afraid that further cuts would exacerbate the situation.

The Ontario government moved in early September to investigate school funding in general. They appointed an Educational Equality

Task Force, headed by the president of the University of Guelph, Mordechai Roazanski, to hold hearings and make recommendations on the possible revision of the funding formula. He was to report by November. At hearings in London soon after the opening of the legislature, among those who addressed Dr Rozanski was Training, Colleges and Universities Minister Dianne Cunningham, who conceded that more money needed to be pumped into the system. Notably, she did not claim to be speaking for the government.

In early October Minister Witmer did move to put some additional funds into the system for teacher recruitment and training. She announced $11 million for teacher recruitment and professional development – $5 million for distance education for teachers, $5 million for professional development in the teaching of early reading skills, and $1 million for recruiting, especially in mathematics, science, and technology. Canadian Press quoted Emily Noble, president of the Elementary Teachers Federation, as saying that the money was 'a drop in the bucket' – not nearly enough to offset cuts made by the government, estimated by some critics to be as much as $2 billion since 1995.

A coalition of parents, unions, and trustees in Toronto moved in November to launch a court challenge to the provincial takeover of the Toronto District School Board and the appointment of Paul Christie as supervisor. By the end of the month, however, Christie had submitted a budget that cut $90 million from the Toronto School Board's planned expenditures.

On 10 December Mordechai Rozanski submitted his report and recommended an infusion of $1.8 billion into the school system. Before the legislature rose for the Christmas recess (and the government retired to consider Rozanski's report), the premier announced a grant of $341 million for teacher salary increases.

Money was at issue in the world of post-secondary education as well. In January five students invaded the office of the principal of Queen's University to protest that institution's support for a proposal to deregulate tuition fees – allowing universities to charge what the market would bear. Although Queen's was not alone in its position on fees, the universities of the province were divided on the question, and on 24 January it was reported that the government had rejected the deregulation request from Queen's and would keep the 2 per cent cap on tuition fee increases in most program for 2002–3. In February, during the leadership campaign, Jim Flaherty expressed his view that post-secondary tuition was a bargain and was quoted by Canadian Press as saying that students were paying about 35 per cent of the costs of their education. The figure seemed out of date at many provincial universities, where tuition now accounted for between 45 and 55 per cent of operating expenses.

In May the government made three significant moves in the post-secondary field. Ryerson Polytechnic University was renamed Ryerson University, completing the process begun several years earlier to recognize Ryerson's transformation into a full-service university. At the same time, the government authorized the Ontario College of Art and Design to begin granting university degrees, and they established a new post-secondary institution – the University of Ontario Institute of Technology, located adjacent to the campus of Durham College of Applied Arts and Technology. The president of Durham College became the first president of UOIT. The new university was designed to take advantage of projected demand for technological education at a university level. The model frequently cited was the Massachusetts Institute of Technology, but it was too early to tell if that comparison was realizable or overly ambitious.

In August the government invited Ontario's Community Colleges of Applied Arts and Technology to apply for the right to offer 'applied degrees.' It was assumed that not all community colleges would apply or be granted the right, and some observers predicted a division of the CAATs into two tiers – those with applied degrees and those without. The degrees would be four-year technical program, rather than the two-and-three-year diplomas and certificates currently being offered. The opening of new 'degree' opportunities was thought to be part of the government's response to the 'double cohort' resulting from the end of Grade 13. In mid-October Canadian Press quoted Queen's professor Alan King as saying that there was a secret government report that predicted more than seven thousand qualified university applicants would not be admitted in September 2003 because of inadequate planning. Government representatives denied the problem was of that magnitude, and university officials sought to reassure parents and potential students that space would be available for qualified applicants. Later in October the government revealed its plan to provide $40 million to the post-secondary system – $27 million to universities and $13 million to colleges – to renovate facilities to accommodate the double cohort demand.

In addition to concerns that there would not be room for those who wished to continue their education after high school, there was also a fear that new testing requirements in the schools would make increasing numbers of students ineligible to graduate. (In January, when Grade 9 mathematics testing was under way, it was reported that in the previous year that only 44 per cent of students had met the 70 per cent standard on the standardized test.) In late September Liberal leader Dalton McGuinty had proposed a new high school diploma that would combine academic achievement with workplace experience. In October Education Minister Witmer said that she was willing to consider an alternative diploma for those not going on to post-secondary education, but no action had been taken in that direction by year's end.

Perhaps the most ironic moment for education in 2002 came when the Ontario Labour Relations Board responded to parents of blind, deaf, and otherwise disabled children who wanted special schools reopened that had been closed by the OPSEU strike. They argued that the workers in the schools provided an essential service. The schools *should* be reopened, said the board, but not for the purposes of teaching. Education for the disabled was not deemed an essential service, but health care for the disabled students was.

Health

As health care delivery continued to account for the largest proportion of provincial government expenditure, issues of health remained at the forefront of political consideration during the year. With one or two exceptions, however, no aspect of health care took up the public's attention for any great length of time. Waiting times for emergency care and surgical procedures, the quality and availability of medical personnel, the government's plans to develop Family Health Networks, the funding of hospitals, the refusal of paramedics to accept mandatory flu shots, and specific outbreaks of communicable diseases all made headlines at one point or another. Of somewhat more durability than all of these, however, was the report of the Walkerton water contamination inquiry. In early January the government announced it was providing $2.6 million to Walkerton "to rebuild," but critics observed that the bulk of the funding was going to service an industrial park, rather than to address issues of water quality in particular (Canadian Press, 10 January).

In the third week of January the Liberals and NDP both called on the Conservatives (then heavily engaged in their leadership race) to recall the legislature to deal with the first report of the Walkerton inquiry. Canadian Press quoted Justice Minister David Young's response on 21 January, 'The last thing the people of the province need is more debate from politicians. They want action.' No one expected that the report would result in action without any legislative debate, but clearly, such debate was not to occur until the PCs had selected their new leader.

Late in May Justice O'Connor released the second report of his inquiry into the Walkerton water tragedy. In it he included ninety-three recommendations for improving the safety of the water treatment system and to prevent a recurrence of events such as those that had resulted in the Walkerton tragedy. He called on the province to enact a safe drinking-water act, related to treatment and distribution. In addition he recommended that a branch of the environment ministry be devoted to drinking water and another to watershed management. The ministry, he said, should be in charge of regulating the impact of farms on water sources. (The contamination that resulted in seven deaths in Walkerton had come from the manure generated by a nearby farming operation.) The report also addressed the responsibility of municipal governments for aspects of drinking water safety and called for the accreditation and periodic inspection of water-testing laboratories. The government took the report under advisement and promised legislative action later in the year.

In late October the government made good on its promise, introducing safe water legislation that contained many of the elements recommended by Justice O'Connor. The bill had drawn some inspiration from a private member's bill introduced earlier by NDP environment critic Marilyn Churley, but Churley was critical of the fact that the government bill did not adequately address the issues of cost (especially for municipalities). The premier opined that much of the additional cost would have to be borne by consumers, noting that people were apparently willing to pay more for cable television than they were for water. Some of the actions contained in the legislation had already been implemented; others were to be put in place in the future. While the Opposition was critical of the bill (including asking why it had taken so long), the *Globe and Mail* called it 'a bold step back from Harris cuts' (30 October).

One potential victim of the Harris government's restructuring of the hospital sector was given a final reprieve in February. The government had proposed the closure of the Montfort hospital in Ottawa, but the Ontario Court of Appeal had agreed with the assertion that the hospital – providing services largely in French – was vital to the survival of the French-language community in that city. On 1 February it was reported that the government had decided not to pursue an appeal to the Supreme Court of Canada, and the hospital was thus saved from closing.

In late January the province announced – as a public health measure – that it would require paramedics working with ambulance services in the province to have flu shots each year. Perhaps because of scepticism about the efficacy of such inoculations, and noting that they were already required to take many other shots, the paramedics voted in February not to comply. Negotiations continued for several months, until in early October the government relented and lifted the requirement.

Public health issues appeared on a few other occasions during the year. In January an E. coli outbreak occurred in several towns, with a total of twelve cases, but the cause was undetermined. Later in the month several hospitals reported outbreaks of the Norwalk virus, but all of them reopened on 1 February after taking precautions to control and eliminate the infection. In August, after the province had experienced numerous cases of the mosquito-borne West Nile virus, the government promised $9 million for program for largely preventive measures to fight the disease.

Much of the government's attention during the year 2002 was directed to improving the delivery of health care and of ensuring that necessary medical personnel were available. In mid-January nurses in the province agreed to a salary settlement that provided 10 per cent salary increases over three years. The difficulty of retaining skilled nurses remained a concern, but the settlement of a salary agreement promised to alleviate the worry in some measure. One use that the province had made of nurses, in an effort to provide health advice more efficiently, was through the development of its Telehealth project, sometimes colloquially called 'dial-a-nurse.' In February Canadian Press reported that the service had logged half a million calls in its first year of operation, mostly from people reporting nausea, vomiting, abdominal pains, fever in children, colds, coughs, and rashes. About one-third were advised to see a doctor; about 40 per cent were repeat calls. Critics called it 'cookbook medicine' and worried about liability. Proponents argued that if it prevented many people from clogging emergency rooms unnecessarily, it was worth the investment (Canadian Press, 15 February).

In a different use of technology, the Registered Nurses Association announced in February that it had created a website at which people could get answers to some of their questions about health policy, and at the same time they invited MPPs to provide their positions on health issues so that the nurses could publicize them. This effort came at a time when the PC leadership race was focused on health care, as Ernie Eves had expressed his possible openness to measures that other candidates dubbed 'two-tier medicine.' April Lindgren of Southam News quoted Eves as saying it made no sense that one could pay for magnetic resonance imaging (MRI) for one's pet at 2:30 in the morning but could not pay for a similar test for one's mother. In early July the *National Post* reported that the Ontario government would permit twenty new MRI machines and five new computed tomography (CT) scanners to be operated privately, provided that they accept Ontario Health Insurance Plan (OHIP) payments for all medically necessary services.

The issue of private provision of health care had also arisen in February, when provincial Auditor Erik Peters said that private cancer treatment clinics were proving more expensive than those operating under the auspices of Cancer Care Ontario. Two business professors, Murray Bryant of the Ivey School at the University of Western Ontario and Ramy Elitzur at the University of Toronto's Rotman School, took issue with his findings, saying that Peters had made 'accounting errors.' Peters countered that Elitzur, in particular, was ignoring the fact that the private clinics dealt with an inherently cheaper subset of treatments (for breast and prostate cancers). The debate remained lively, and in October Health Minister Tony Clement (who had, in the leadership campaign, criticized Eves for promoting two-tier medicine) pointed with favour to the role of privatization in the health care system. Then in December Lewis Auerbach (a former director in the federal auditor-general's office) issued a report in which it is asserted that hospitals that the government was proposing be built as public–private partnerships might result in higher costs and/or reduced service. While Minister Clement agreed that such proposals should be subject to review by the provincial auditor, he denied that they would cost more. Andrea Baillie of Canadian Press quoted Auerbach as saying that there was 'a disturbing lack of the most basic information' available about the government's decision. It appeared that the debate over the role of private provision in health care would continue into the future.

Throughout the year 2002 there were frequent announcements of new government expenditures in support of improving health care. In February the Ontario government announced it would approve \$800,000 to fund fifteen post-graduate medical training positions for Canadian citizens or permanent residents who completed medical training abroad and would return to Ontario and agree to work in underserviced areas. In April it was announced that hospitals in three cities (Sudbury, Ottawa, and North Bay) would receive some \$200 million in funding. Critics were quick to observe that over half the money was going to North Bay, in the last days before the Nipissing by-election. In August the government proclaimed that it would invest \$32.5 million to improve ambulance response times. In September it announced federal and provincial funding of \$213 million for health care, and in November it promised Ontario hospitals \$300 million in new funding.

Towards the end of November the premier announced a plan to 'fast-track' qualification of foreign-trained doctors so they could practise in Ontario. The aim was to encourage doctors to serve for at least five years in underserviced areas of the province. The target was to attract another 650 doctors to serve in Ontario – 150 in the first year. The Ontario Medical Association, however, asserted that there was a world-wide shortage of physicians, so Ontario could not rely on foreign-trained doctors to alleviate its own shortage, estimated at over 1,500.

In an effort to provide primary health care with greater efficiency, the government had urged the creation of Family Health Networks in which physicians, nurses, and nurse-practitioners would combine their efforts collaboratively to treat patients who were enrolled in them. Payment would be on a per patient or 'capitation' basis, rather than by fees for services. In September Health Minister Tony Clement pointed with pride to the growth of participation in FHNs as an indication of the increasing pace of primary health care reform. Critics, however, asserted that only a handful of doctors had signed up and they called for scrapping the scheme. The plan came under attack in October, when the Coalition of Family Physicians of Ontario expressed their view that the FHNs were not an improvement on the fee-for-service system. They cited a survey of their members in which 98 per cent of respondents had rejected the scheme, and they called instead for giving doctors a raise in the fee schedule.

Despite the promises of increased funding, and efforts to attract needed personnel, the rising demand for health care continued. In January Canadian Press reported the creation of a new organization called Communities for Home Health Care that was calling on the government to release $295 million in home health care funding that had been frozen pending the overhaul of municipal Community Care Access Centres. In March the Ontario Hospital Association predicted more emergency room backlogs unless the province put $1 dollars into hospitals. At the same time, manufacturers of generic drugs asserted that the government was wasting millions of dollars because they were slow to approve generic drugs. Although both of these claims were arguably self-serving for the organizations making them, they nonetheless highlighted two areas of continuing concern with regard to the rising cost and allegedly diminishing availability of important elements of health care delivery. In mid-March a group of midwives and pregnant women protested that the government was delaying entry to practice for graduates of a new midwifery program. The government reconsidered in light of this protest and announced that the graduates could begin immediately.

In September a Peel-Toronto Task Force headed by former federal

Conservative cabinet minister Michael Wilson called for a major reform of the mental health treatment system. What was needed, it said, was a system of regional mental health boards with dedicated funding to provide services. Towards the end of October the parents of an autistic child petitioned the legislature to allow the intensive behavioural intervention treatment that they had been receiving for their child to continue. The legislation then in place provided OHIP funding only to age 6, and the parents argued that it was needed much longer. The cost of treatment was such that parents could ill-afford it, but they argued that the treatment was effective and medically necessary. By year's end no action had been taken, and the parents contemplated court action to try and force the government's hand.

Energy and environment

The province struggled throughout the year 2002 with plans to open the electricity market to competition and to ensure an adequate supply of electric power. The breaking up of Ontario Hydro into component parts, and the intended privatization of significant parts of the resulting organizations, was a cause of much debate during the year. The tension between developing the energy capacity of the province and maintaining an affordable energy supply remained a troubling issue at year's end.

When Ontario Hydro was broken up, it was left to consumers to pay off the 'stranded debt' of the corporation. In January Canadian Press reported speculation that households might each pay $4 a month extra for electric power, as local utilities found themselves required to pay off the debt through payments to the province in lieu of taxes. By September the unfunded debt, held by the Ontario Electricity Financial Corporation, was seen to be increasing, and electricity bills were therefore likely to continue their rise.

Another concern born of the restructuring was the impact on employment. The *Toronto Star* reported on 15 January that Ontario Power Generation, one of the companies resulting from the Hydro breakup, would have to cut 2,000 jobs over the coming two years in order to be competitive after the electricity market opened on 1 May. OPG was at that point responsible for generating 72 per cent of Ontario's power. Given this projected job loss, the NDP called on the Ontario government to fight an election on the future of the electric power system. Towards the end of February NDP leader Howard Hampton issued what he called an alternative energy plan that would have halted the proposed opening of the electricity market to private competition and would have stopped the selling of Ontario Hydro assets to private firms.

In the meantime, as the opening of the market approached, there was concern expressed (by Energy Minister Jim Wilson among others) about the tactics being used by energy marketers who were trying to sign up as many consumers as possible to long-term electricity contracts before the market opened. The confusion of consumers about these contracts, and the high pressure sales approach of marketers, was reflected in the revelation in early March that many households (some estimates went as high as half a million) had signed long-term electricity supply contracts with more than one supplier. The complexity of operating in the new market environment was highlighted by the case of Toronto Hydro, revealed in September. The company had been fined by the Ontario Energy Board after it had been determined that the regulated arm of the corporation, Toronto Hydro Electric System (which owns the wires carrying electricity to homes and businesses) had improperly conveyed information about consumers to the deregulated arm of the corporation, Toronto Hydro Energy Services (which sells fixed-price electricity and natural gas contracts). It was also alleged that some door-to-door sales personnel had led customers to believe that they represented the utility rather than the unregulated retailer. Toronto Hydro Energy Services stopped selling contracts door-to-door as a consequence and relied on direct mail, advertisements, and call centres instead.

It was announced in late February that Ontario Power Generation would be required to rebate to consumers any additional revenue it received if the electricity price rose above 3.8 cents per kilowatt hour after the market opened. OPG estimated it would be rebating about $425 million, as the price was expected to be 4.3 cents per kilowatt hour. Perhaps in an effort to calm fears about price increases in the new privatized market, the Independent Market Operator (which would regulate the market after 1 May) predicted in early April that demand for power would be modest and that supply would increase. By 18 April, however, the same body was predicting that Ontario might be subject to brownouts and blackouts under a worst-case electricity scenario.

Somewhat earlier, NDP leader Howard Hampton pressed the government to reveal any dealings it had with the U.S. energy trading firm Enron, which had gone bankrupt towards the end of 2001 amid allegations of executive corruption. On 22 February Colin Perkel of Canadian

Press quoted Hampton saying, "Enron had an influential role in shaping the [Ontario] government's privatized, deregulated electricity program." Energy Minister Wilson, however, said that the only representation that the government had received from Enron was from its Canadian subsidiary, which Wilson claimed had nothing to do with its failed U.S. parent and was 'one of our great energy companies.' Enron Canada had sought an injunction in a Calgary court to prevent clients from cancelling their contracts with the company, in light of the parent company's failure. Enron Canada claimed it needed the injunction to survive as a stand-alone company, but the court refused to grant it.

In late March the NDP complained to the Advertising Standards Canada about a government-sponsored news supplement concerning the planned deregulation of Ontario's electricity market published in the *Globe and Mail*, which the NDP described as 'propaganda masquerading as news' (Canadian Press, March 26). Much of the debate throughout the remainder of the year concentrated on two issues: the privatization of electric power and the price of electricity.

In early April two unions (the Canadian Union of Public Employees and the Communications, Energy and Paperworkers Union) had taken the Ontario government to court to prevent the sale of Ontario Hydro assets to private owners. On 19 April Justice Arthur Gans of the Superior Court of Justice ruled that the government did not have the legal right to sell the electricity power grid. In response, the government suggested on 30 April that it might instead lease the grid to private firms. When the market opened on 1 May it did so without the sale of the electricity grid. In late May, the government introduced legislation that would put in place the legal authority Justice Gans had said was missing. On 12 June, however, it was announced that Ontario would *not* sell the grid. On 4 July Canadian Press reported that the Ontario Court of Appeal had refused to hear an appeal against Justice Gans' lower court decision. Since the legislature had now passed a law permitting such a sale, the appeal would have been moot. Nevertheless, it now appeared that the government had decided to retain a controlling interest in the province's electric power grid. A side issue in the privatization discussions was the assertion in mid-May that some Hydro One executives might be pushing privatization since it would result in their receiving expensive severance packages. Six executives, it was suggested, were in line for severance totalling some $12 million. Whatever the truth of the assertion, the government moved in early June to introduce legislation that would limit severance packages for Hydro One executives.

In mid-July the board of directors of Hydro One (the operator of the power grid) announced that it had fired its Chief executive officer, Eleanor Clitheroe, asserting that she had misused company resources for personal needs. The board was a new one appointed by the government after the original board had supported the CEO. Clitheroe filed suit alleging wrongful dismissal a month later and also asked that the court overturn, as unconstitutional, legislation rolling back salary increases of Hydro One executives. Hydro One challenged her right to sue, but in December the courts agreed that she could sue to seek fulfilment of her contract. The case remained unresolved at the year's end.

When the electricity market opened on 1 May, prices were initially lower than they had been, but price fluctuation began soon thereafter. The new energy minister, Chris Stockwell, sought to assuage fears by asserting that blackouts or brownouts were unlikely. By July, however, the unusually hot summer was leading the Independent Market Operator and political figures to urge conservation of electricity to avoid just such eventualities. By October the high energy use in the summer had led to fears of service interruptions, as well as demands from consumers for protection from price increases. John Baird (by then the energy minister) asserted that Ontario had sufficient generating capacity but he would not guarantee there would be no brownouts or blackouts. It was Baird who responded for the government (on 30 September) to the report of an all-party committee on "green" fuels and energy sources some four months after the issuance of the report. He promised a progress report on the 149 recommendations by the end of the year. Canadian Press quoted critics Marilyn Churley (NDP) and Jim Bradley (Liberal) as saying that the response was 'totally inadequate' and 'absolutely pathetic' (Canadian Press, 1 October). The premier speculated about limiting the authority of the energy price regulator. When the Ontario Energy Board threatened to cut the rebate to consumers, the premier promised that the rebate would go ahead. In an unrelated event, former NDP finance minister Floyd Laughren announced that he would retire from his post as chair of the Ontario Energy Board at the end of December.

By November criticism of the government's energy policy was seen as threatening its success in the next election. The hoped-for expansion in generating capacity had not materialized, because private firms had shown reluctance to build the necessary plants. In the meantime, it was announced that the renovation of the Pickering nuclear generating station would be delayed until 2006 and that it would be some $2 billion over budget. Liberal leader Dalton McGuinty, with a focus on air pollution rather than energy generation, promised to close all coal-fired generating plants if he were elected Premier. Energy retailers were complaining that government price freezes had killed the open energy market. Nevertheless, in December, just before the Legislature went into recess, the premier announced that Ontario electricity rates would be frozen for the next four years.

In the area of environmental protection, the government had a relatively quiet year. To be sure, there were isolated incidents of threats to the environment, such as the announcement by the *Globe and Mail* in February that it had uncovered environment ministry documents alleging dangerous levels of polychlorinated biphenyls (PCBs) in the Grand River from the site of a manufacturing plant once owned by General Electric Company. The government's biggest exposure to criticism, however, came in three reports released in June, July, and September, from the Canadian Environmental Law Association, the Sierra Legal Defense Fund, and the province's Environmental Commissioner Gord Miller respectively.

The first report, from the CELA in June, accused the Conservative government of gutting the process for environmental assessment. The second, from the Sierra Fund in July, asserted that lax enforcement and low transparency had made Ontario a haven for polluters. The government took issue with the latter allegations, saying the organization had underreported charges laid against polluters and convictions secured. The report from the province's own environmental watchdog was perhaps harder to dismiss.

Gord Miller's third annual report, issued in late September, found inadequacies and room for improvement in areas of water quality, biodiversity, air quality, and land use planning. He cited reductions in water monitoring stations and a consequent lack of information on water pollution in southern Ontario rivers and streams. The threat of acid rain and the risks to ecosystems were inadequately addressed, in his opinion, and emissions from electricity generation and automobile traffic were threatening air quality without hindrance. He indicted the government for an inability to measure the protection of the natural heritage in southern Ontario.

The particular issues arising from the Walkerton inquiry probably took most of the government's environmental attention throughout the year, although they did promise $50 million in April for clean-up program for the Great Lakes. Critics complained that this was not enough. In March the government announced a sweeping ban of development on the ecologically sensitive Oak Ridges Moraine; however, the *Toronto Star* reported that a backroom deal had been concluded to permit the building of 7,000 homes on the moraine.

Other issues

The province dealt at various times with issues outside the three main areas of concern. There were disputes in the early spring around the continuing issue of Quebec-based contractors seeking construction work in Ontario, as well as questions for the federal government about support for the provincial role in immigrant resettlement. In February an inquest into the death of Gillian Hadley, shot and killed by her estranged husband who then killed himself, made fifty-eighty recommendations to help prevent further such occurrences of domestic violence. The response from the office of the attorney general was to express concern about costs. Later in the year, an inquest opened into the death of Kimberly Rogers, a young woman who had died of a drug overdose while confined to her home because of a conviction for welfare abuse. The government introduced legislation to ensure Ontarians would be prepared for possible terrorist attacks. It also addressed issues of pension reform, doing so in an unusual way. The government introduced a bill, parts of which it promised not to proclaim, and then withdrew those parts before final passage.

None of these matters occupied the front pages for long, but all were of considerable importance to some part of the community, and some promised to be of greater importance at a later date. All served to highlight the diversity and complexity of Ontarian political issues.

Legislative politics

The Speech from the Throne, delivered at the opening of the legislature on 9 May, spoke of the government's plans in the area of education, health care, water quality, and energy, and those indeed were the matters that commanded the greatest attention throughout the year. When Finance Minister Janet Ecker presented the budget on 17 June, it was the fourth balanced budget in a row, in spite of fears expressed in February that the government might have to plan for a deficit. When the minister produced an economic statement in the fall, however, things appeared somewhat less rosy, and she elected to postpone some promised tax cuts to 2004.

There was speculation in the fall about the date of a provincial election, given that the government had elected a new leader in the spring and might soon be ready to go to the polls. In September all three party leaders appeared at an international plowing match in Glencoe. In the province's more agricultural past, such a gathering was often the prelude to an election campaign, and traditionalists wondered whether the event might still have that function. A week later, the legislature reconvened, and the premier identified the session as 'make-or-break,' suggesting to many that an election might be called for the spring of 2003. In late October, however, a poll showed that the governing party had suffered a 9 per cent decline in popularity, and although the premier dismissed the poll, saying government popularity went up and down all the time, he began to talk soon thereafter about a *fall* 2003 election.

Perhaps it was a preview of electioneering when in May the Opposition accused Chris Stockwell and his staff of filing extravagant expense claims, including sizable bar tabs. At first Minister Stockwell said that he would not file such claims in future but refused to refund the money. A week later, as Opposition and press comment continued, Stockwell agreed to repay $3,000 of the expenses. In early October, similar accusations were levied against Tourism Minister Cam Jackson, and he was told by the premier's office to repay some $7,600 of unjustified expenses. Following allegations that Jackson and his officials had run up expenses of over $100,000 in twenty-six months, he resigned his post. Canadian Press quoted Jackson as saying, in his defence, that when he was hosting tourism ministers from across Canada, he should not be expected to take them to Swiss Chalet. Predictably, several Swiss Chalet managers complained at this slight, and Jackson's successor, Frank Klees, was quick to observe that he had been a fan of Swiss Chalet for many years. A couple of days later, it was the premier's turn to be accused of filing illegitimate expense claims (during the time he had been finance minister). A few days after that his staff undertook to repay 'inadvertent' erroneous claims.

The government sought to turn the tables on the Opposition by accusing some Liberal members of having similarly filed improper expense claims. Then in late November, legislation was introduced to allow the Integrity Commissioner to review the expense claims of Opposition leaders and their staffs.

Partisanship was clearly increasing, and observers presumed an election could not be far off. Following the usual December revelations by the provincial auditor of wasteful government spending, the legislature recessed, with Canadian Press headlines calling the government 'bruised but still standing' (12 December). Seasoned Ontario politics observer Graham White of the University of Toronto was quoted by Colin Perkel of Canadian Press as saying, 'What they did was respond to crises, fix up problems they'd inherited from Mike Harris and react. They didn't set out why they should be re-elected' (12 December). It remained to be seen whether the Conservatives could remedy that over-sight before they called on the people for their votes.

DANIEL SALÉE

Quebec

Was it the wear and tear of power? Despite his vast experience of Quebec politics and his undeniable competence as public manager, Bernard Landry's premiership in 2002 failed to excite and bring the Parti Québécois back into popular esteem. The Opposition never stopped picking up steam all through the year: Mario Dumont's Action démocratique du Québec gained substantial ground with right-wing, soft nationalists, and Jean Charest's Liberal Party looked more and more like a credible alternative.

It did not help that the Parti Québécois continued to suffer from the perennial internal tensions between moderates and hardliners over the best strategy to achieve sovereignty – a debate with less and less resonance with the general population. Just like his predecessors at the helm of the PQ, Bernard Landry could scarcely avoid being caught in the crossfire. In addition, his leadership, initially uncontested when he took over from Lucien Bouchard a year earlier, was now subject to backroom criticisms from other possible contenders who felt that they had all too summarily been overlooked in favour of his candidacy, as well as from several party members generally unhappy with Landry's governing style. Quite a few high-profile cabinet members even left the party and politics altogether.

Strangely, though, despite its waning political fortune, the government was nevertheless able to score a few significant points on the public policy front, as a number of its achievements got a fairly positive reception from the public. The general consensus over fiscal imbalance, the signing of important treaties with Indigenous peoples, and the legislation against poverty were high points and much appreciated moments in an otherwise bumpy year for Bernard Landry and his administration.

Waning political fortune

After nearly a year in the premier's seat, Bernard Landry had yet to put his own stamp on government. The cabinet he appointed as he took office as premier in March 2001 brought in a few new faces, but stood by and large in continuity with the Bouchard government. On 30 January he proceeded to remedy the situation and reorganized his cabinet with a comprehensive shuffle and the creation of a number of new ministries. In all, his new cabinet, the largest in Quebec history, comprised thirty-eight ministerial positions – thirteen of which went to inexperienced newcomers. It provided Landry with an opportunity to reward faithful supporters and keep on side a few others who were liable to work against him. But it also led to the departure of three veteran ministers and long-serving members of both the Parti Québécois and the government: Guy Chevrette, Jacques Brassard, and David Cliche, all associated with the more nationalistic wing of the party. Uninterested in and unhappy with the rather minor and peripheral roles that Landry reserved for them in his new cabinet, Chevrette and Brassard resigned their seats in the National Assembly the day before the shuffle was announced. Cliche, for his part, was completely excluded from the new ministerial line-up and resigned the next day as well.

The resignation of these three pillars of previous Parti Québécois administrations infused Landry's shuffle with rancour and bitterness, and did little to alleviate tensions and resentment within the party, let alone consolidate Landry's leadership. Later in the year, on 28 October, Paul Bégin, minister of justice and Quebec's attorney general, also resigned, ostensibly unhappy with Landry's governing style and unconvincing commitment to Quebec sovereignty. Bégin and Landry had disagreed publicly over the former's handling of a labour dispute between the government and its Crown prosecutors. This incident seemingly played a part in Bégin's decision. In his public statement explaining the reasons for his resignation, however, he explicitly insisted on his dissatisfaction with what he saw as the government's unwillingness to foster sovereignty or create opportunities to push the option forward. He concluded that he could no longer be part of such a government.

Paul Bégin's was the last in a fairly long string of political resignations – six in all – that plagued Landry's administration in 2002. Two more had occurred earlier in the year, although for reasons that had less to do with internal party rifts than with imprudent governance. On 9 February, barely ten days after the cabinet shuffle, news of financial wrongdoings involving the executive director of the Parti Québécois broke out. Raymond Bréard, a close friend, adviser, and former chief of staff of Bernard Landry when he was minister of finance, was alleged to have benefited from his position in Landry's cabinet to pocket over

$200,000 in commission on public grants to a private public relations and lobbying firm, Oxygène 9, mandated to organize cultural events. Bréard resigned his post as director general of the PQ two days later. The next day, Gilles Baril, newly appointed minister of state for natural resources and the regions, also tendered his resignation and announced his intention not to seek re-election. Baril's unexpected, decision was officially motivated by 'family reasons,' but hounding pressures from the media to account for his close relationship with the owner of Oxygène 9 proved unbearable.

Those were particularly trying days for Landry and his entourage. Both Bréard and Baril were ardent supporters and trustworthy collaborators; in a highly emotional declaration to the press, Baril even evoked the quasi-filial nature of his relationship with Landry. But more importantly for the government, the allegations of conflict of interest surrounding this whole episode, whether founded or not, left the devastating perception in the public's mind that the holier-than-thou image that the Parti Québécois had always cultivated with regard to misappropriation of public funds was highly overrated. Members of the Parti Québécois, it would appear, were not necessarily above the kinds of impropriety they so indignantly decried.

All those resignations were in fact symptomatic of a deeper political malaise. To a number of observers and critics, they spoke of unresolved issues within the Parti Québécois, of the smugness of power, and in the end, of Bernard Landry's inability to steer his party and his government in a controlled and effective fashion. In the weeks following the Bréard-Baril episode, public opinion polls indicated that the premier was quickly losing the public's confidence. In the fall of 2001, in the aftermath of 11 September, Landry's confidence rating was at 33 per cent, while that of his opponents was at 26 per cent for Liberal Party's Jean Charest, and at 16 per cent for Action démocratique leader Mario Dumont. By mid-winter 2002 the premier was trailing Charest, who had become the favourite of 29 per cent of the population. With a confidence rate of 28 per cent, Landry was just slightly ahead of Mario Dumont, whose popularity, at 25 per cent, literally skyrocketed, and would only get stronger in the following months. By and large, 53 per cent of the electorate were dissatisfied with the government's performance. Had there been an election at that point, the Liberals would have won with 44 per cent of the vote against 34 per cent for the PQ and 22 per cent for Action démocratique (*La Presse*, 23 February).

The results of seven by-elections held later in the spring only confirmed the Parti Québécois and Bernard Landry's growing unpopularity.

On 15 April the government lost the riding of Saguenay, a PQ stronghold, to the Action démocratique candidate, who won with nearly 48 per cent of the vote. The PQ candidate came last with less than a quarter of the vote, behind the Liberal candidate who got 28 per cent. The Parti Québécois also did poorly in the other two ridings in contention that day, Viger and Anjou, where the Liberal candidates won as expected. On 17 June, as the four ridings formerly held by the ministers who resigned earlier in the year were at stake, the Parti Québécois only succeeded in clinging to the riding of Lac-Jean, the other three, Vimont, Berthier, and Joliette, switched over to Action démocratique. The defeat in Berthier was particularly upsetting for the government. Premier Landry had great hopes of seeing star recruit David Levine elected in that riding: Levine, a high-profile, public health care administrator had been appointed to the cabinet by Landry in the January ministerial shuffle as a non-elected minister of health. Clearly, a victory was essential for Levine's legitimacy, but more importantly, unable to get a sitting minister elected, the government was losing face. Levine had to resign his ministerial post the day after his defeat. Things could have been worse: according to electoral sociologist Pierre Drouilly, had a general election taken place instead, the outcome of these by-elections suggests that not only would Action démocratique have taken power, but the Parti Québécois would have failed to get one single MNA elected (*La Presse*, 28 June).

Mario Dumont and the rise of Action démocratique du Québec

The electoral successes of Action démocratique, although more significant than anticipated, came as no surprise to political observers. Since the fall of 2001 the standing of Mario Dumont's party in public opinion polls was improving by leaps and bounds. A poll commissioned by *Le Soleil* and *La Presse*, and released on 11 May, indicated that 33 per cent of the electorate would support the Liberal Party, 31 per cent would favour Action démocratique, and less than 25 per cent would go for the Parti Québécois. The poll also showed that among francophone voters nearly 37 per cent were ready to support Action démocratique ahead of the PQ (27.5 per cent) and the Liberal Party (26.8 per cent). In fact, practically every poll taken throughout the summer and fall continued to show sustained and even increasing support for Mario Dumont and his party, peaking at 45 per cent among francophone voters in September.

The rise of Action démocratique du Québec was undoubtedly the most astonishing political phenomenon of the year. Its leader, Mario

Dumont, founded the party in 1994, following the constitutional debates of the early 1990s over the future of Quebec and the Canadian federation. Dumont had been quite active within the provincial Liberal Party as president of its youth wing during the late 1980s, and along with a number of others had grown frustrated with at party's ambivalent stance on the national question. He left the Liberals to create Action démocratique ostensibly to mark his distance from the federalist position of the party, but also to offer a neoliberal, nationalist alternative to the PQ. Despite Dumont's support of the Yes side in the 1995 referendum on sovereignty, his youthful image – he is only thirty-two – and his own personal popularity, his party has essentially remained on the margins of the Quebec political landscape, garnering hardly more than 12 per cent popular support at any given time since the mid-1990s. Until the party's electoral successes in the spring of 2002, Dumont was the only Action démocratique representative to be elected in the National Assembly, sitting for his eastern Quebec home riding of Rivière-du-Loup.

Action démocratique's platform includes the idea of school and day care vouchers (to allow parents more freedom of educational choice and to compensate mothers who stay at home to raise their children), greater involvement of the private sector in the delivery of health care, proposals for a 20 per cent flat tax, and substantial decreases in income tax. On the issue of Quebec sovereignty, Dumont has called for a ten-year moratorium on constitutional matters in a bid to rally those who are put off by the more uncompromising nationalism and constitutional politics of the Parti Québécois.

Dumont's and his party's meteoric rise in public favour was particularly worrisome for the government and the Parti Québécois. It became painfully clear by mid-year, as the support for the Liberal Party only increased slightly and tended to remain relatively stable, that Action démocratique made its remarkable gains in public support essentially by winning over large portions of the Parti Québécois's traditional electoral base. Dumont and his party appeal to middle-class and relatively young (aged 25 to 44 years), upwardly mobile, largely suburban francophones. These supporters might have voted for the Parti Québécois and Quebec sovereignty at one point, but they were now tired of constitutional wrangling, no longer convinced by the PQ's unfulfilled dream of an independent nation, and exasperated with the fiscal burden and financial demands that they feel the state unduly imposes on them: they are an emergent constituency, comprised both of soft nationalists and guarded federalists, who feel unjustly blocked in their social ambitions by the baby boomers who preceded them, and stifled in their economic and entrepreneurial aspirations by what they see as the obsolete social democratic pursuits of the Quebec state.

A few weeks before the 17 June by-elections the Minister of Energy Rita Dionne-Marsolais went on to say publicly that Action démocratique caters to 'a young generation that is very individualistic, that thinks only of itself' (http://www.thecommentary.ca/archives/20020607.html), implying that her generation – the generation that is currently in power – was driven by collective projects and social solidarity, and was hence morally superior. Dionne-Marsolais' remark – which followed others by PQ colleagues who compared Action démocratique's platform with that of France's right-wing leader Jean-Marie Le Pen, or hinted that Mario Dumont's supporters were de-politicized – was clearly insulting to a large constituency and unavoidably stirred controversy. Pressed by Dumont to take his distance from his minister's statement and fire her, Bernard Landry retorted that today's youth were indeed less collectivistic and less engaged socially, and that Dumont was only encouraging the cult of his personality within his own party. In the end, the whole incident only served to reinforce the political popularity of Action démocratique and its leader and showed how troubled and nervous the government was with Dumont's standing in the opinion polls.

Questioning the Quebec model

The ever-swelling wave of favourable public opinion in support of Action démocratique crested on 23 September, when Mario Dumont received a warm welcome as keynote speaker at the elite and influential Canadian Club in Toronto. A few weeks later, on 17 October, a new poll suggested that Action démocratique was still ahead in popular support, but losing ground in favour of the Liberal Party. By year's end, the party had slipped further in the polls. Both the PQ and the Liberals began to regain the support lost in the preceding months and started to move progressively ahead of Dumont's party.

Was the amazing and unexpected political ascent of Action démocratique merely an inexplicable incongruity? Clearly, the political arrogance of the Parti Québécois, the apparent ineffectiveness of the Liberal Party, and the inability of both these traditional parties to offer new, viable sociopolitical projects made Action démocratique seem like an attractive alternative for a while. But, the new party's lack of experience, the indeterminate nature of some elements of its platform, and Dumont's reticence to commit clearly to either Quebec sovereignty or

Canadian federalism led some people to reassess their initial enthusiasm. But there is another dimension, less easy to pinpoint: the general feeling of ambivalence that has come to shroud Quebec's traditional policy paradigm probably contributed significantly to the fickleness of public opinion. By calling for a serious reconsideration and reduction of the role of the state, and thus by questioning the very foundation on which much of Quebec's political emancipation and economic accomplishments have been made possible, Mario Dumont and Action démocratique challenged Quebecers to embark on a path that seemed both tempting and daunting. Although many might have agreed with Dumont that the Quebec state had become an impediment to individual freedom and free initiative, what he proposed – that is, a fairly radical departure from the model of state intervention that has served Quebec for decades – did not necessarily appear to all as the most desirable alternative. In the end, Quebecers' indecisiveness as to the proper way to rein in an overwhelming state might have played both for and against Action démocratique du Québec.

Be that as it may, the deep-reaching, if temporary, interest in Mario Dumont and in his vision was real and politically compelling. The government and the Parti Québécois as well as the Liberal Party had to pay heed to the vehement, neoliberal clamour it underscored; they were pushed to take position with respect to the future of what has come to be known as the *modèle québécois* – the Quebec model.

Under the PQ government the idea that there is a Quebec model has worked as a metaphor for the notion that since the Quiet Revolution successive Quebec governments have conformed to a well-entrenched policy paradigm that holds that social solidarity is a central value of policymaking; that the Quebec state must be actively involved in promoting economic development, along with the cooperative movement, the labour movement, and all those who are committed to the social economy; that this model is unique and a defining characteristic of the only francophone jurisdiction in North America; and that it has been beneficial to all Quebecers by allowing them to grow as a united political community. Since the late 1990s some intellectuals, academics, and politicians have occasionally raised doubts about the effectiveness and the appropriateness of the Quebec model, much to the dismay of the government. The rise of Action démocratique in 2002, though, forced the issue. The possibility that such an ardently neoliberal political formation might soon come to power brought the political class to address the broad policy concerns raised by Dumont's vision, and confront itself with what for some was a heart-wrenching question: should the Quebec model be preserved or reconfigured? Should policymakers opt for a more individualistic approach and abandon the values of social solidarity that have long informed Quebec's policy choices?

The most surprising – and unexpected – contributions to the political debate on the Quebec model came from within the government. In the days following the electoral upset of the 17 June by-elections, a number of high-profile ministers hinted that the Quebec model had run its course. André Boisclair, minister of state for the environment and water, declared, 'Ordinary people in everyday life require that the Parti Québécois situate itself more towards the centre.' The PQ, he added, must take note of 'a very big concern on the part of ordinary people of the middle class, who demand more freedom in the relations that they are able to have with the Quebec state.' Similarly, Health Minister François Legault said, 'There is no need to be afraid of challenging the Quebec model without throwing overboard the gains of the Quiet Revolution' (www.wsws.org/articles/2002/aug2002/queb-a15.shtml). President of the Treasury Board Joseph Facal articulated the most forceful and direct indictment of the Quebec model and called publicly for a major review of Quebec's dominant policy paradigm. He urged his ministerial and PQ colleagues to re-think the notion of social solidarity. The concrete application of that notion, Facal argued, has led to social rigidities and the entrenchment in the policy process of the interests of certain lobbies – namely, the union bureaucracy closely associated with the Parti Québécois – to the detriment of the interests of the general population. In his view, the political impasse that the Parti Québécois was facing stemmed in part from its inability to recognize the inherent weaknesses of the Quebec model, namely, the extreme dependency of individuals on the state and the astronomical public debt that it has generated over the years. Although Facal stopped short of endorsing Action démocratique's policy platform, he expressed clearly his sympathy for a more neoliberal and less interventionist approach to the formulation of public policies in Quebec (www.wsws.org/articles/2002/aug2002/queb-a15.shtml).

Premier Landry was clearly displeased with his minister's declaration. It came barely a week after the government announced a $1.5 billion, five-year plan to fight poverty and social exclusion; it could easily be interpreted as a break from ministerial solidarity and as yet another indirect sign of distrust in his leadership. Landry immediately took issue with what he saw as Facal's mistaken analysis of the Quebec model. He maintained that the model's record of achievement was impressive, that it had been a key factor in Quebec's social and economic accomplishments and that it constituted the best synthesis yet between the imperatives of the market economy and state intervention.

Facal did not relent. On 6 September, at the height of Action démocratique's popularity in public opinion polls, he published a lengthy article in Montreal's French daily, *La Presse*, in which he reiterated his position and further explained his criticism of the Quebec model. Using typical neoliberal notions, Facal decried Quebec's reliance on the state as financially untenable, economically inefficient, and socially stifling. He advocated downloading state functions to the private sector and community organizations and a greater involvement of the private sector in the delivery of the various services currently under the responsibility of the state. In his view, there has to be a middle course between the radical neoliberalism of Mario Dumont's Action démocratique and the old ways of the Quebec model. He never made it entirely clear, however, how his appeal for a renewed policy paradigm differed from that of Mario Dumont.

A little before Facal's first public declaration, Liberal Party leader Jean Charest launched a vigorous attack against the policy platform of Action démocratique at a party convention held two weeks before the 17 June by-elections. Charest, who clearly saw Dumont as his main political opponent at the time, flatly denounced the key policy proposals of Action démocratique, which, he argued, would set Quebec back to the 1950s and widen the socioeconomic divide between the haves and the have-nots. He did not explicitly come to the defence of the Quebec model, but his call for renewed investment in health, education, and regional economic development might have led one to believe that he and his party would continue to adhere to that broad policy paradigm. In the ensuing months, however, at various Liberal Party functions and public meetings, Charest and other high-profile party members clarified their position: while they acknowledged that the policy paradigm that Quebec inherited from the Quiet Revolution largely and positively contributed to the socioeconomic fulfilment of Quebecers, the functions and bureaucratic processes of the Quebec state were now too unwieldy; they need to be re-engineered and made more in tune with the needs of the population.

In the end, the qualitative differences between the three major political parties with respect to the future of the Quebec model were fairly minimal. Following Facal's *cri du coeur*, others — politicians, journalists, academics, and ordinary citizens — joined the fray, arguing either side of the debate with equal conviction in public forums and newspapers. Except for those within the Parti Québécois, who, like Premier

Landry, remained unconditionally committed to the policy paradigm and value set of the Quebec model, many across the mainstream political spectrum tended to agree that a significant overhaul of state practices was in order.

The debate over the Quebec model is typical of the questioning that confronts most Western societies with regard to the nature, legitimacy, and future of the modern welfare state. But in Quebec such questioning has a particular political resonance that strikes at the heart of the collective identity of Quebecers. Being critical of the Quebec model implies indirectly that one is also disparaging of their achievements and the choices they made to assert their existence as a distinct political community. When couched in those terms, there can clearly be no easy solution to the conundrum posed by the challenges of state and societal transformation.

Federal–provincial relations: consensus over fiscal imbalance

On the federal–provincial relations front, the question of fiscal imbalance between the federal government and Quebec was by far the most important issue in contention in 2002. On 7 March Yves Séguin, chair of the commission on fiscal imbalance set up a year earlier by Premier Landry, released his report. The mandate of the Commission was three-pronged: Séguin and his team had to identify the causes of fiscal imbalance between Ottawa and Quebec, analyse its actual consequences, and propose practical solutions to correct the situation.

The work of the commission rested on a major prospective study of the Conference Board of Canada projecting the budgetary situations of the two governments over the next twenty years. Based on deliberately conservative assumptions on growth in spending and revenue for each government, the Conference Board estimated that over the next two decades the federal government will be posting ever greater budget surpluses: by 2020 the federal government's surplus will reach $90 billion, while Quebec will post a deficit of $5 billion. For the period as a whole, the federal government would reap an accumulated surplus of $570 billion, while Quebec's debt will rise by close to $60 billion.

The commission argued that the federal government occupies too much tax room in comparison with its responsibilities: it controls 60 per cent of the personal income tax, which yields the fastest growing revenue. As a result, it can run a sizeable surplus, which, in turn, it can apply in part to intervene unilaterally in provincial fields of jurisdiction. Meanwhile, the provinces, have insufficient resources to fund their own expenditures in those same fields. They face a precarious budgetary situation, repeated deficits, and extreme financial pressures particularly with respect to their commitment to maintaining quality health care services. According to the commission the causes of this imbalance have to do with the increased demand for provincial governments' services, the inadequacy of two major federal transfer programs – equalization and the Canada Health and Social Transfer – and the abuse by the federal government of its spending power. The consequences of fiscal imbalance, noted the commission, are many and problematic. Most of all, it curtails the ability of the provinces to fund and deliver key services, particularly in areas of high social, health, and education needs. The impact is not only financial, but it also affects negatively the quality and coherence of social programs and public services for which the provinces are responsible.

The commission concluded that fiscal imbalance constitutes a major dysfunction of the Canadian federal system and correction can be brought only through substantial transformation of the existing dynamics of fiscal relations between the federal and the provincial governments. The commission made the following five general recommendations to achieve this transformation: (1) provinces need and must have access to additional financial resources; (2) the terms and conditions under which financial resources are currently divided within the federation must be radically changed, which implies that the CHST be eliminated and new tax room be freed for the provinces; (3) the equalization program must be completely reviewed so that the tax bases used to determine equalization entitlements be better defined in collaboration with, and with the approval of the provinces; (4) a restriction on, or reduction of the federal government spending power must be imposed, and any future federal initiative in a provincial jurisdiction must be limited; (5) mechanisms meant to respond rapidly to any new causes of fiscal imbalance must be implemented, and public information concerning intergovernmental fiscal arrangements must be made more available and more transparent.

Fiscal imbalance has been a major bone of contention for all the provinces for quite some time. Most have intimated on several occasions and in no uncertain terms their unhappiness with the way the federal government has allocated monies that they believe are rightfully theirs. Under the Parti Québécois, the Quebec government has been the most vocal about the situation and the most adamant that it be corrected quickly. To sovereignists, fiscal imbalance is just one more proof that the Canadian federal system does not work and that Quebec as a distinct political community and sociological entity is necessarily hard done by it. Premier Landry's decision to set up a commission of inquiry on fiscal imbalance was as much a politically and ideologically driven gesture as it was, on the surface, an executive move to shed light on a given public management problem. Fiscal imbalance has been in recent years the principal rallying cry of Quebec sovereignists to mobilize popular support in favour of their political project.

The strategy of the Quebec government has met with vigorous opposition on the part of Ottawa. On a number of occasions during the year, Stéphane Dion, the federal minister of Canadian intergovernmental affairs, and Prime Minister Jean Chrétien locked horns with their Quebec counterparts. They engaged in often arcane public debates over the reality of fiscal imbalance and defended the political and administrative legitimacy of the central government. As one might expect in this context, Dion and Chrétien essentially argued that fiscal imbalance was a myth: federal surpluses are not what Quebec and other provinces make them out to be, and if the provinces have less financial resources than they would like, it is all because of their own budgetary choice to reduce income tax. As far as the federal spending power was concerned, they disagreed that the federal government impinged on provincial jurisdiction and argued that the proportion of federal expenditures in all government programs in Canada has in fact diminished by 20 per cent over the past four decades. According to Dion and Chrétien, the Canadian federal system is highly flexible and allows provinces to tap into and have control over a multitude of income-generating sources (e.g., royalties from natural resources, lotteries, etc.).

The political animosity between Ottawa and Quebec reached a new high in the fall. On 7–8 October the Quebec government held a forum on fiscal imbalance in which the three major political parties and nearly thirty civil society organizations (business lobbies, unions, and the community sector) were invited to take part. All the participants, including the Liberal Party and Action démocratique du Québec unanimously endorsed a resolution denouncing the fiscal imbalance between Ottawa and the provinces (although the Liberals accused the government of using the fiscal imbalance issue for electoral purposes, and both they and Action démocratique disagreed with the government's idea of holding a referendum on the recuperation of taxation points). Prime Minister Jean Chrétien responded to this unanimity by denying once more the existence of fiscal imbalance. He added that if Quebec is strapped for cash it is only because the government does not know how to manage its financial resources well; it squanders it on opening so-called embassies (mostly business or trade offices) all over the world – a clear jab at Quebec's will to be an independent actor on the international scene. The federal government is doing well, Chrétien concluded, simply because it is a better manager of the public purse than Quebec's current administration.

Chrétien's declaration was greeted with indignant howls of displeasure in Quebec where everyone, including Opposition parties, rallied behind the government to denounce the prime minister's remarks. Premier Landry demanded apologies from Chrétien and other federal ministers who also made similar public statements, noting that the prime minister should be more flexible and more sensitive to Quebec's claims, given that a majority of his own constituents voted Yes in the 1995 referendum on sovereignty. The apologies, of course, never came. The Quebec government could not make the federal government change its mind, but it did succeed in getting all major social and political stakeholders to adhere to its view on the inequity of current fiscal relations with Ottawa. Floundering as it was in public opinion polls, this was a moral victory for the PQ of no negligible import.

The policy agenda

The previous two years had been rather difficult on the government's policy agenda. The reform of municipal governance and the attendant mergers of small, independent towns into larger urban agglomerations in particular stirred stiff opposition from several quarters. Similarly, the government's stance on health reform and education often met with disapproval. In 2002 several policy decisions also irritated a number of different constituencies. For example, the exceptional measure (Bill 114) adopted by the National Assembly in July to force physicians to contribute their time in understaffed or overburdened emergency wards throughout the province was strongly condemned by various medical professional associations as a direct assault on the freedoms and civil rights of doctors. The obligation made to schools (Bills 123 and 124) to develop a *plan de réussite scolaire*, a success or performance plan, was received by many stakeholders in the field of education as another encroachment of the state on local mechanisms of decision, and as a deleterious attempt to quantify academic achievement.

Despite opposition and its declining fortune, the government stood fast. With time, unpopular policies receded somewhat from public notice, and the government managed to focus on a few policy and legislative accomplishments that, by most accounts, shed a more favourable light on its actions. Two dossiers likely to usher in new standards of policymaking stand out and deserve particular attention: the treaties with Indigenous peoples and the anti-poverty legislation.

Indigenous land claims and treaties

On 7 February Bernard Landry and Grand Chief of the Grand Council of the Crees Ted Moses signed a major landmark agreement. Dubbed Paix des Braves (Peace of the Braves), the agreement made official the agreement in principle signed earlier on 23 October 2001. It is in fact a comprehensive treaty detailing the territorial and economic rights of the Cree nation in Quebec. It updates the 1975 James Bay and Northern Quebec Agreement, and establishes a new relationship between Quebec and the Cree nation by providing for increased management by the Crees of their own economic and community development. It is premised on the abandonment by the Crees of pending multibillion dollar lawsuits against Hydro-Québec and the Quebec government, and on the promise on their part not to seek redress for past (possibly inappropriate) applications of the James Bay and Northern Quebec Agreement. This opens the way for the government to ensure the completion of major hydroelectric projects within the James Bay territory, which had been interrupted in the 1990s following successful legal and political contestation by the Crees. Plans were in the works to get two projects under way in April on the Eastmain and Rupert rivers. Together, they are expected to generate $4 billion in investments and create 10,500 new jobs over the next nine years.

In return the Crees will be more directly involved in the development of forestry and mining resources so as to guarantee the harmonization of natural resources exploitation with their traditional activities. To prepare the Crees to assume increased responsibilities in land and resources management, the government has agreed to $23 million in 2002–3, $46 million in 2003–4, and $70 million in 2004–5, as well as $70 million annually (or an amount corresponding to the indexed value of $70 million as of 2005–6 in accordance with a formula that reflects the evolution of the value of hydroelectric production, mining exploitation production, and forestry harvest production in the territory) until the year 2052. In all, over a fifty-year period, the Quebec government is committed to turn over more than $3.5 billion to the Cree nation.

Although the agreement met with opposition from environmentalists, and conservationists as well as a number of Cree people, it was largely and enthusiastically supported by the chiefs of the Cree communities.

Referenda held in all the Cree villages showed that more than 70 per cent of the local population was also favourable to it. Both Premier Landry and Grand Chief Moses hailed the agreement as a great opportunity for partnerships and the development of harmonious relationships between the Cree and Quebec nations.

Two months after the Paix des Braves, the government announced on 9 April a similar agreement with the Inuit. Again in this case the state was highly motivated to access the great hydroelectric potential of Nunavik (as much as 7,200 megawatts according to some estimates), which could result in investments of $18 billion and employment of up to 50,000 person-years in all Quebec regions over many years. This new agreement, known as Entente Sanarrutik provides for the Inuit to assume responsibility for economic and community development (which had been the responsibility of the Quebec government under the James Bay and Northern Quebec Agreement). The Quebec government commits to pay the Inuit $7 million in 2002–3, $8 million in 2003–4, and $15 million per year until the end of the twenty-five-year agreement. Over the life of the agreement, more than $360 million will have been paid to the Inuit. In addition, Hydro-Québec will allot $50 million to environmental impact assessments and other technical and economic studies.

In the ensuing months both Quebec and Cree officials travelled the world to publicize the agreements with the Crees and the Inuit as exemplary showcases of how to improve relations between indigenous peoples and the state. The Quebec government took great pride in these treaties and insisted at every opportunity that they reveal the strong democratic and pluralist spirit of the Quebec state and society.

Events surrounding yet another major agreement, this one with the Innus, dampened somewhat the government's self-congratulatory spirit. In July Bloc Québécois MP Ghislain Lebel vehemently denounced the negotiation process between four Innu communities, Quebec, and the federal government, and the agreement put forward for ratification by their respective negotiators a month earlier. As a Quebec sovereigntist, Lebel felt that the government was prepared to give too much to the Innus and feared that if the agreement was ratified it would open the door to endless territorial claims by other Indigenous nations, and Quebec would lose its essence as a nation. This agreement, known as Approche commune, came after nearly twenty-five years of acrimonious and all too often inconclusive negotiations between the Innu and the state over land rights and administrative autonomy. Given the history of problematic relationships between the Innu and the state, this agreement in principle was considered a major breakthrough by all parties concerned. The negotiators proposed full recognition of ancestral rights, including Aboriginal title; the non-extinguishment of Innu land rights; the creation of a new land regime with two types of territory, *Innu Assi*, limited areas roughly corresponding to current reserves upon which the Innu would have full ownership of the land and could exercise a large measure of self-government, and *Nitassinan*, 300,000 square kilometres of land from Lac-Jean to Labrador to remain under the jurisdiction of the Quebec government, but upon which the Innu can maintain their traditional activities and participate in partnership with the state to development projects that affect their rights; direct cash transfer of $275 million ($102 million from Quebec); financial support to Innu enterprises and manpower training; the creation of non-judicial mechanisms for the settlement of disagreements over specific issues; the extension of the land under the direct jurisdiction of band councils; and 3 per cent royalties derived from the exploitation of natural resources on Innu territory.

Ghislain Lebel was publicly reprimanded by Bloc Québécois leader Gilles Duceppe and castigated by a number of individuals sympathetic to the Quebec government for voicing his position; he eventually left the party to sit as an independent. Former premier and Parti Québécois leader Jacques Parizeau, however, echoed Lebel's sentiments with more nuance in a letter to newspapers in which he too denounced the agreement in principle, taking issue with the fact that Innu land rights would not be extinguished (contrary to what had been done in other similar agreements), with the judicial and legal chaos that, in his mind, it would create, and finally with the unwarranted legitimacy it brings to the Constitution Act of 1982, which Quebec has never recognized. In the following weeks others joined the voices of Lebel and Parizeau. From Lac-Jean to Sept-Iles, individuals and groups from the non-Indigenous towns, villages, and communities that would be touched by the proposed agreement mobilized against it with enough vigour that the government appointed former Minister for Aboriginal Affairs Guy Chevrette to tour the region during the fall and inform the population and hear the concerns of those who opposed it. The government also announced that it would hold a parliamentary commission on the agreement in February 2003. Although the government remained unwavering in its commitment to Approche commune, it seemed clear by year's end that seeing it through would not be as politically unproblematic as things were for Paix des Braves and Entente Sanarrutik.

Bill 112, the law against poverty[1]

According to the National Council on Social Welfare, Quebec's post-tax poverty rate for all individuals is the highest in Canada. Although other measurements of poverty – such as Statistics Canada's low income cut-off adjusted to reflect provincial cost of living and modify other biases – suggests that the situation is not as negative as may appear, the fact is that 'Quebec remains collectively poorer than the Canadian average and its history as a relatively poorer and less educated society has left important legacies for the older age groups and, possibly, for some in the next generations.'[2] As a result, since the mid-1990s, a variety of Quebec civil society groups and organizations devoted to the elimination of poverty and socioeconomic exclusion have been particularly active in lobbying the government to remain true to its traditional social-democratic orientation and pay greater heed to the plight of the Quebec poor. A broad-based coalition of unions and anti-poverty groups founded in 1998 and calling itself Collectif pour une loi sur l'élimination de la pauvreté (Collective for a Law on the Elimination of Poverty) has led several collective actions and undertaken a process of public deliberation that resulted in a full-fledged proposal written as a draft legislation laying out the content of what would be an ideal law against poverty. Throughout the process, it sought with some success the support of politicians from all parties, and in November 2000, three MNAs tabled the collective's proposal in the National Assembly.

Under Lucien Bouchard, the government, though not totally unresponsive to the plea of anti-poverty activists, was somewhat reluctant to commit fully to a formal policy. In the wake of the 1996 socioeconomic summits on the economy and employment, a temporary tax on business and high-income earners was instituted for a three-year period, with the expressed purpose of financing a special fund to combat poverty and assist the unemployed to reintegrate into the labour market. Similarly, in 1997, a new family policy introduced several innovations that were meant to ease the economic burden of the poorest families. But by and large the Bouchard government did not act directly on poverty, and Bouchard himself uttered doubts that any government could ever adopt the kind of legislation that the anti-poverty collective was proposing.

1 This section draws in part from Alain Noël, *A Law Against Poverty: Quebec's New Approach to Combating Poverty and Social Exclusion*, Background paper – Family Network, Canadian Policy Research Networks, December 2002.

2 *Ibid.*, p. 4.

In contrast, as he succeeded Bouchard as premier, Bernard Landry made the fight against poverty a personal priority. In June 2002 his government presented its own assessment of the situation and introduced a new legislative project, bill 112, inspired in part by the collective's proposal. Bill 112 was designed as a general framework and strategy to combat poverty and social exclusion. Its overarching objective is 'to progressively transform Quebec over a ten-year period into one of the industrialized societies with the least poverty, according to recognized methods of international comparison.' In addition the new law is meant to protect the dignity and improve 'the economic and social situation of people living in poverty and marginalized by society,' reduce 'inequalities that hinder social cohesion,' favour the participation of persons living in poverty in Quebec's collective life and in the development of society, and develop a sense of social solidarity.

To achieve these goals, the legislation targets the following five specific action areas and commits the government to implement: (1). better measures of prevention and empowerment to support families, promote access to education, and support skill development; (2). a strengthened social and economic safety net that improves incomes, work opportunities, and individual assets, and expand social housing; (3). improved access to work and employment through greater labour market integration, the development of the social economy, and the creation of quality employment; (4). greater opportunities for the involvement of all social actors via measures that encourage participation, local development, socially responsible enterprises, and community actions; (5). an institutional framework that generates information and improves evaluation and accountability, supports social innovation, and facilitates participation and more consistent and coherent actions at all levels.[3]

The law was adopted unanimously by all three parties in the National Assembly on 13 December 2002. It did not move forward unopposed, however, even in cabinet. Sceptics dismissed the legislation as a desperate attempt of the government to regain the favour of public opinion as it approached the end of its mandate. Critics described it as 'a proposal long on symbols and institutions but short on specifics and commitments.'[4] Still, most of the 130 groups heard by the Social Affairs Commission of the National Assembly generally spoke in favour of the law. The Collective for the Elimination of Poverty greeted the draft legislation as a good step forward and a good basis for discussion, but pro-

3 Ibid., p. 6.
4 Ibid., p. 7.

posed a number of amendments which found their way into the law. The anti-poverty collective was relatively happy with the end result, observing that the law should be seen as a starting point, but that it has little immediate impact on the living conditions of the poor. The greatest gain of this law is to have brought social actors in Quebec to accept that poverty is neither the consequence of personal failure nor a social inevitability. The government derived a great sense of pride in this legislation. It remains to be seen whether Quebecers as a collective are truly willing to commit resources to reducing poverty and to supporting a more generous distribution within society.

Turning a page?

The Quebec government's moral victory on the issue of fiscal imbalance, the positive inroads made in mending relations with Indigenous peoples, and the substantial social-democratic good will shown in the legislation against poverty are not without import on the long run. Fairly significant breakthroughs were made in 2002 in these critical policy areas. To many who remain unimpressed with the Parti Québécois's overall record, those were too little, too late. At year's end, the PQ's standing in public opinion polls had improved somewhat, but it was still lagging behind the Liberal Party who, by then, had also sailed past Action démocratique. As the perspective of an unavoidable general election weighs in, little time is left to change course. The tension between the social-democratic and nationalistic ideals that has long characterized the Parti Québécois, on the one hand, and ever more intractable neoliberal imperatives, on the other, has proved quite hard to address to everyone's satisfaction. Judging from the political scars it left, it may well have taken an irredeemable toll on the government.

RICHARD WILBUR

New Brunswick

The most critical and unresolved problem facing the government of Premier Bernard Lord continued to be how to finance and staff the health care sector. Finding the money was not the only issue. The government's determination to keep control of hospital administration was another, as was the question of whether there should be a degree of privatization. The touchy bilingual question continued to fester in Moncton, where a strong French lobby emerged to ensure that one of the city's two hospitals continued to provide services *en français*. Strikes and threatened walkouts of health service personnel compounded the volatile situation. Continuing issues involving NB Power, education, the pros and cons of provincial lotteries, and rising motor vehicle insurance rates reaffirmed that governing New Brunswick is a constant challenge.

Hospital woes

In January the Lord government passed legislation creating regional health authorities with limited control inasmuch as their chief executive officers would be appointed by and report to the government – a move strongly criticized by the Liberal Opposition (*Daily Gleaner*, 8 January). Two weeks later, in accepting the report of the Health Quality Council, while making no specific references to its 122 recommendations including one creating community health centres, Premier Lord said, 'If we don't adopt some of these changes, we will hit the medical wall' (*Telegraph-Journal*, 23 January). Noting that the health department intended to establish its first community health centre later in the year, Lord said that the plan was to locate it in a community with a high volume of traffic but where people are having difficulty accessing the system.

The spending estimates tabled in late April by Health Minister Elvy Robichaud earmarked $2.1 million to implement health centres in at least two sites, but he added that this might not happen until 2003 pending the necessary legislation to give greater authority to nurses and to create the nurse practitioner category. Richard also revealed that the overall debt for the seven hospital corporations had been reduced to $7.6 million, down from $50 million when the PC government took over. Earlier, while in Vancouver attending a premiers' meeting on health care, Lord said that he had asked Ontario to provide him with more details about its privately built but publicly financed hospitals: 'Maybe it's something that we need to explore' (*Telegraph-Journal*, 25 January). He emphasized that regardless of who does the construction, 'the care will always be provided by the government, the same way it is now.' Lord expressed these same sentiments in April when the Romanow Commission on the Future of Health Care in Canada visited Fredericton: 'If it doesn't create a parallel system then we should be open to those ideas'(*Daily Gleaner*, 19 April). Elizabeth Weir, the NDP leader and its only member of the Legislative Assembly, told the Commission that 'there are ways to help the Canadian health system without turning to corporate Canada.' She added that 'we are the only province ... to have contracted out our seniors' drug program to the private sector – Blue Cross ... [Those] who are not part of the low income government plan have the worst and the most expensive drug plan in the country' (*Daily Gleaner*, 20 April).

Two weeks earlier, the emergency room at the hospital in Sussex had had to close from 7:00 a.m. to 7:00 p.m. because no doctors were available, a situation that the health minister said 'is not a province-wide problem' (*Daily Gleaner*, 12 April). Acting Liberal leader Bernard Richard responded by noting that surgery waiting time had doubled in the Moncton region over the previous three years and that the hospital in Dalhousie was flying in doctors from Quebec to staff its emergency room. In January the government finally released a report completed the previous September by a Nova Scotia specialist, Dr Robert Martel, who had been asked to examine the status of rural emergency rooms following the death of a child in June 2001. The child died while travelling to the hospital in Caraquet because the emergency room in his home town of Tracadie was closed, again because of a staffing problem. Dr Martel urged the government 'to add a premium of 20 per cent above current fees to attract doctors to work ER shifts in areas with fewer than eight doctors on the on-call roster'(*Telegraph Journal*, 31 January) On 30 April Health Minister Robichaud rose in the Legislative Assembly to deny media reports that the francophone Georges L. Dumont Hospital in Moncton might close (*Telegraph-Journal*, 1 May). The Société des Acadiens et Acadiennes du Nouveau Brunswick had launched a civil suit against the Lord government on grounds that Bill 17, designed to reform the provincial health care system, was unconstitutional because it would not guarantee that all services would be available in French – in conformity with New Brunswick's Official Languages Act (*Times & Transcript*, 18 April). On 17 May Premier Lord, responding to a citizens' group called the SOS Dumont Committee, acknowledged that because of rising health care costs, the Dumont and other hospitals 'will likely be sharing some of their services with other hospitals,' but he emphasized that users of the Dumont 'will be served in the official language of their choice no matter what the evolutionary path of health care in New Brunswick' (ibid., 18 May).

The role and the pay of New Brunswick nurses remained a major health care issue throughout the year 2002. In April contract talks between the government and 350 civil service nurses broke off when the dispute went before a conciliation board. In early November, with still no settlement, 150 members of the New Brunswick Nurses Union protested outside a Miramichi hotel where the Progressive Conservative Party was holding its annual meeting. They talked briefly with the health minister and a settlement was reached a few days later, giving the nurses a contract for the first time in two years. Details announced after the union members had ratified the terms showed that the agreement included a 2 per cent wage increase each year over four years. On 7 May Minister Robichaud introduced legislation outlining the role of nurse practitioners, a concept first suggested by the former Liberal government. When the Lord government assumed power in 1999, it delayed any further action pending the results of a two-year study by the Premier's Health Quality Council. On 4 November the government and the Nurses Union agreed to a wage scale ($58,870 to $65,000 a year) for nurse practitioners but by year's end, the first nurse practitioner was still to be hired.

In the rapidly growing nursing homes sector, which was under the legislative jurisdiction of Family and Community Services, the minister, Joan MacAlpine, in her budget estimates on 10 April, allotted $12 million more to hire sixty-five additional full-time staff and another $10 million to cover 50 cent an hour wage increases. This would bring the average hourly wage to $7 and the annual wage before taxes to $15,600 – still the lowest wage in Canada for such workers. A month later MLAs learned that agencies running home care services were increasing their monthly fees to seniors by between $50 and $100, a move that the Liberals claimed meant that seniors on fixed incomes and special needs clients in effect were paying for the pay hikes.

In another sector closely linked to health care, government social workers, members of of the Canadian Union of Public Employees Local 1418, went on strike 4 September, affecting those in non-emergency mental health services, and public health nutrition programs, as well as sport, recreation, and arts consultants. About 350 of 900 workers were designated essential, ensuring that emergency cases would be handled. The dispute was settled on 3 October, when the striking workers 'voted solidly but not enthusiastically to accept the latest contract,' giving all members a 12.5 per cent increase over four years and 4.8 per cent bonuses for child protection workers and psychologists (*Daily Gleaner*, 4 October). CUPE members returned to work the next day.

Overworked Crown prosecutors and overpaid judges and executive?

'A desperately needed overhaul of the province's justice department is stuck in limbo because the government can't spare the cash to hire more staff.' That was how one reporter began her story on a report completed eight months earlier by Cleveland Allaby, a former Tory leadership candidate, who was paid $112,000 to study how the department could address recruiting problems and retain its existing staff (*Telegraph-Journal*, *Daily Gleaner*, 2 March). Deputy Justice Minister Roger Bilodeau told the legislature's Public Accounts committee that the department could only follow the recommendations if it got more staff. On 17 January the province's forty-four Crown prosecutors ended their work-to-rule campaign as a sign of good faith that action would be taken to reduce their heavy workload. Bilodeau revealed that four retiring lawyers had to be rehired on part-time contracts. Sixteen experienced lawyers would be taking early retirement at the end of March, and while about half had been replaced, the deputy minister admitted that 'they didn't have as much experience and it's difficult to attract veteran lawyers' (*Telegraph-Journal*, 2 March).

In May a ruling by the Court of Queen's Bench upheld the government's decision rejecting a recommendation by the Judicial Remuneration Committee that would have increased the salaries of twenty-five provincial court judges from $141,206 to $159,101 immediately and to over $170,000 by 2003. The judgment said there was no evidence that the government tried to 'manipulate the bench or politically interfere with it' (*Times & Transcript*, 15 May).

In mid-December the annual release of public account figures giving the salaries of every public servant earning over $40,000 showed that, a year after leaving his position as president and CEO of NB Power, James Hankinson still received for the fiscal year 2001–2 a salary of $328,832, well above the $172,821 paid to the next highest officer in the facility. Two executives in another crown agency, the Investment Management Corporation, received $255,033 and $192,867 respectively, while several senior personnel in the seven Regional Health Authorities received annual salaries of between $141,000 and $145,000. Clearly, the wage disparity phenomenon was alive and flourishing in New Brunswick's public service.

NB Power's continuing problems

As January ushered in one of the coldest winters in a decade, New Brunswickers collectively kept one eye on their fuel bills and the other on the future of their publicly owned power utility. Two weeks into the new year the Power Utilities Board began hearings on the request by NB Power to spend $747 million to replace the heavy oil currently used to fuel the Coleson Cove facility outside Saint John with orimulsion, a slurry made of water and bitumen, an ingredient that is similar to crude oil and found only in Venezuela. NB Power officials said the change, 'to be completed by 2008, will help meet our environmental obligations and it will put downward pressure on our rates' (*Daily Gleaner*, 15 January). Converting to a blend of natural gas and oil, on the other hand, would increase rates by 8.7 per cent and cause a 'cumulative net loss of $220 million.' On 28 January the board recommended in favour of the conversion, although it was 'disappointed that the province was unable to provide a definite policy with respect to the management of emissions' (*Daily Gleaner*, 29 January). One day later a faulty circuit shut down the Lepreau nuclear facility, the fourth such interruption since mid-December (*Times and Transcript*, 30 January). For the next few weeks Opposition MLAs, especially NDP leader Elizabeth Weir, kept asking for a decision as to whether the aging facility, which provides 22 per cent of New Brunswick's electricity, would be refurbished to give it another twenty years of life. The government and power officials remained mum on the facility's future, but on 13 March before the legislature's Crown Corporations Committee, Weir said that the fact that NB Power had spent $40 million on a feasibility study and had already 'paid millions of dollars for special tools to refurbish the nuclear power plant ... indicated the decision ... was made well before last year' (*Daily Gleaner*, 14 March). On 7 March the utility announced rate increases, effective 1 April. Residential users would pay 3 per cent more, compared with a 1.5 per cent hike for industry and business customers. Together, the two increases amounted to 2.1 per cent, just below the 3 per cent threshold that would require NB Power to justify an increase before the Utilities Board. Energy Minister Jeannot Volpe said the government supported the rate increase: 'We've seen their numbers and we feel it's needed' (*Telegraph-Journal*, 8 March).

The government's long-range plans for NB Power were finally unveiled at a news conference on 30 May, when Premier Lord outlined plans to restructure the debt-ridden facility. Although government control would be retained, by April 2003, 'NB Power will operate as four distinct companies, generation, distribution, nuclear and transmission, and if a private company places the right offer on the table, the province will consider selling Point Lepreau and Coleson Cove' (*Telegraph-Journal*, 31 May). The utility's current debt was $2.9 billion and another $1.6 billion would be required to cover the costs of a proposed refurbishing of the Lepreau and Coleson Cove facilities. Each of the four companies would be responsible for any money that they would borrow and the province would not guarantee their loans. Premier Lord said that the province 'just can't afford to increase its debt by borrowing the money. We want someone else to put their money on the line' (*Telegraph-Journal*, 31 May). He admitted that there were no offers 'on the table yet,' but concluded, 'Our decision can be summed up in one overriding objective: to minimize financial risk to taxpayers and maintain affordable and fair electricity rates to ratepayers' (*Daily Gleaner*, 31 May).

On 24 September the Public Utilities Board recommended against the utility's plan to spend $845 million to refurbish Point Lepreau, saying that the project was financially risky and not in the public interest (*Times & Transcript*, 25 September). Noting the board's suggestion that NB Power take another look at building a plant powered by natural gas rather than refurbishing Lepreau, Ken Little, a vice-president at the utility said that 'there are no guarantees of a long-term gas supply from offshore Nova Scotia.' Expressing his surprise at the Power Utilities Board's recommendation, Energy Minister Volpe said, 'We have opened the door for the private sector to produce power in New Brunswick, so if we don't go ahead with refurbishing Point Lepreau, that will create a vacuum for the energy need for New Brunswick.' Premier Lord noted that 'it will be months and months' before a final position is taken ... In the meantime, the government will continue on its search for alternate energy sources to replace or supplement the power now created by the nuclear plant' (*Times & Transcript*, 26 September). On 17

October Volpe, in an editorial board meeting with the Moncton *Times & Transcript*, said that construction of the Coleson Cove orimulsion project would begin 1 November and would cost $747 million by the time of its completion in November 2004 (ibid., 18 October). The largest generator in the province, the Coleson cove facility provides about one-third of New Brunswick's power needs during the winter. Volpe said that more than half the conversion costs would be spent on environmental improvements so that sulphur dioxide emissions would be reduced by 77 per cent, nitrogen oxides by 70 per cent, and carbon dioxide by 3 per cent.

The legislature's continued diminishing role

Ever since the former Liberal premier Frank McKenna introduced an executive-style government with major policy announcements being issued from his office in the Centennial Building, while others were made outside to assembled media people, the historic old legislature has never regained its paramount role. In the first week of January 2002, Premier Lord extended the sitting time to the same schedule as in the McKenna era, with evening sessions three nights a week plus an extra sitting Thursday morning. Throughout the year, the Tory leader followed the other McKenna approach: holding major news conferences not only outside the chambers but often in his home constituency of Moncton. The fall session, which began the previous November, finally ended on 11 January after giving royal assent to twenty bills, none of which could be considered major with the exception of the Regional Health Authority Act. At the end of the session, Liberal leader Bernard Richard expressed his disappointment at a government he considered 'increasingly secretive' (*Telegraph-Journal*, 12 January).

The Legislative Assembly resumed sitting on 26 March. The new finance minister, Peter Mesheau, presented his first budget, which reflected the higher revenue achieved by tax increases announced late in 2001 on gasoline and tobacco. These tax increases helped the Lord government close the books on the 2001–2 fiscal year with a $37 million surplus. For the new budget year, however, the government would have to withdraw $80 million from the recently established Stabilization Fund in order to deliver the mandatory balanced budget. Health care spending would be increased by $80 million, including $4.5 million for a new system of community health services; public education would get an additional $36 million, while another $15 million was set aside to improve university infrastructure. Small businesses would see their corporate taxes reduced by 1 per cent, while the general corporate tax would be cut incrementally to 13 per cent by 1 January 2003. The latest Tory budget continued the trend begun in 2000 by making further small cuts in family income taxes. Over the next two years, individuals earning less than $12,000 a year, and families with an income of less than $20,000 a year, would no longer have to pay provincial income taxes. Mesheau predicted the provincial net debt would increase by $58.7 million, but in his budget address he made no mention of any payment on the overall debt of $6.57 billion. Liberal financial critic Marcelle Mersereau accused the government of wasting $70 million on its voluntary retirement program, noting that the new budget revealed that the size of the civil service had not decreased. In fact, thirty-three more full-time equivalent positions had been added since the retirement program was started. Earlier, before the Public Accounts Committee, Auditor General Daryl Wilson suggested that the government could have achieved the same savings in money and personnel through attrition and normal retirement. Two days after the budget was tabled, Sharon MacFarlane, vice-president of NB Power, warned that, due to a variety of negative factors, the net income that the government had expected to receive from the utility had been revised downward to $19 million instead of about $30 million. 'In the past, the positives offset the negatives ... In this current fiscal year, it's been mostly negative' (*Telegraph-Journal*, 29 March).

On 4 June Premier Lord introduced new official language legislation to replace the original act passed thirty-three years earlier by the Liberal government of Louis Robichaud. Designed to quiet the protests among vocal francophone groups, the new bill 'broadens guaranteed access to services in both official languages to policing, health care, municipalities and even municipal planning and solid waste commissions' (*Telegraph-Journal*, 6 June). It also creates the position of an official language commissioner with power to investigate complaints under the Official Languages Act. During the ensuing debate the government accepted two Liberal amendments, and on 7 June tears flowed on all sides of the legislature when Louis Robichaud was ushered to his old seat, where he made a short speech after the bill received royal assent. It was a far cry from the scenes in 1969 when the original bill was finally passed after what one observer, Robert Pichette, who was its principal author, remembered as a 'nasty and difficult' debate (*Daily Gleaner*, 8 June). In mid-December, in Moncton, Premier Lord and federal Minister of Canadian Heritage Sheila Copps publicly signed a joint agreement authorizing $2 million in funds to cover the cost of translating municipal laws into French (*L'Acadie-nouvelle*, 9 December).

Outlining details of his department's estimates, Education Minister Dr Dennis Furlong told the legislature on 15 May that nearly 85 per cent of this year's funding increase of $39 million would be spent on higher teachers' salaries. Of the remaining $6 million in additional funds, $2.5 million would pay for the second instalment of a three-year program to provide high-speed computer band width to all schools. At the post-secondary level, the government would add $1.4 million to its bursary and scholarship fund.

During the lacklustre session political attention was diverted to the Liberal leadership campaign in April and May, even though it, too, lacked any real spark as the results were never in doubt. MLA Shawn Graham handily defeated his only opponent, party executive director Jack MacDougall in the first ballot at the convention held in Fredericton on 11 May.

After seventy days, the second-longest legislative session in New Brunswick's history, and the first to be carried live on the Internet, ended on 7 June, with the new Official Languages Act its most notable piece of legislation. Another more controversial item called for the government to pay an additional $24.5 million to MRDC, the firm originally contracted to build a toll highway linking Fredericton and Moncton. Removal of the tolls was the main campaign promise on which Bernard Lord and the Conservatives were swept into power in 1999. Another even more vital transportation issue, sharply rising motor vehicle insurance rates, prompted the Lord government to use a now-familiar ploy aimed at defusing a potentially divisive question: it formed a select committee on car insurance, which would hold hearings at five major centres to find the views of 'concerned New Brunswickers.'

The Speech from the Throne opening a new legislative session on 19 November reaffirmed the Lord government's 'commitment to set up the $20-million New Brunswick Innovation Foundation ... based on developing knowledge industries, life sciences, advanced manufacturing and value-added natural resources' (*Times & Transcript*, 20 November). The speech also promised 'targeted tax incentives to spur on job growth for small businesses, a mandatory business impact test for new legislation or regulations and a repatriation project to bring New Brunswickers back to work in the province.' The president of the New Brunswick Teachers Association, Mary Wilson, said she hoped that the education minister would announce the learning agenda's specifics with-in the next few months: 'They've got to put more money in education; they have to hire more teachers and they have to look at the composition of classrooms. Our teachers are really struggling' (ibid.). On 6 December, Education Minister Dennis Furlong released a study that the government had commissioned on the state of the province's school system. Alberta educator Elana Scraba had handed in her report seven months earlier, but despite requests through the Right to Information Act by several groups, its release was delayed. Scraba found that the dismal results achieved by New Brunswick students in international examinations in 2001 could be blamed on 'the constant educational change and experiment that has characterized education in New Brunswick over the last dozen years' (ibid., 7 December). Speaking for teachers, Mary Wilson urged the government to use the report 'as a tool to make some good decisions for teachers and students.' Furlong acknowledged that students 'suffered through one poorly thought out strategy after another. Our government will ensure the next generation and subsequent generations of New Brunswick students do not suffer the same results' (ibid.).

With a general election expected within the next twelve months, the Lord government's fourth budget, introduced on 10 December, increased gas and tobacco taxes for the second consecutive year, while increasing spending for health care, education, and transportation. The projected surplus, a mere $7.5 million from an overall expenditure of $5.4 billion, depended on withdrawing the $108 million remaining in the Fiscal Stabilization Fund. Liberal finance critic Bernard Richard said the latest gasoline tax hike 'is just a way to pay for the 1999 election promise of taking off the Moncton-to-Fredericton highway tolls ... This is over four cents increase in fuel taxes in two years ... These are shadow tolls'(*Times & Transcript*, 11 December). The government's spending policies received sharp criticism from the auditor general, when he released his annual report on 17 December. He questioned the need for a Fiscal Stabilization (or Rainy Day) Fund, which had been drained the week before his report was released: 'Given the significant amounts the province owes ... it is difficult to imagine how the amounts accumulating in the Fiscal Stabilization Fund will be able to stabilize the fiscal position of the province from year to year ... It was merely taking money from one pocket and stuffing it into another' (ibid., 18 December).

The overall economic picture

Moncton enforced its reputation as New Brunswick's fastest growing area by adding another 600 jobs in February 2002, when Rogers Communications unveiled plans for a $30 million call centre. Figures released three weeks later by Statistics Canada showed that Moncton's employment rate stood at 63.1 per cent, up from 61.5 per cent a year earlier. By contrast, the employment figures for the Acadian peninsula had dropped from 44.6 to 42.7 per cent, while unemployment was 20.1 per cent compared with 16.8 per cent a year ago. In July the federal Labour Minister and MP for Moncton-Riverview-Dieppe Claudette Bradshaw announced the details of federal grants for four research and development projects in her riding. Micro Optics Design received $6 million, the Université de Moncton $5 million, the Beausejour Medical Research Institute $6 million, and the Genie Concept, a non-profit research group $1.2 million. Moncton and its neighbouring suburb, Dieppe, became the first major centres to receive provincial approval for year-round shopping seven-days a week, beginning 3 March. This prompted civic officials in Fredericton and Saint John to announce that they would not file complaints under the Days of Rest Act for Sunday shopping violations. Moncton also scored when a local firm, Spielo Gaming International, announced in late February that it planned to hire up to thirty more workers after winning a $60 million contract to replace 6,100 video lottery terminals for Loto-Quebec. Snow crab fishermen on the Acadian Peninsula welcomed news that their annual quota would be increased by 40 per cent to 22,000 tonnes, but a subsequent decision by several plant owners to shift their processing to other factories, in southern New Brunswick and Nova Scotia, brought loud protests from 1,200 Acadian workers, most of them women, who claimed that they would not earn enough to collect Employment Insurance benefits in these circumstances. In August Premier Lord and Prime Minister Jean Chrétien donned hard hats in St Leonard to announce a cost-sharing plan to spend $400 million to twin a dangerous section of highway between the Quebec border and Fredericton. No similar good news awaited owners of the St Leonard airport, who learned a few weeks later that Air Canada Jazz was ending its service linking this northwest region to central Canada. The same day, officials at the Charlo airport, near Campbellton, announced that the airport would close on 28 September, while on the same page, *L'Acadie-Nouvelle* reported that federal Transport Minister David Collenette would be arriving to announce that Moncton's expanding airport would be re-designated as an international facility. If New Brunswickers needed further proof of the lopsided economic picture, they got it from the latest national census figures. The Moncton suburb of Dieppe was the fastest growing centre in New Brunswick, increasing in population by more than 19 per cent between 1996 and 2001, while the population of Moncton itself grew by 2.9 per cent. Both increases reflected the steady migration from the predominantly French-speaking areas in the northern counties of the province. Overall, New Brunswick's population declined by 1.2 per cent or by more than 8,000 individuals, for a total population of 729,498.

PETER E. BUKER

Prince Edward Island

The year 2002 was one of solid economic growth across most sectors for Prince Edward Island with good recovery in agricultural production and exports compared with the previous year. Some significant legislation was passed, and provincial budget expenditures exceeded $1 billion for the first time. PEI made news beyond its boundaries on the issues of pesticide use, child abuse associated with a religious commune, and factors leading to the resignation of Cardigan MP Lawrence MacAulay from his cabinet position of solicitor general.

The economy

Prince Edward Island's population, as of 1 July 2002, was estimated by Statistics Canada to be 139,913, which represents an increase of 1,009 people or 0.7 per cent from a year earlier.

The province's gross domestic product expanded from 2001 by 5.6 per cent, in constant dollars, to $3,767 million at 2002 market prices. Growth was helped by the recovery of potato crops and potato processing, and GDP per capita was $23,807. Fishing income grew by 23.1 per cent, agriculture income increased by 20.2 per cent, information and culture services, as well as construction incomes were up by 9.1 per cent, business services expanded by 7.9 per cent, and manufacturing went up by 7.5 per cent.

Manufacturing shipments totalled $1,316 million. Food shipments (excluding fish products) totalled $413.5 million, an increase of 2.4 per cent, while processed fish products increased 14 per cent to $363.5 million, following a decade-long trend of their increasing importance in the Island economy. Manufacturing accounted for 9.4 per cent of employment in the province.

Favourable growing conditions led to a 57 per cent increase in potatoes harvested for a record $197 million in sales. Livestock receipts fell by 5.8 per cent. Government support payments to farm operators in total declined 60 per cent from 2001, but compensation payments related to potato production were at a historic high.

Total retail sales were $1.3 billion, an expansion of 3.4 per cent from 2001 but considerably lower than the 6 per cent national average increase. The wholesale and retail trade sector was PEI's largest private-sector employer with 9,500 people.

Fish landings fell by 0.4 per cent to $164.3 million; herring landings declined 21 per cent because of quota restrictions. The lobster catch was 19.9 million pounds, up only slightly from the previous year, but giving a record high value of $105.4 million because of strong prices.

Partly because PEI was exempt from the countervailing duties imposed in the Canada–U.S. softwood lumber disputes, the volume of primary forest products rose by 8.8 per cent, and the value of shipments was up 14.1 per cent, at $60 million.

Tourism showed a 3 per cent decrease in numbers of visitors but a 7.5 per cent increase in revenues compared with 2001, breaking previous records. There were an estimated 1.1 million tourists and 45,417 business visitors. No doubt because of the lingering effects of 11 September 2001, air travel was down in 2002, but the ferry service to the Magdalen Islands, Quebec, had 17.4 per cent more passengers and the PEI to Nova Scotia ferry service saw a modest increase. The Confederation Bridge to the mainland had 1.6 million vehicles cross (in both directions), up 3 per cent from the previous year. Housing starts reached 775 units, a 15 per cent increase from 2001, although non-residential construction declined by an enormous 70 per cent from 2001's record-breaking year to $47 million. Still, total public and private investment in 2002 increased by 9.2 per cent to reach $652.4 million.

The public sector accounted for 28 per cent of the province's employment: there was a 2.6 per cent overall decline in public sector employment, although education services grew by 2.7 per cent.

Total revenue for the province for the fiscal year 2001–2 was up 2.3 per cent to $973.6 million; provincial tax revenues increased by 4.1 per cent; equalization payments increased by 4.4 per cent; and Canada Health and Social Transfer payments increased by 15.9 per cent. Federal transfers accounted for 41 per cent of provincial revenues. Total expenditures increased by 2 per cent, reaching $981.9 million, rendering a $17 million deficit after pension adjustment. Estimates by bond-rating services brought out in the autumn put provincial government debt at about $1.3 billion.

With increases in labour force participation, an all-time average high of 67,100 people were employed in PEI, representing a 1.8 per cent increase in employment and a 6.3 per cent growth in labour income compared with 2001. Unemployment increased to an average of 12.1 per cent, up from 11.9 per cent in 2001.

The Atlantic Technology Centre, a high-technology office building heralded as 'five levels of information technology, television production and software development space' opened in Charlottetown on 8 September. The centre was a $21 million construction and engineering project, 'aimed at providing a heart to' PEI's 'growing technology sector.' Also in Charlottetown, a $60 million revitalization project for the downtown core, funded by the three levels of government, was announced. The City of Charlottetown had 92 new homes built in 2002, a 34 per cent increase over 2001. Building permits issued until the end of November represented an historically unprecedented $45 million, giving the city a three-year average of close to $40 million.

Summerside, the province's other city, was considered one of the fastest growing communities in the Maritimes, with an estimated $20 million in building permits issued for 2002. The year also saw the beginning of a $7 million project to eliminate the long-standing problem of the stench of rotting eel grass, which had long hindered economic development in the west end of the city.

Fiscal events

Prince Edward Island's government was considering becoming the first North American jurisdiction to license Internet-based gambling, but a court ruling led to the proposal's abandonment. PEI's Lottery Commission reported that the province had made $15,190,587 in the previous fiscal year by games operated by the Atlantic Lottery Corporation. Taking into account all gaming, Islanders received over $17 million in that fiscal year for prizes, while $7.7 million was paid out in gaming-related commissions. In 2002 the government decided to eliminate all privately owned video lottery terminals in the province, about 500 machines owned by five companies, and to take over all of the video lottery business. The province purchased new machines, and there continued to be public controversy surrounding the whole issue of video lottery gambling.

In January the federal government informed the PEI government of the misallocation of federal income tax as a result of a federal accounting error in the administration of capital gains tax from mutual fund trusts; this had led to an overpayment of equalization to PEI of $6 million. On 31 January Provincial Treasurer Patricia J. Mella warned that the provincial government could no longer afford its current level of services.

A voluntary work adjustment program was announced on 8 February to reduce the provincial public service by encouraging early retirement or fewer work hours; the program projected savings of $3.75 million.

On 26 March the third session of the sixty-first general assembly reopened for the spring sitting with the presentation of the budget. (Mella's sixth), entitled 'A Balanced Response in Difficult Times.' It contained expenditures of approximately $1 billion, and forecast that the provincial economy would grow 1.2 percent in 2002. Health and social services continued to account for the largest share of provincial expenditure, at just over $389 million, or 38.9 per cent of the total, followed by education at $203 million or 20.3 per cent. Tax measures included raising the health tax on tobacco by $5 per carton of 200 cigarettes, and an increase in the gasoline tax of 1 cent per litre. The Canada Health and Social Transfer was announced to be about $89 million for the fiscal year 2002–3, a 2.8 per cent increase over the previous fiscal year but short of the over 7 per cent growth in provincial health costs.

The 2002–3 budget set overall spending at 1.4 per cent higher that the forecasted expenditures of 2001–2, with a predicted deficit of $28.8 million, $17.2 million attributable to the province's $21 million investment in the East Prince Health Facility. Expenditures announced included magnetic resonance imaging (MRI) and linear accelerator services with an investment of $9.6 million in capital and $1.6 million in start-up costs, and a $1.1 million expansion to the O'Leary Community Hospital. Additional health funding were promised: $480,000 for private nursing homes, $1.5 million for home and palliative care, and $1.5 million for the Disability Supports Program.

Expenditure reductions of $39.5 million or 4 per cent of overall spending were announced, including $12.5 million in the highways budget through delayed capital spending and $5.2 million saved by delaying the Summerside Intermediate and the Bluefield (phase II) schools. Later, however, on 13 September, $11.6 million in highway improvement funding for PEI was announced through a joint funding agreement between the province and Transport Canada following their Strategic Highway Infrastructure Initiative Program.

The government announced a number of changes in 2002. On 27 March Premier Pat Binns announced a process to standardize the adjustment of deputy ministers' salaries; previously there had been no such mechanism in place. On 27 June federal funding of $5.2 million was announced, based on 60/40 cost-sharing with the province, for an

'Agricultural Policy Framework' intended to enhance food safety, innovation, and environmentally responsible production in agriculture. A four-year $3.8 million 'Building on Success: Best Start Program' was announced on 1 November by Premier Binns; it was intended to enhance the overall well-being of children from birth to three years of age, and used a variety of screening, assessment, and in-home support methods that built on previous government initiatives for this age group. On 16 December, a major tourist development was announced for North Cape; the project was to include an interpretive centre focusing on the Atlantic Wind Test Site, as well as the expansion of existing tourism infrastructure. This development was to be funded by a number of partners, with the bulk of the money, $1.5 million, committed by the Atlantic Canada Opportunities Agency. Finally, the advertisement of PEI government tenders, available on the national MERX service since 1998, was changed in response to MERX fee increases; tenders were moved to the official government homepage, where documents were available at no charge, although they could still be accessed as a MERX Opportunity Search.

The legislature

Governor General Adrienne Clarkson presented an augmented coat of arms for Prince Edward Island at a ceremony at Province House 13 December, in honour of the 150th anniversary of the granting of responsible government to PEI in 2001. The grant of arms was made by the Office of the Chief Herald of Canada, based on the artwork of Charlottetown's David Webber. This Full Achievement of Arms recognized PEI's co-sovereign status in the Canadian federation, and Queen Elizabeth II approved the use of the Royal Crown in the new Armorial Bearings.

In January Dr Herb Dickieson announced his intention to resign as leader of PEI's New Democratic Party. Gary Robichaud, a 39-year-old Acadian high school teacher from Summerside who billed himself as a moderate, was elected as the new party leader 13 April by winning 60 of the 82 votes cast.

The Freedom of Information and Protection of Privacy Act was proclaimed 1 November. The Act's intention was to make the provincial government more open and accountable to citizens and to ensure the privacy of personal information held by government. It excluded some parts of government, with school boards and health regions slated to come under the Act later. Also in 2002, however, an Act to Amend the

Freedom of Information and Protection of Privacy Act was passed; it expanded cabinet confidentiality by removing the exception regarding background documents, among other changes. This act also specified the process for appointing the information and privacy commissioner; the appointment was to be made on the recommendation of the Standing Committee on Legislative Management to the Legislative Assembly, supported by at least two-thirds of the members present. Karen Rose of Charlottetown was appointed Prince Edward Island's first information and privacy commissioner on 19 November 2002.

Several other notable acts were passed. An Act to Amend the Health and Community Services Act was passed that provided for the establishment of a new Provincial Health Services Authority and a new Advisory Council. The Act to Amend the Family Law Act was passed, replacing references to 'a man and a woman' with references to either 'two persons' or to a 'common-law partner' with respect to domestic contracts. Also, The Smoke-free Places Act was passed, prohibiting smoking in a public place or workplace unless it is carried out in an area designated for smoking in accordance with the Act, including posting of signs and complaint investigation by inspectors. On 1 August, the government announced the appointment of twenty volunteer provincial police constables to monitor activity on the Confederation Trail. The trail is part of the Trans-Canada Trail system and runs the length of Prince Edward Island. On December 6 legislation was tabled making it mandatory to wear bicycle helmets for everyone cycling on Island roads. And finally, The Companion Animal Act, passed by the assembly in the autumn of 2001, allowed intervention to prevent abuse to companion animals and for the licensing and inspection of businesses that sell or display companion animals.

The provincial government charged its Standing Committee on Agriculture, Forestry, and Environment with examining the events surrounding the potato wart fungus crisis, which had led to the closure of the U.S. border to PEI potato exports in 2000 and 2001. As part of this investigation, the committee had, in December 2001, subpoenaed two representatives of the federal Canadian Food Inspection Agency to appear before them. This action had followed CFIA's repeated refusal to volunteer their employees. In January 2002 the federal government made application to have the subpoenas stayed. Legal wrangling concerning the committee's rights to require testimony continued, and had not been resolved by the end of 2002. In October there was another conflict brewing between the provincial and federal governments; the boundary of the exclusion zone along the northeastern shore of PEI where herring seiners were not allowed to fish became an issue between Island fishers represented by their provincial government and the federal Department of Fisheries and Oceans. An uneasy compromise agreement was reached, which moved the boundary farther offshore in attempts to protect the lobster habitat and future herring stocks.

On 19 April in a debate in the Legislative Assembly concerning a motion dealing with child pornography, Belfast-Pownal Bay MLA Wilbur MacDonald made comments that associated the decline of Canadian society with immigrants; these comments resulted in several days of furore in the local and national media. MacDonald later gave an emotionally charged unqualified apology in the legislature for these comments, resigned from the Standing Committee on Social Development that he chaired, and resigned from the government's Strategic Planning Committee.

On 22 August Premier Binns made several changes to the provincial cabinet; he created a Department of Fisheries and Aquaculture, gave new responsibilities to four existing ministers, and introduced a new member into the cabinet. On 5 December Environment Minister Chester Gillan announced that two potentially cancer-causing pesticides, Telone C-17 and Vapon, used by strawberry plant operations, were to be banned after being found in four private wells in Alberton. Only the day before Gillan had said in the media that the province was in no rush to ban the chemicals.

The third session of the sixty-first general assembly prorogued on 10 May after a total of forty-five sitting days (fall and spring sittings). The fourth session of the sixty-first general assembly of Prince Edward Island opened on 14 November with the reading of the Speech from the Throne by Lieutenant Governor J. Léonce Bernard and adjourned on 18 December after nineteen sitting days.

In the Speech from the Throne the government announced an independent commission to consult on and consider changing PEI's electoral system by reviewing methods of proportional representation. Norman J. Carruthers, retired chief justice of the Supreme Court of PEI, was appointed to head the Prince Edward Island Commission on Electoral Reform.

Auditor General Wayne Murphy, FCA, announced his intention to retire as of 31 July. A new procedure to appoint Murphy's successor was proposed by Opposition leader Ron MacKinley that would reinforce the message that the position was independent, impartial, and directly accountable to the Legislative Assembly. MacKinley proposed amending the Audit Act to give selection authority to the speaker, the provincial treasurer, and the opposition leader in consultation with the Standing Committee on Public Accounts. Colin Yonker, CA, was appointed Prince Edward Island's auditor general on 7 October using the procedures of the original Act; however, the 14 November Speech from the Throne indicated that the government would introduce measures to 'enhance the autonomy of the Auditor General.'

Finally, the most prominent story of 2002 centered around Lawrence MacAulay, MP for Cardigan and solicitor general of Canada. In the last week of May MacAulay was under attack by opposition MPs, who charged that he used his position in attempts to secure $3.5 million from the RCMP for a police-training program at Holland College in Charlottetown; MacAulay's brother Alex was president of Holland College. The RCMP turned down the application. On 22 October MacAulay resigned as solicitor general after several weeks of renewed allegations in the national media that he was involved in conflicts of interest and patronage, although he maintained that he had done nothing wrong and retained the confidence of Prime Minister Jean Chrétien. Ethics Counsellor Howard Wilson reported on 18 October to the prime minister that MacAulay had violated cabinet guidelines by intervening in an application for federal funding by Holland College, although he cleared MacAulay of other allegations centred on an untendered $100,000 government contract to two of his political associates in Prince Edward Island. Many Islanders came to MacAulay's defence, claiming that the popular politician was simply doing what he was elected to do in trying to bring some prosperity to his riding and to his province. Earlier allegations of improprieties had been levelled against MacAulay by both Conservative and Alliance MPs regarding to the awarding of the approximately $17 million contract for the Parks Canada Greenwich Interpretive Centre project to the development company APM, in turn owned by Tim Banks, who was for a short while in 2002 the PEI Liberal Party president. There were also questions raised about APM's landing a contract for renovations to the Confederation Centre and how Montague was chosen for the solicitor general's Addiction Research Centre. Malpeque MP Wayne Easter was sworn in as solicitor general the same day that MacAulay resigned.

Businessmen Tim Banks was narrowly defeated as president of the PEI Liberal Party by University of Prince Edward Island Professor Tim Carroll, on 2 November at the party's annual general meeting, following much public bickering between Banks and the Liberal's one elected MLA, Ron MacKinley.

Other events

On 2 January Senator Heath Nelson Macquarrie died. Senator Macquarrie was elected eight times to the House of Commons in the period from 1957 to 1974, as MP for the former federal riding of Queen's and later for Hillsborough. Prime Minister Joe Clark appointed him to the Senate in 1979. Macquarrie retired from the Senate in 1994. Prominent Island businessman Harry W. MacLauchlan passed away on 27 March; MacLauchlan was very active in community service, owned and operated a wide range of Island-based businesses, and employed hundreds of Islanders over the years. On 10 October Premier Pat Binns dedicated the Province House Annex, built in 1872, as the J. Angus MacLean Building, after the legendary former premier and Island MP who died in 2000. In another dedication on 19 June, Premier Binns designated the 216 kilometre Route 2 that spans the Island as the 'Veterans Memorial Highway' commemorating Island servicemen and servicewomen.

PEI's first poet laureate, Dr John Smith, author of five volumes of poetry and professor emeritus at the University of Prince Edward Island, was announced on 5 December; the appointment was for a two-year term. In a presentation on 10 December, Douglas B. Boylan was named the first recipient of the Institute of Public Administration Canada – Lieutenant Governor's Award for Excellence in Public Administration. Boylan was secretary to the cabinet and clerk of the executive council for sixteen years, clerk of the Legislative Assembly for three years, and clerk assistant for eighteen years.

Water quality was an issue in 2002. Charlottetown and Stratford had repeated cases of home wells contaminated by coliform and *E. coli* bacteria. *E. coli* also hospitalized two boys attending Camp Abegweit in Augustine Cove in mid-August; thirteen of seventy people attending the camp became ill. The source was not found. Starting 19 October, there was an *E. coli* outbreak at the Hillsborough Hospital in Charlottetown that originally affected fourteen patients and thirty-one staff; a later epidemiological investigation identified 101 people who were probably affected, and at least one patient died from the bacterium. In a media release of 26 November, Chief Health Officer Dr Lamont Sweet indicated that the likely source of the bacterium was the hospital kitchen.

Several items in 2002 brought Prince Edward Island into the national and international news spotlight. PEI was subject to national media scrutiny in late summer when the current affairs television program W-Five aired a critical report on the Island potato industry's use of pesticides. Another sensation was created by a PEI trial reported in news media around the world of the former nun and self-described prophet Lucille Poulin, age 78, who was convicted and sentenced to eight months in jail and to three years probation for savagely assaulting five children at the religious commune that she operated at Hazel Grove. Also prominent in the news was the unsolved murder of Chrystal Beairsto, a 23-year-old mother of two, found dead in Charlottetown along the Confederation Trail on 28 July. Media attention focused as well on the strike of six female caregivers at the non-profit Southern Kings Group Home Inc. in Montague. These women were represented by the Canadian Union of Public Employees and had been on strike for the last seven months of 2002. At the end of the year, the strike remained unresolved.

Other things of note in Prince Edward Island in 2002 included the completion of the province-wide implementation of Waste Watch. In 2002 mandatory crop rotation and soil conservation measures took effect for PEI's farming industry. Charlottetown became part of a 'Smart Communities' project – one of twelve communities in Canada – that saw the introduction of an electronic council chamber and direct delivery system for some city services. In late November a ground-breaking ceremony was held at the University of Prince Edward Island campus for an $18 million sports facility that includes two rinks, two pools, and a senior's active living centre. The decision to locate it at UPEI was made after public opposition to a previous decision to build the facility on the 88-acre green space of the Experimental (Home) Farm property in Charlottetown.

ROBERT G. FINBOW

Nova Scotia

The international conflict with terrorists after the 11 September 2001 attacks affected Nova Scotia directly in April 2002. Two Nova Scotians, Private Richard Green of Mill Cove and Private Nathan Smith of Ostrea Lake near Musquodoboit Harbour, were killed by 'friendly fire' when U.S. warplanes mistook them for Taliban forces. Two other Canadian soldiers were also killed. There was dismay at the lack of communication between Canadian and U.S. personnel and alleged overzealousness by the U.S. pilots. President George W. Bush was criticized for his belated apology to the families, but charges were brought against the pilots. Numerous Nova Scotian service personnel served in the conflict, designed to prevent Afghanistan from remaining a safe haven for terrorists. Canadian naval ships maintained surveillance operations in the region to prevent potential escapes by Al Qaeda and Taliban forces.

Globalization affected Nova Scotia in other ways. The G7 finance ministers' meeting in Halifax turned ugly when police used tear gas to disperse protestors, prompting complaints of police misconduct. Lithuanian refugees were mysteriously dropped off by a small boat on the province's Eastern Shore after a trans-Atlantic journey. The provincial economy managed to ride out the post 9/11 economic downturn in the United States with a credible performance. Overall, the province experienced a relatively quiet political year despite the global tumult.

The legislature

The spring legislative session, broadcast on the Internet for the first time, opened with no Speech from the Throne. The Opposition claimed the government lacked a plan for the future. Premier John Hamm emphasized a balanced budget and three core spending priorities: health, education, and roads. The government claimed a milestone when it introduced a balanced budget, the first in the province in decades. The budget sought $80 million in additional revenues, from taxes, user fees, and alcohol sales, to bring in a surplus of $1.3 million despite $47 million in new spending. According to Finance Minister Neil LeBlanc, the budget would reduce debt servicing costs and allow more funds for education, health, and other services. The Opposition alleged that the government's omission of capital borrowing for new schools and hospitals from the budget was dishonest, allowing it to claim a surplus even though the province's debt would actually increase by more than $100 million.

Hikes in gas and cigarette taxes and higher fees for drivers' licences, ambulances, and ferry transport drew criticism. Amid controvery, $30 million in revenues was to be raised from new video lottery terminals, $10 million more from lotteries, and a further $4 million from casinos, which critics asserted risked increasing problem gambling in the province. The Tories postponed a 10 per cent cut in personal taxes but promised to reduce debt without cuts to health or education. By the year's end the finance minister had announced that the projected surplus had increased to $8.3 million from stronger economic growth, higher tax intakes, and reduced deficits in district health authorities. But a decrease in transfers from Ottawa, particularly $60 million in equalization payments, reduced the surplus.

Overall, twenty-nine bills were passed in the spring session. Premier Hamm described an anti-smoking bill, which he claimed was the strongest in the country, as a 'real coup' that would reduce long-term health costs, but the Opposition sought a complete public smoking ban. Healthcare spending, which consumed 40 per cent of the provincial budget, was up in excess of $130 million over the previous year. But the Opposition charged that this increase in spending was only enough to cover wage hikes and would still mean reduced services in some communities. In particular, critics claimed that increased premiums for pharmacare would negatively affect seniors on fixed incomes. Protestors chanted 'People will die' as they called for funds to reduce hospital bed closures and cancelled surgeries. Many protestors were from the Annapolis Valley, where the health district's $7.2 million deficit forced cutbacks; some regional hospitals faced permanent closure of intensive care or emergency rooms, and patients and families were forced to commute distances of up to 120 kilometres for care.

Post-secondary students staged protests in Halifax and Sydney over escalating tuition, which they claimed limited access to higher education. Students briefly occupied Royal Bank offices to protest the inadequate student loans managed by that firm. Critics feared that cuts to family violence programs could force transition houses to close and expose more women and children to violent situations; the minister of community services acknowledged that one-third of the transition house beds might close, but promised to deliver these protective services in new ways. Another bill expanded the jurisdiction of small-claims court to include landlord–tenant disputes.

The fall session was short and inactive, with only a few minor provisions adopted, including adjustments to workers' compensation. The sessions were often brief or postponed altogether, prompting charges that the Hamm government was avoiding controversial issues. One sitting lasted only forty-two minutes. Legal experts questioned a bill that allowed police to use broader investigative techniques on violations of provincial laws; NDP justice critic Kevin Deveaux feared that the vagueness of the bill could allow the police to use surveillance, wiretaps, and other tactics that could violate privacy. The Opposition criticized increased fees under the Freedom of Information and Protection of Privacy Act, which, they asserted, limited public access to critical information. Applications for access dropped by 25 per cent following the increase; a government committee reconsidered the fees, and a decision was pending at year's end.

The redistribution of electoral districts also proved contentious, as the committee responsible, bound by tight rules, left Metropolitan Halifax underrepresented and gave more than a per capita share of seats to rural districts. The all-party committee, with a Conservative majority, allowed riding populations to deviate by up to 25 per cent from the average, undermining the principle of one person, one vote. Even so, Halifax gained a seat at Cape Breton's expense, and rural politicians feared decreased representation in the future in light of the capital's strong growth. A Liberal proposal to reduce the eligible age to run for provincial elected office to 18, consistent with the age of majority, was approved in the hope of dispelling youths' apathy towards politics.

Politics

The two opposition parties selected new leaders. The NDP sought a replacement for Helen MacDonald, who led the party briefly but resigned after she lost a by-election bid. The NDP selected Dartmouth–Cole Harbour MLA Darrell Dexter, the interim leader, whose low-key style had been well received. Dexter handily defeated Hants East MLA John MacDonell, who based his campaign on his considerable charisma, his appeal to rural voters, and his advocacy of increased accountability in the party. His campaign was, however, hampered by his role in the MacDonald ouster, which eroded his support among Cape Breton delegates. In other NDP news, federal NDP leader Alexa McDonough announced that she would step down, although she would remain as MP for Halifax.

The NDP kept the issue of health care costs for nursing home patients on the front burner. Seniors had to submit all their assets to a government audit and were, in some cases, asked to turn over savings, pensions, insurance plans, and even cars to pay for services normally provided under the province's Medical Services Insurance. Many seniors and their spouses confronted poverty and uncertainty when income and savings were turned over to cover health care costs. Many citizens signed a petition calling for an end to these practices. The government promised only vague improvements and did not guarantee to address the issue before the next election. This debate helped Dexter appear as a moderate concerned for families' well-being, with appeal to elusive rural voters; but he trailed the other leaders in popularity in year-end polls nonetheless.

Meanwhile, the Liberals selected Danny Graham, son of Liberal Senator Al Graham, as their leader on the first ballot. He defeated businessman Francis Mackenzie and Halifax broadcaster Bruce Graham. The party backed off a planned $20 fee for members to cast a leadership ballot after a food-bank worker from Cape Breton alleged that an agent for Mackenzie offered to pay the $20 plus a $10 membership fee to secure his vote; the unproven allegation caused a stir in the campaign and possibly harmed the candidate's chances. The Liberals, under youthful leader Graham, positioned themselves as a party of reform and proposed a fixed date for provincial elections. A poll near the end of the year showed Graham rivalling Hamm in popularity and the Liberals moved into second place behind the Conservatives. Former Minister and Deputy Premier Don Downe decided to leave provincial politics, depriving the Liberal caucus of an experienced member.

The Liberals were embarrassed by a human rights case pressed by a Halifax lawyer who charged that he was not awarded government jobs in the 1990s because he was not a member of the Liberal Party. Prominent politicians for all three parties were called before the Human Rights Commission to examine charges of patronage and discrimination made by the plaintiff. The government reached a settlement, promising to spend on education about mental health and political discrimination, and to advertise positions more fully to discourage political favouritism. But the government missed an opportunity to demonstrate its commitment when it appointed a Conservative Party member to head the Human Resources Committee, which oversees appointments to agencies, boards, and commissions. The Opposition proposed a review to determine which agencies required non-partisan appointments and which positions might be appropriately deemed political. MLA Graham Steele proposed that quasi-judicial tribunals dealing with utilities, rents, pay equity, and health and safety should remain outside the government's patronage network.

The NDP queried the government's hiring of high-priced officials at Nova Scotia Business Inc., which had been created to reduce administrative overhead. It replaced the Department of Economic Development, which had only one deputy minister paid more than $100,000 a year. NSBI had four officials salaried in excess of $90,000. Economic Development Minister Gordon Balser said the high salaries were required to compete with private sector positions and that the province's growth rate – second only to Alberta's – indicated the success of NSBI. A loan deferral granted to Ocean Nutrition Canada Ltd., a company owned by one of NSBI's most prominent private sector board members, generated controversy. NSBI's president declared that the decision to extend Ocean Nutrition Canada's payment deadline was reviewed by an independent group comprised of prominent businessmen, under guidelines that prohibited conflicts of interest on the part of board members. But NSBI's refusal to release the names of the purportedly independent observers generated scepticism about the process by which Ocean Nutrition Canada Ltd. was given a four-year reprieve on its loan repayments.

The Opposition also alleged that the premier's claim that he employed a staff of twelve at $750,000 annually, overlooked six speech writers and policy researchers who were billed under the Treasury Board, effectively concealing another $297,000 in staffing expenses. The premier's chief of staff was also guaranteed a salary and severance package for a period exceeding the government's mandate. The NDP also criticized nearly $500,000 in legal and consulting fees for the premier's "campaign for fairness." The rehiring of a senior civil servant who had earlier received a severance package was also condemned.

The arts community was upset when the government dismissed staff from the Nova Scotia Council for the Arts and curtailed its budget. The council was later replaced by a new Arts and Culture Council in the tourism ministry, headed by a civil servant with no arts background; the government emphasized regional cultural advisory boards in place of the council. The arts community sought a return to the former arm's-length Nova Scotia Council for the Arts to avoid political interference regarding grants, which should, many proclaimed, be awarded solely on artistic merit.

Nova Scotians marked the tenth anniversary of the Westray mine disaster with a solemn ceremony at the site. After the failed prosecution of mine owners and managers, the Opposition pressed for a prosecutor with training in health and safety issues to pursue violations. The minister of justice noted that the Criminal Code made these matters a subject for federal prosecution. Westray's final assets were sold at public auction

Premier Hamm had back surgery in April and again in December. His health and age (64) sparked speculation about his pending retirement, but he seemed determined to remain for a spring election in 2003. Hamm shuffled his cabinet in December to reinvigorate his team for the coming election. Critics decried the shuffle as a cynical means to move ministers from core portfolios so that they could avoid accountability for prior mistakes. For instance, Education Minister Jane Purves, who was moved to health, had been criticized for the closure of a popular French immersion school and contentious contract talks with teachers that were resolved only after the appointment of a conciliator. The premier made announcements on health care spending and other popular programs, which indicated that an election was imminent. As the year 2002 drew to a close, the Tories revived questions about the Liberal Party's trust funds, allegedly secured under previous governments by kickbacks from contractors; this renewed attack was widely interpreted as indicating concern within Conservative ranks about the Liberals' improved poll numbers.

The economy

Provincial economic performance remained steady in 2002, but with minimal job growth. Overall, economic figures for the year were positive, despite disruptions from the U.S. economic slowdown. The economy grew 3.1 per cent, with employment up by 1.1 per cent. Only 5,000 new jobs were created, however, and these consisted of mostly part-time positions filled by women. Employment in Halifax decreased slightly for the second straight year. The unemployment rate in the metropolitan era edged up to 7.6 per cent, with job losses in the civil service, health care, and education. This was offset somewhat by a strong housing market that, driven by low interest rates, fuelled construction and strengthened consumer confidence, which in turn bolstered retail sales. Manufacturing growth was limited, but some jobs were created, especially by rail orders and offshore contracts at Trenton Works Ltd. Exports decreased by 6 per cent, with corresponding drops in commodity prices.

Natural gas replaced fish as the province's top export. But gas development suffered a blow when Sempra Atlantic Gas, selected by the government to be the commercial distributor of natural gas in the province, pulled out over the potential costs of safety regulations for pipeline construction. Regulators accepted Sempra's decision to cede distribution rights when the province would not let it build pipelines in highway shoulders, a cheaper but arguably hazardous approach. The changing energy market made the proposal to ensure delivery of gas to 75 per cent of residences in the province unviable. To encourage distribution, the government allowed firms to bid for rights in limited areas and permitted municipalities to seek local distribution rights. The Opposition supported the changes, although expressing concerns about rural access. While Nova Scotia waited for royalties and supplies, its gas was already available in New Brunswick and Maine.

Estimates of reserves on the Sable field were reduced by one-third, and a decision on the Deep Panuke project was delayed. There was pessimism about additional reserves, although successful tests by Marathon Oil in the Annapolis field revived interest. Other companies resumed deep water drilling. Complaints about the awarding of contracts on offshore projects to firms based outside the province were partially addressed when Irving's Halifax Shipyards was chosen for part of the Sable Tier II development. But despite continued spin-offs, the slow pace of development frustrated provincial leaders, who felt that firms were not providing enough local benefits; industry blamed uncertain supply and convoluted regulations and approval procedures.

The forestry industry remained divided over sustainable practices in harvesting timber and pulp resources. A split emerged within the Nova Scotia Forest Alliance, a federally funded group designed to promote sustainable practices. Small woodlot owners and environmentalists pulled out over alleged insincerity on the part of large firms and the provincial government. The dissidents claimed that the decline in mature and old-growth trees reflected unsustainable clear-cutting, but industry blamed natural causes, such as spruce-budworm infestation. While pulp and paper production and exports decreased, lumber shipments were strong; the region received a partial exemption from U.S. duties on softwood lumber, although prices decreased by 17 per cent because of the ongoing trade dispute.

Tourism was affected by the U.S. slowdown, bad weather, and poor transportation links. Revenues were up 5 per cent, led by an increase in cruise ship visits. The return of some discount air carriers produced hope for future expansion. The province considered buying the Cape Breton portion of the railway line to see if new private investors could be found after its U.S. operator abandoned the unprofitable route.

The opposition criticized the government for not requiring Nova Scotia Power to retain more linesmen after lengthy power outages caused by storms; the firm had cut 20 per cent of its linesmen since 1997, when the Utilities and Review Board warned it lacked sufficient personnel to cope with major outages. The government resisted calls for an inquiry, arguing that the company had improved response times by bringing in personnel from neighbouring jurisdictions.

Projects based on new technologies and the information economy proceeded. These included call centres in Cape Breton, investments in research and universities, and a magnetic resonance imaging (MRI) clinic in Halifax. A disappointing poll showed that high-technology investors and executives avoid Nova Scotia, which they consider backward, overtaxed, and depressed (*Daily News* [Halifax], 12 July).

Intergovernmental relations

Halifax hosted the annual meeting of provincial and territorial leaders in August. The premier and his counterparts called on Ottawa to address funding shortfalls in health care by increasing its transfers and strengthening equalization. The premiers cited a Conference Board of Canada report to illustrate the growing 'fiscal imbalance' between Ottawa and the provinces and the chronic shortfall in provincial coffers for essential services. Premier Hamm cited this report as evidence of the need for 'fairness' in intergovernmental finances via improved equalization that addressed provincial needs and the instability of provincial incomes based on volatile resource revenues. The province collaborated with its neighbours to find ways to cut health care costs, including a joint review process for the approval of medicines.

The premier continued to press Ottawa for more favourable treatment regarding revenues generated from offshore projects. Under the status quo, Ottawa receives 81 per cent of Nova Scotia's offshore royalties through clawbacks applied to the province's equalization payments: Hamm hoped to reduce or eliminate these deductions. Federal Intergovernmental Affairs Minister Stéphane Dion criticized the premier for targeting equalization payments for redress, since, were the federal government to accede to Nova Scotia's demands, other provinces would want similar adjustments. Dion rejected the notion that the province had been treated 'unfairly' but promised to consider other modifications. Federal Industry Minister Allan Rock proposed that Ottawa channel its share of offshore revenues to business development initiatives in Atlantic Canada, but Nova Scotia and Newfoundland both rejected this proposition.

Premier Hamm joined his regional counterparts in welcoming Roy Romanow's royal commission report on health care. Hamm supported Romanow's recommendations for long-term stable funding, arguing that this would allow the province to modernize equipment, hire more health care professionals, and reduce wait times for essential procedures and care. Health Minister Jamie Muir wanted Ottawa to go beyond the report to fund nursing home care – a sensitive issue, given the province's aging population. Nova Scotia, like other provinces, resisted federal restrictions on the use of health care funds, although the province agreed to account for how it spends the federal transfers. But Ottawa resisted provincial demands for $25 billion in new funding for health care; federal officials suggested that even the Romanow Commission's proposal for $15 billion in federal health care transfers to provinces would not be realized in the near future.

Nova Scotia lost a battle over offshore boundaries with Newfoundland, which affected offshore energy exploration on the Laurentian Shelf. An arbitration panel awarded the province only 10 per cent of this potentially lucrative area. Companies were not quick to begin exploratory drilling. Cape Breton environmentalists planned to fight any exploration or sonic testing, which could harm these sensitive environs. The province also tussled with New Brunswick, which wanted a "Canada first" approach to its neighbour's offshore gas, shipped directly to U.S. markets at this time. Although the pipelines went through New Brunswick, Nova Scotia wanted to be able to sell its gas to the highest bidder regardless of nationality.

On environmental issues, Nova Scotia joined in calling for a first ministers' meeting on federal plans to fulfil Canada's commitments under the Kyoto Protocol on climate change. The province pulled out of a December meeting, when it appeared that Ottawa would ratify the Kyoto Protocol without addressing provincial concerns about economic effects and funding for efforts to reduce greenhouse gases. Provincial officials feared economic slowdown and higher electricity bills if the use of coal for power generation was phased out under Kyoto.

The province and Halifax Regional Municipality contested funding for cleaning up Halifax Harbour. In correspondence with Ottawa, the premier initially ranked the sewage treatment project as a low priority for federal infrastructure dollars in favour of highway projects. The city and the province then accused each other of undermining the project. The premier later clarified that the harbour project was a priority along with four major highway upgrades. With $2 billion budgeted nationally for the Canada Strategic Infrastructure Fund, Halifax had to settle for a federal contribution of $30 million for the $315 million sewage treatment system. The city signed a deal with a private group to construct treatment facilities despite a shortfall of some $45 million.

The province and Ottawa collaborated on rural water and highway upgrades. The Opposition charged that these agreements were given priority because they improved the government's prospects of re-election, given the Conservatives' rural electoral base. But the government countered that concerns about highway safety and rural water contamination, including boil water orders in several communities, made these deals vital.

In other intergovernmental ventures, Mi'kmaq leaders commenced negotiations with the province and Ottawa on treaty rights and access to natural resources, including unresolved disputes stemming from the Marshall decision on the fisheries. Ottawa and the province announced a plan, in partnership with the private sector, to attract skilled immigrant workers and entrepreneurs, as well as a program to retrain older workers. The two governments also agreed to give $4 million to hog farmers to compensate for decreased pork prices. But major federal–provincial agreements on business and research promotion came to an end, and were replaced with the five-year Atlantic Investment Partnership and the Strategic Community Investment Fund, unilaterally directed by Ottawa. The provincial Liberals blamed the provincial government for slashing its contributions to the previous partnerships.

Federal Canadian Alliance Party leader Stephen Harper raised hackles when he described the Atlantic region as suffering from a 'culture of defeat.' The Nova Scotia Legislative Assembly voted unanimously to condemn the comment, which Harper suggested had been misinterpreted. Federal Conservative House Leader Peter MacKay declared that the remark reflected Harper's 'ill-informed and antagonistic attitude' and 'demonstrates the thinly veiled biases and provincial prejudices in the Alliance party.' MacKay rejected calls for a joint leadership race for the two right-of-centre parties.

MELVIN BAKER AND PETER NEARY

Newfoundland and Labrador

The management – past, present, and future – of natural resources dominated public discussion in Newfoundland and Labrador in 2002. Early in the year public attention focused on a possible operations restructuring by Fishery Products International, of St John's, the province's major fish-processing company. The proposed change threatened the well-being of several communities. Following the election in May 2001 of a new board of directors, supported by Clearwater Fine Foods Inc. of Nova Scotia, FPI had sought to reassure the Government of Newfoundland and Labrador about the effect of the corporate takeover that had occurred: 'Our goal is to grow our Company in a manner which provides security to our current workforce while at the same time increasing employment in Newfoundland and Labrador' (Fisheries and Aquaculture, News Release, 10 January 2002).

On 9 January, however, FPI, which was now planning to take over Clearwater, made known its plan to eliminate 580 jobs at three plants – in Fortune, Marystown, and Harbour Breton. This in turn derailed contract talks with the Fish, Food and Allied Workers Union, which represented over 2,500 of the company's plant workers. The government responded by declaring its intention to hold the company to the commitment it had made following the corporate restructuring of 2001. In pursuit of this objective the government launched an all-party committee of the legislature that toured the province, beginning in late January, seeking public input on the difficulty that had arisen. The first public meeting was held in Marystown on 28 January. On this occasion FPI was represented by former provincial and federal cabinet minister John Crosbie, now a prominent member of the company's new board of directors. Crosbie received a rough reception, but told the meeting that the company had abandoned its plan to cut jobs. Then, on 15 February, faced with a rising tide of political and public opposition, FPI and Clearwater cancelled their plan merger. Next, the legislature amended the 1987 legislation that had launched FPI as a private company (it had previously been publicly owned). The amendment strengthened the existing share ownership rule to ensure that no person or corporation could hold more than 15 per cent of the issued and outstanding securities of any class of the company. This change received royal assent on 14 March.

Jobs had been saved in rural Newfoundland, but life there was anything but static. In April Municipal and Provincial Affairs Minister Oliver Langdon announced that the province would provide financial compensation if all 120 residents of Great Harbour Deep agreed to move from their physically isolated community on the Great Northern Peninsula. Until both the northern cod fishery and the local fish-processing plant closed in 1992, about 300 people had lived in the community. But it did not have a road connection to the rest of the province and depended for transportation on a government-subsidized ferry service, which operated in summer and fall only and involved a three-hour journey to Jackson's Arm. Over the years many local residents had voluntarily left to seek employment elsewhere, and after 1992 the remaining residents tried to get the government to resettle them at public expense. In 2002 their wish was granted and they thereby became part of the resettlement history of modern Newfoundland.

In St John's the fourth session of the Forty-Fourth General Assembly opened on 19 March with the reading of the speach from the Throne by Lieutenant Governor A. Maxwell House. The highlight of the speech was the announcement that a Royal Commission on Renewing and Strengthening Our Place in Canada would be appointed forthwith. The commission, the speech explained, would have 'a broad mandate' to do research and consult the public throughout the province (House of Assembly, Speech from the Throne, 19 March). 'The Commission's mandate will be to involve the people of the province in seeking a ... consensus on a vision to position ourselves in the global community ... renew our relationship with Canada ... complete a critical analysis of our strengths and weaknesses and ... promote direction for the decade to come. It will address, among other things, who we were when we joined Canada in 1949, how we have changed over the past five decades, our relationship with other governments, our contribution as a society and where we see ourselves in the future' (Ibid.). On 19 April the government issued the terms of reference of the royal commission and appointed its members. Victor Young, former chief executive officer of FPI, was named chair. His associates were Sister Elizabeth Davis, former CEO of the Health Corporation of St John's, and Judge James Igliorte, a former negotiator for the Labrador Inuit Association in its land claims discussions with the province. The commissioners were instructed to file their report no later than 30 June 2003.

The Speech from the Throne also reaffirmed the province's determination to campaign with the other provinces to reform Canada's equalization program: Newfoundland and Labrador should no longer be disadvantaged because of its growing natural resources revenues. The budget speech for the fiscal year 2002–3, delivered on 21 March by Finance Minister Joan Marie Aylward, forecast total expenditures of approximately $4 billion and a deficit of $93.3 million. The budget provided additional funding for healthcare and education (including a 10 per cent tuition reduction for undergraduate students at Memorial University), and funds for improved transportation in Labrador.

The province's economy grew again in 2002, thanks mainly to a whopping 92.1 per cent increase in offshore oil production. During the year oil production reached 104.3 million barrels and was valued at $4.1 billion. Petro-Canada's Terra Nova field produced its first oil on 20 January, and production for the year was 38.5 million barrels. On 28 March Husky Energy and Petro-Canada announced that they would proceed with development at a third offshore site – White Rose – with production scheduled to begin in late 2005. For several years oil production had been inflating gross domestic product numbers in the province, but much of the newly created wealth actually went as profits to the oil companies and as taxes to the federal government. Oil-related activities were, however, providing a big stimulus to the housing market in metropolitan St John's, where housing starts in 2002 reached their highest levels since 1992. The housing performance was driven by employment gains, higher incomes, and low mortgage rates. Total fish landings for 2002 grew by 2.5 per cent over 2001, with the crab and shrimp fisheries at the fore.

There was also very good news for the province in the decision of the federal arbitration tribunal, established on 31 May 2000 to settle a long-simmering offshore boundary dispute with Nova Scotia in the Laurentian Basin. The tribunal was appointed under the settlement provisions of the Canada–Newfoundland Atlantic Accord Implementation Act (1987) and the Canada–Nova Scotia Offshore Petroleum Resources Accord Implementation Act (1988). The chair of the tribunal was the Honourable Gérard La Forest, a retired justice of the Supreme Court of Canada; its other members were Leonard Legault, chairman of the Canadian section of the International Joint Commission; and Dr James Richard Crawford, professor of international law at the Cambridge University. Their decision, rendered on 26 March, and final and binding on the parties, favoured the Newfoundland and Labrador position and confirmed the province in possession of about 70 per cent of the 60,000 square kilometres of seabed in dispute.

Tourism remained another bright spot in the economy in 2002, with expenditures by non-resident travellers up by 5 per cent during the year to an estimated $304.5 million. On 27 January and 3 and 4 February television viewers across Canada saw something of the province's early settlement history when the CBC featured the mini-series *Random Passage,* based on two historical novels by local author Bernice Morgan. The provincial government advertised heavily during this series as part of its campaign to attract visitors eastwards. On 14 April the Juno Awards ceremony was held at Mile One Stadium in St John's. This was only the second time that the event had been held outside Ontario, and the occasion was made possible by a provincial government sponsorship contribution of $550,000. In September the province hosted and sponsored North America's first Targa-style international car rally. This week-long event attracted international collectors of historic, classic, and modern sporting cars, with the vehicles being seen in various communities in eastern and central Newfoundland. The government hoped that the rally would become an annual event on the provincial tourism calendar. With another future attraction in mind, Premier Roger Grimes announced on 4 October that provincial funding of $150,000 would be given to the 2004 Society, which was promoting the celebration of five centuries of French presence in the province. An appropriate year for this is 2004 because it marks the centenary of the Anglo-French Entente Cordiale, which settled the tangled French Shore question in Newfoundland.

From a tourism marketing perspective in 2002, the province highlighted the attractions of Labrador through a Labrador Access North program of events. Specifically, the province honoured the 250th anniversary of the Moravian presence among the Inuit of northern Labrador. This important anniversary was marked with a symposium on the history and progress of the Moravian Church in the region, held 8-10 August in Makkovik and Hopedale. There was also a travelling photo exhibition, which featured pictures from the Moravian archives in Hernhut, Germany, taken by Moravian missionaries. Sponsored by the provincial government, the symposium and exhibit were organized and led by Dr Hans Rollmann of Memorial University's religious studies department, a leading international scholar of Moravian history and life.

On 11 June, with summer delights in prospect around the province, the government announced that it had reached agreement with Inco for the development of the Voisey's Bay nickel deposit in northern Labrador. According to a statement of principles between the two parties, Inco agreed to construct a $710 million mine and mill and concentrator at Voisey's Bay, build an $85 million hydrometallurgical (hydromet) processing plant at Argentia to determine whether this advanced technology was suited to the processing of Voisey's Bay concentrate, and establish a $10 million research centre at Memorial University and provide this facility with operating funds of $1 milion per year for ten years. Inco was not permitted to ship nickel concentrate from Voisey's Bay until the Argentia facility was ready to begin testing. Thereafter it could ship concentrate from Labrador to its plants in Sudbury, Ontario, and Thompson, Manitoba, but beginning in 2012 concentrate would have to be processed at a commercial hydromet plant to be built at Argentia at an estimated capital cost of $800 million and completed by 31 December 2011. If (this was considered unlikely) hydromet technology proved not to be feasible for Voisey's Bay concentrate, a state-of-the-art commercial plant using a proven technology would be built at Argentia according to the same schedule. Inco also guaranteed that, before the cessation of mining operations at Voisey's Bay, it would commence replacement of concentrate shipped out of the province for refining. The company likewise undertook to enter into impacts and benefits agreements that it had negotiated with the Labrador Inuit Association and the Innu Nation.

Over its thirty-year lifespan, the government estimated, the Voisey's Bay project would provide 76,000 direct and indirect person-years of employment in the province and add $11 billion to the provincial gross domestic product. 'Government,' said Premier Grimes at the news conference announcing the deal, 'made a commitment to the people of the province that the Voisey's Bay nickel deposit would be developed in a manner that maximizes benefits for Newfoundland and Labrador. We had fundamental requirements that Voisey's Bay nickel concentrate would be processed in the province to a finished nickel metal product and that any concentrate shipped out would be replaced for processing. We have achieved each of these objectives ... Today's announcement confirms that this government will only sign deals that achieve maximum benefits for the people of Newfoundland and Labrador. It also demonstrates that this province continues to be an attractive place to invest and to conduct business' (Executive Council, New Release, 11 June).

On 18 June the House of Assembly met for three days of debate on the proposed agreement. Introducing the resolution to ratify and endorse the statement of principles, Premier Grimes waxed eloquent on what had been achieved. 'We believe,' he said, 'we have negotiated a great deal. We believe there is a great business case that makes sure that Inco can succeed. We believe they will be able to raise the financing because it is a great project. It is good for them. It is good for us' (*Hansard*, 19 June). By contrast Opposition Leader Danny Williams told the House that he had 'a sick, nauseated feeling' in his stomach, 'that feeling that you have when something wrong is about to happen, something terribly wrong' (Ibid.). Williams described the scheme embodied in the statement of principles as a 'giveaway': 'We have given away too much too often ... We have given away our hydro and the Upper Churchill to the tune of $1 billion a year. Our fish are gone to foreigners. Our iron ore has gone to Quebec. Our oil is going to the States. Now it is going to be our nickel ... Why, on this particular project, are we creating jobs for people in Ontario and Manitoba?' (Ibid.) It was amazing that Premier Grimes had agreed to a scheme that, because of the way equalization worked, would allow '95 per cent of the royalties' from Voisey's Bay to go to Ottawa (Ibid.). 'What has happened here,' Williams concluded, 'is that Inco's objectives, the objectives of a mega corporation that has more assets than we have debt in this Province, have taken priority over the interests of the people of Newfoundland and Labrador. Their cheerleader [Premier Grimes] has said: Inco comes first, Newfoundland and Labrador comes second' (Ibid.). The province could 'do much better than this eighteen page Statement of Principles,' and the House should postpone voting until 30 September to allow the government to table 'the definitive and binding agreements' rather than the document now under debate (Ibid.).

These were strong words, but the government was undeterred, and on 20 June the resolution was approved by a vote of 28 to18. The majority included two opposition members: Randy Collins (Labrador West), a New Democrat, and Fabian Manning (Placentia and St Mary's), a Progressive Conservative member whose district included Argentia. Premier Grimes had not only carried the day but had divided his opponents in the legislature. On 7 October Grimes, Mines and Energy Minister Lloyd Matthews, and Scott Hand, president and CEO of Inco, signed the legal documents that completed the complex Voisey's Bay deal.

The government's continuing efforts in 2002 to promote power development on the Lower Churchill River in Labrador – an old provincial objective – produced a very different outcome. In July 2001 Newfoundland and Labrador had launched a joint study of Lower Churchill possibilities with the U.S. aluminum producer Alcoa Ltd. Negotiations between the two parties continued in 2002, but on 29 July Lloyd Matthews and Alcoa vice-president Alan Renken announced that the feasibility study had shown that it was not economically attractive for the company to proceed with the construction of an aluminum smelter in the province. The focus next shifted back to Quebec, the province's most obvious development partner in relation to the Lower Churchill. Talks had continued intermittently with Quebec, and on 1 August Premier Grimes announced that he and Premier Bernard Landry had reached agreement on the fundamentals of a Lower Churchill deal between the two provinces. Newfoundland and Labrador would own the production and transmission facilities in Labrador, and a long-term contract would include a clause giving the province additional revenues if energy prices increased. The electricity produced on the Lower Churchill at Gull Island would be sold to Hydro-Québec but Newfoundland and Labrador would have recall rights. The two parties would also respect the interests of the Innu Nation in the development and proceed in an environmentally sound manner. As envisaged, the project would cost $4 billion and take six years to complete.

Opposition in Newfoundland to the proposed agreement was immediately heard and came from both expected and unexpected quarters. Danny Williams criticized the plan because no transmission line would be built from Labrador to Newfoundland, because of the long-term commitment to Quebec, and because of the vagueness of the recall rights that would accrue to Newfoundland and Labrador. Charles Furey, former liberal mines and energy minister, spoke out in opposition because the proposed deal excluded renegotiation of the 1969 Churchill Falls power contract, which so favoured Quebec and so disadvantaged Newfoundland and Labrador. Most damaging to the government's purpose, however, was the resignation on November 25 of two members of the board of directors of the publicly owned Newfoundland and Labrador Hydro: board chair Dean MacDonald and St John's businessman Mark Dobbin. Another director, Bill Kelly from Labrador, also made his opposition known but did not choose to resign.

The torrent of criticism, much of it close to home, forced the government into an unedifying retreat, which heightened speculation, already rife, about its electoral prospects. Federal and provincial by-elections during the year also cast doubt on the future of the government. On 2 April Deputy Premier and Industry, Trade and Rural Development Minister Beaton Tulk, who had been premier between Brian Tobin and Roger Grimes, resigned from the cabinet and the House of Assembly to seek the federal Liberal nomination in Gander–Grand Falls. This seat had become vacant on 26 March when the sitting Liberal member, George Baker, was appointed to the Senate. Tulk won the nomination but lost the by-election, which was held on 13 May: Rex Barnes (PC), received 9,273 votes (48.49 per cent); Tulk, 8,552 votes (44.72 per cent); John Lannon (NDP), 873 votes (4.56 per cent); and Garry Hartle (Canadian Reform Conservative Alliance), 422 votes (2.20 per cent). Tulk next ran for re-election in Bonavista North, the provincial seat that he had vacated so that he could run federally. But when a by-election was held there on 24 July he lost again, this time to Progressive Conservative Harry Harding. By contrast, the PCs handily held Conception Bay South in a by-election held on 12 November. In this seat Bob French, who died on 2 August, was succeeded by his son Terry. At year's end interest was rising in the heavyweight electoral title match to come between Grimes and Williams. As the last provincial election had been held on 9 February 1999, this contest could not be long delayed.

Obituaries

ADAMSON, ANTHONY (3 May, age 95). Architect and writer who designed Upper Canada Village and refurbished Hamilton, Ontario's Dundurn Castle.

ADASKIN, MURRAY (6 May, age 96). Violinist and composer.

ARLOOKTOO, GOO (30 April, age 38). Former premier of the Northwest Territories.

ARNOLD, GLADYS (29 September, age 96). Author, former director of information at the French embassy in Ottawa, a member of France's Legion of Honour, and the only accredited Canadian journalist in France at the outbreak of the Second World War.

BALFOUR, ST CLAIR (9 May, age 92). Former chairman of Southam Inc., former governor of the Toronto Stock Exchange, and former chair of the University of Toronto's governing council.

BARCLAY, WILLIAM (11 February, age 67). President of the Royal Canadian Legion.

BARLOW, LADY JACQUELINE (29 March, age 73). Founder of the Monarchist League in Newfoundland.

BELL-IRVING, HENRY (21 September, age 89). Former lieutenant governor of British Columbia.

BELLIVEAU, MICHAEL (26 January, age 59). Secretary of the Maritime Fishermen's Union and labour organizer for the National Farmers Union and the Canadian Auto Workers.

BLACK, GEORGE MONTAGU (10 January, age 60). Businessman, a member of various corporate boards, and older brother of media magnate Conrad Black.

BLACKMAN, TED (2 October, age 60). Journalist and radio broadcaster.

BOGGILD, KAI (28 November, age 82). Naval officer who charted the western Arctic.

BOREHAM, JOHN FRANCIS (10 January, age 72). Pioneer of wheelchair basketball.

BOYD, EDWIN ALONZO (15 May, age 88). Toronto bank robber and Don

Jail escapee, sentenced to eight consecutive life sentences for the killing of a police officer.

BROWN, ARNOLD (26 June, age 88). Former leader of the world Salvation Army.

BROWN, HAROLD ANDREW (30 March, age 72). Radio broadcaster.

BURGHARDT, JACK (28 September, age 73). Former broadcaster, Liberal MP, and deputy mayor of London, Ontario.

CAMP, DALTON (18 March, age 81). Journalist and Conservative strategist.

CAMPBELL, GEORGE (17 July, age 82). Former Vancouver prosecutor, veterans' advocate, and father of former Conservative Prime Minister Kim Campbell.

CARTER, ALEXANDER (17 February, age 92). Catholic Bishop of the Diocese of Sault Ste Marie, who was prominent on the Second Vatican Council.

COMOR, HENRY (9 March, age 71). Actor, writer, former president of the Alliance of Canadian Cinema, Television and Radio Artists, and media adviser who worked with former Prime Minister John Turner.

COSGROVE, STANLEY MOREL (30 April, age 90). Painter.

COSTELLO, LES (10 December, age 74). Priest, former Toronto Maple Leaf, and co-founder of the Flying Fathers hockey team.

COTÉ, JEAN-PIERRE (10 July, age 76). Former federal cabinet minister and lieutenant governor of Quebec.

COX, KENNETH (18 August, age 80). Former president and chief executive officer of NBTel and a community leader in Saint John, New Brunswick.

CROMWELL, GEORGE (30 January, age 88). Radio broadcaster who founded in Saint John, New Brunswick, the first radio station in Atlantic Canada.

DOLIN, SAMUEL (13 January, age 85). Musician, teacher, and composer.

DUHAMEL, RON (30 September, age 64). Senator, former minister of veterans' affairs, and former MP.

DREWERY, JOHN (4 February, age 77). Former parliamentary reporter for CBC.

EGGLESTONE, TOM (3 April, age 57). The highest ranking officer in Manitoba and vice-president of the Canadian Association of Chiefs of Police.

ELDER, JUDY (28 March, age 47). General manager of Microsoft Canada's consumer division, chair of the Canadian Marketing Association's Board of Directors.

ESTEY, WILLARD (25 January, age 82). Former Supreme Court justice.

EWEN, PATERSON (17 February, age 76). Painter.

FORD, JOHN (1 January, age 68). Conductor emeritus of the Oriana Singers and former high school teacher.

GARDINER, WILF (3 October, age 78). Former Liberal MPP in Saskatchewan and provincial public works minister, the son of former Saskatchewan premier and federal cabinet minister Jimmy Gardiner.

GIGUÈRE, LOUIS (15 June, age 90). Former Liberal senator, Quebec fundraiser for the Liberal Party, and adviser to Pierre Trudeau who was charged and then acquitted in the Sky Shops case.

GILLAN, MICHAEL (29 June, age 64). Former speechwriter and adviser for Pierre Trudeau, journalist, and the husband of Senator Joyce Fairbairn.

GOODIS, JERRY (8 November, age 73). Former publicist for Pierre Trudeau, a one-time Communist, and the songwriter who wrote Canadian lyrics for "This Land Is Your Land" in 1955.

GREENHAIGH, TED (20 January, age 83). Actor.

GZOWSKI, PETER (24 January, age 67). Journalist and radio and television broadcaster.

HAIG, DON (2 March, age 68). Filmmaker known as the 'godfather of Canadian film.'

HARE, KENNETH (3 September, age 83). Environmental scientist and meteorologist who was a leading expert on global warming.

HARRIS, CHRISTIE (4 January, age 94). Children's author, novelist, and chronicler of Haida folklore.

HAYTHORNE, GEORGE VICKERS (22 November, age 93). Former civil servant and deputy minister of labour who played a key role in the establishment of the Canada Labour (Standards) Code in 1965.

HEMSWORTH, WADE (19 January, age 85). Folksong writer who composed several iconic songs about life in the Canadian north.

HENDERSON, LORNE (7 February, age 81). Former Ontario Conservative MPP and cabinet minister under Premier Bill Davis.

HNATYSHYN, RAY (18 December, age 68). Former Conservative MP, federal cabinet minister, and governor general.

HOGAN, ANDY (10 April, age 78). Former NDP MP and the first Roman Catholic Priest ever elected to the House of Commons.

HUGHES, SAMUEL (26 April, age 88). Former Ontario Supreme Court justice who authored the report on abuses by Christian Brothers at the Mount Cashel orphanage in Newfoundland.

HUNTER, IAN (14 August, age 41). British Columbia marijuana activist.

JOLLEY, DAVID (4 November, age 60). Engineer, geologist, former publisher of the *Toronto Star*, and former president of the Canadian Press news agency.

JUNG, DOUGLAS (4 January, age 77). Lawyer and former Conservative MP who was the first Chinese Canadian accepted to the British Columbia bar, the first to appear before the B.C. Court of Appeal, the first to be elected to Parliament, and the first to represent Canada at the United Nations.

KARSH, YOUSUF (13 July, age 93). Photographer.

KAYFETZ, BEN (15 February, age 85). Former director of community relations for the Canadian Jewish Congress.

KECK, JENNIFER (12 June, age 48). Social activist and professor at Laurentian University who launched the campaign to raise awareness about the death of Kimberly Rodgers when she was under house arrest for welfare fraud in 2001.

KIRCK, HARVEY (18 February, age 73). Former CTV news anchor.

LABERGE, LOUIS (18 July, age 78). Former President of the Quebec Federation of Labour.

LAPOINTE, LOUISE MARGUERITE RENAUDE (11 May, age 90). Journalist who was named Canadian Journalist of the Year in 1965, and former Liberal senator who was the first French-Canadian woman to serve as speaker of the upper chamber.

LAYTON, ROBERT (27 May, age 76). Former Conservative MP, chairman of the party's caucus, minister of state for mines, and father of Toronto City Councillor Jack Layton.

LEGGAT, STUART (21 September, age 70). Former British Columbia Supreme Court judge, New Democratic MP, and British Columbia MPP.

LEFAIVE, LOUIS (4 July, age 74) Sports administrator who, among other things, helped organized the 1972 ice hockey series between Canada and the Soviet Union.

LOWY, OTTO (28 May, age 81). Former host of CBC Radio's *The Transcontinental.*

MACDONALD, FINLAY (2 March, age 79). Former chief of staff for Robert Stanfield, former adviser to Joe Clark, a founding director of CTV, and a Conservative senator.

MACHAM, DOROTHY ANN (12 July, age 91). Former head of Women's College Hospital in Toronto.

MACLEAN, OSBORNE (5 March, age 76). Merchant seaman and millwright who led a hunger strike on Parliament Hill in 1998 to gain compensation from the federal government for Second World War merchant mariner veterans and their widows.

MACLEOD, STEWART (6 February, age 69). Journalist.

MACQUARRIE, HEATH (2 January, age 82). Former Conservative senator and MP.

MARCH, HAROLD (9 January, age 93). Former hockey player and National Hockey League referee who scored the Stanley Cup winning goal in 1934, the first goal ever scored at Chicago Stadium, and the first one at Maple Leaf Gardens.

MARRIÉ, WILLIAM (16 November, age 33). Former principal dancer of the National Ballet of Canada.

MCDOWELL, STIRLING (5 February, age 70). Former general-secretary of the Canadian Teachers' Federation.

MCLAUGHLIN, ISABEL (26 November, age 99). Painter and the first woman to serve as the president of the Canadian Group of Painters.

MCLEAN, GRANT (19 December, age 81). Filmmaker and pioneer at the National Film Board of Canada.

MITCHELL, ROBERT GRAHAM (4 April, age 64). Criminal who was a member of the infamous "Stopwatch Gang" in the 1970s and 80s.

MOLSON, HARTLAND DE MONTARVILLE (28 September, age 95). Former independent senator, former owner of the Montreal Canadiens, and a former director of Molsons Breweries.

NAKAMURA, KAZUO (26 April, age 76). Artist and Japanese-Canadian detainee during the Second World War.

OLLIVIER, EMILE (10 November, age 62): Haitian-Canadian author and member of the academies of letters in both Quebec and France.

OLSON, HORACE A. (14 February, age 76). Former federal Liberal cabinet minister, former Senate opposition leader, and former lieutenant governor of Alberta.

OUELLET, GARY (8 June, age 57). Magic show producer, lawyer, lobbyist, composer, and writer.

PALMER, JEAN (1 February, age 86). Former executive director of the Toronto YWCA, and social work pioneer.

PASTORE, RALPH (1 February, age 60). Archaeologist who discovered that ecological factors played a major role in the extinction of the Beothuk people of Newfoundland.

PATRICK, KENNETH (1 June, age 86). Businessman and founder of CAE Inc., which became the world leader in the design and manufacture of flight simulators.

PICKERING, EDWARD (17 April, age 94). Former business executive, patron of the arts, and personal secretary to William Lyon Mackenzie King.

POTTLE, HERBERT LENCH (21 September, age 95). Former member of

Newfoundland's British-run Commission of Government, Liberal MPP, and provincial cabinet minister who caused an uproar in 1955 by resigning suddenly from Premier Joey Smallwood's cabinet.

POUND, MARJORIE (12 September, age 91). Executive secretary to Progressive Conservative Prime Minister John Diefenbaker.

POWER, LEONARD (30 June, age 60). Former head of the Royal Newfoundland Constabulary who was in charge in 1998 when the force became the last in North America to arm its officers with firearms.

POY, WILLIAM (3 February, age 94). Entrepreneur, and father of Governor General Adrienne Clarkson.

PRITTIE, BOB (14 January, age 82). Former New Democratic Party MP who was pivotal in the campaign to decriminalize birth control literature and materials.

PUERTA, RAMIRO (4 January, age 48). Actor, writer, and musician who programmed the Latin American and Spanish movie sections of the Toronto International Film Festival.

QUEEN ELIZABETH, THE QUEEN MOTHER (30 March, age 101). Queen Elizabeth II's mother, and widow of King George VI.

RANKIN, HARRY (26 February, age 81). Bombastic former Vancouver city councillor and self-proclaimed socialist.

READ, JOHN HAMILTON (31 May, age 78). Co-founder of the University of Calgary's medical school who led the successful push to make the Olympic Games smoke-free. The father of skier Ken Read.

RITCHIE, ALBERT EDGAR (24 January, age 85). Former ambassador to Ireland and the United States.

ROCKWOOD, ARTHUR AUGUSTUS (18 August, age 55). Newfoundland CBC radio host.

RODOCANACHI, JOHN (27 April, age 71). Retired Canadian admiral and intelligence and security expert.

ROGERS, LOUIS (29 September, age 82). Former high commissioner to India, ambassador to Yugoslavia, ambassador to the Security and Cooperation in Europe, and ambassador to Israel including during the Six Day War.

ROSS, MALCOLM (4 November, age 91). Author, professor, former editor of McClelland and Stewart's influential New Canadian Library series, and a key figure in the creation of such institutions as the Canada Council and the Canadian Federation for the Humanities (later the Social Sciences and Humanities Research Council of Canada).

SAUNDERS, HARRY (8 September, age 69). Former President of Zurich Canada who was instrumental in defeating the Bob Rae's NDP government of Ontario's plan to nationalize auto insurance.

SHEPHERD, REGINALD S. (1 June, age 78). Visual artist who co-founded Newfoundland's first art academy.

SHUSTER, FRANK (13 January, age 85). Comedian and former co-star of CBC's *The Wayne and Shuster Show.*

SNOWDEN, THE COUNTESS OF, THE PRINCESS MARGARET (9 February, age 71). Younger sister of Queen Elizabeth II.

SOCHA, NORMAN (4 December, age 66). Professor, art gallery owner, and patron of Native art.

SPRACHMAN, MANDEL (11 February, age 77). Toronto architect who specialized in altering old movie palaces and theatres.

STANLEY, GEORGE (13 September, age 95). Historian who designed the Canadian flag.

STANTON, JOHN H.F. (1 February, age 87). Author and labour lawyer who helped organize British Columbia's lumberjacks and longshoremen.

STEVENS, HOMER (2 October, age 79). Fisherman and former leader of the United Fishermen and Allied Workers Union in British Columbia.

STORRS, ANTONY HUBERT GLEADOW (9 August, age 95). Much-decorated retired rear-admiral of the Royal Canadian Navy who had once been Canada's highest-ranking officer at sea. He led the 31st Mine-Sweeping Flotilla on D-Day, and became the first director of the Canadian Coast Guard.

TAYLOR, JOHN (28 February, age 84). Former Progressive Conservative MP.

TEILLET, ROGER (1 May, age 89). Former Liberal MPP in Manitoba, federal Liberal MP, and minister of veterans affairs. He was also Louis Riel's grand-nephew.

THOMPSON, JIM (14 August, age 60). Chief executive officer of the Canadian Olympic Committee.

TUTTE, WILLIAM THOMAS (2 May, age 84). Mathematician and Waterloo, Ontario resident who helped decipher the codes by which the German high command encrypted its military communications during the Seconde World War.

UTECK, LARRY (25 December, age 50). Former Canadian Football League player, head coach of the St. Mary's University Huskies, Halifax city councillor, and deputy mayor.

WASHBURN, LARRY (12 August, age 57). Former leader of Local 691 of the Communication, Energy and Paperworkers union in St John's, Newfoundland, who led the unsuccessful 825-day strike of refinery workers at Irving Oil. The strike was the longest in Newfoundland's history.

WEBER, J. FREDERICK (7 May, age 80). Broadcast engineer and entrepreneur who was instrumental in bringing television to northern British Columbia.

WHYLIE, DWIGHT (15 September, age 66). Jamaican-Canadian radio broadcaster and the first full-time black announcer at CBC.

WOSK, MORRIS (9 April, age 84). Vancouver entrepreneur and philanthropist.

ZERAFA, BORIS (2 November, age 69). Architect who designed several landmark buildings including ones in Toronto and Montreal.

Index of Names

Index of Subjects

FSC
www.fsc.org
MIX
Papier | Fördert
gute Waldnutzung
FSC® C083411

Kolibri 360 GmbH
Ferdinand-Jühlke-Straße 7
99095 Erfurt, Deutschland
produktsicherheit@kolibri360.de